SURVIVING MYSELF

The True-Life Adventures
of a
Lucky, Risk-Taking Voluptuary*

FRED FAIR

Voluptuary: a person devoted to sensual pleasure.

Surviving Myself

Cover design by Kelly Pasholk of Wink Visual Arts
Front cover photo of Fred on top of Popocatépetl, Mexico, 1959
Back cover photo of Fred aboard *Mullet* in the Bahamas, 1998

Crescent Press
P.O. Box 2747
Taos, New Mexico 87571
crescentpresstaos@gmail.com

For my children —
Michael, Jana, Cobie, Josh and Daisy.

THE OLD HOUSE

I bought the old adobe house in Taos with my girlfriend, Linda, in the early spring of 1975. We'd been living together, and she had just finished remodeling another old adobe to sell. We planned on sharing the purchase price for our new, old home on five irrigated acres; she would put in the proceeds from the sale of her house and I would put up the initial cash, $20,000, and contribute another $20,000 for renovations.

I, too, had been fixing up yet another old adobe off Taos Plaza with a crew made up of Levinio Martinez and his two sons. We'd bonded over tearing down a warren of old rooms in a long single-story structure that had been dubbed "Old Doc Hollis's office." I had been there years earlier to get a blood test for my second marriage license, when Doc was still practicing. I partitioned the old building into art studios and galleries and soon we were finished. The spaces sold quickly at a substantial profit that gave me enough money to purchase my share of the old adobe.

1975 was a pivotal year for me. I had shut down the flying business I'd started ten years prior. I had watched it dissolve from deaths and bankruptcies as several buyers tried and failed to make a go of the enterprise. I'd successfully resolved a protracted IRS audit that had begun ominously with the phrase *criminal fraud*. I had ended my second marriage. I'd averted bankruptcy and even regained some credit worthiness. And by sheer good luck, I had fortuitously entered the world of real estate development in a market that was just beginning to take off. The old house became a metaphor for my personal and financial development. It grew and improved as I did. Or so I like to think.

The territorial adobe house we bought was originally built in 1892 by the sheriff and his prisoners from the county jail. He would get them out working with the invitation, "Want a little sunshine and barbecued pork today, Boys?" For a foundation, the prisoners dug a shallow trench and then filled it with field rocks. Cedar logs were laid down above a caliche base and more rocks were placed here and there to stabilize the floor joists. They then erected an L-shaped structure from adobe bricks stacked and mortared on top of that. Over a hundred years later the logs and stone foundation are still stable and the two-foot wide, two-story adobe walls are still vertical.

The house had stood derelict for years off in the fields a third of a mile from the main highway on a dirt road that goes over four cattle guards and around five ninety-degree turns. I had often seen it there, tall and stark with several large ditch-bank cottonwoods softening its imposing edifice. Two apricot trees, planted when the original structure was completed, were still producing bushels of fruit when we took ownership. Now the ancient trees serve to support hammocks while the giant cottonwoods tower above them, providing shade. There are half a dozen volunteer apricot trees on the property now, descendants of the original two. On the rare occasion a spring frost doesn't kill the blossoms, they, too, produce delicious fruit.

Sometime in the early '70s, an acquaintance had purchased the long-vacant house from its first owners. He began making initial renovations, acquired legal access in from the highway and installed electricity and drilled a well. He also built a large concrete foundation for an addition that doubled the square footage of the old house. There was no indoor plumbing and no heat save for a dilapidated chimney lined with tin that rose thirty feet through the center of the building. A 200-year-old acequia, or irrigation ditch, ran along the southern property line in the back of the house. When there is sufficient winter snowpack in the mountains, water flows every spring and well into summer.

Although the window glass had long since broken, the deep casement window frames of the old house were still intact on both floors. Even the roof was structurally in good shape although its covering was in tatters. I had the house plumbed and added a pot belly stove that eventually gave way to a retro-fitted central heating system, which solved the problem of having to break through ice in the toilet bowl on winter mornings. Plumbers worked from the ground up and the crew and I worked from the roof down all that summer. We shoveled two feet of encrusted pigeon shit out of the second floor and stripped the rotten cedar shingles from the roof.

By late summer Linda and I had moved into the downstairs that consisted of a small living room, kitchen, dining room, and half bath. Up some ladder-like stairs to what had been the pigeon rookery were two bedrooms and a full bath. We had created pitched wood ceilings with skylights in both bedrooms. All the original 6-inch by 12-inch beams for the bottom-floor ceiling were still in good condition, as were the ceiling planks over which I had plywood laid and carpeted. On the bottom floor the crew laid plywood over the original log joists, then put down locally cut pine tongue and groove. With the addition of a couple of new windows for more light, the old house became a lovely, tight little home ready for the birth of our daughter.

Linda and I got married that fall, and Daisy was born in April of 1976. She enjoyed the luxury of growing up and living in the old house until she turned eighteen and left for college. The marriage lasted until 1997. The house had morphed substantially during that time as we had finally finished the massive addition. The same crew built adobe walls from the top of the concrete foundation to create a ten-foot ceiling for a new living room. It was finished just in time for my fortieth-birthday celebration.

Ten years later, I brought the crew back to add a master bedroom, master bath, and an office on top of the living room. The old house is the second one I have owned in Taos and, like the first, it is strategically situated to take in a commanding view of Taos Mountain, perfectly framed in the main bedroom window, rising over 5,000 feet a couple of miles to the east.

Now, in 2017, at age eighty, I have lived more than half my life in the old house. I have been here for forty-two years and have been joined by my fourth wife, Brigid Meier, whom I married in 2006. Brigid has done much to beautify both the inside and outside of the house. She has planted extensive gardens, dozens of fruit trees, hundreds of raspberry canes, and many vegetables, as well as medicinal and culinary herbs. She keeps bees, goats, and chickens and has created a permaculture demonstration site where groups hold classes. While I don't share her passion for farming, I do appreciate how she has made the desert bloom, and I like to graze for strawberries and fresh snap peas. No doubt the healthy food she grows has contributed to my longevity.

Through it all I feel the old house has been my good friend —a living being and a bemused observer of the many vicissitudes that have made up my wild and crazy, wonderful life in Taos, New Mexico. I am grateful to have survived myself long enough to have gotten some of the tales down in writing.

CHILDHOOD

My mother and I fled from our family home just before Christmas in 1948, as she was putting an end to her twelve-year marriage to my father. I was an excited eleven-year-old, off on an adventure. I had known about our departure for a week, since my mother had asked me to pack up my favorite books because we would be moving to Alberta. I was thrilled, because part of the change would bring personal prosperity—a new red bike.

We had lived in genteel poverty in Vancouver, compared to the opulence of living in my grandparents' large home in Calgary. My father was a constable in the Royal Canadian Mounted Police (RCMP) and although he did have his dress uniform with the big hat and red coat and magnificent large pistol, belt, and holster, he went to work dressed in a suit like all the other fathers in our neighborhood. Dad was from Ontario and had left his past behind. I have a vague idea of his childhood which I gleaned from stray comments—there were two older brothers who, by the time their father had fled the family, had gone to good private schools and later into the military. I met one of my uncles just after the war; he was a colonel, escorting Lord Mountbatten on a Canadian tour. Dad took me to see him at the Hotel Vancouver where he presented me with a ballpoint pen, which was broken in half by the class bully the next day. The other brother was a pilot in the RCAF, and there had also been a sister who might have been an opera singer.

On my mother's side, my grandmother was a proud descendent of the Mayflower and a member of the DAR (Daughters of the American Revolution). She was born in Chicago but moved with her husband to Revelstoke in central British Columbia where my mother was born in 1912. They came with American investor money to start a logging operation that grew into several building-supply stores scattered throughout the prairie provinces.

My full name was Frederick Arnold Cleugh Fair, but I have long since shortened it legally to Fred Fair. Arnold was my father's first name although he was known as Bud. The Cleugh came from a distant knighthood in the family. When his father disappeared for mysterious financial reasons, Dad dropped out of high school and went off to the coal mines in northern Ontario where he played semi-pro hockey and then joined the RCMP.

My father did not suffer fools, myself included. He was a stern disciplinary figure, which counterbalanced my mother's unconditional love. Unfortunately, they shared little love and I remember only constant tension between them.

When I was born, my parents were living in a lovely rental house on the water in West Vancouver. Dad's recreation was in a sea canoe that, when not in use, was pulled up on the moss-covered rocks below the house. My first four years were spent on the waterfront or exploring a forest of huge cedar and fir trees right behind the house. My earliest memories are of the rocky coast of Vancouver.

When I was five we moved to a brand new house closer to town on the side of Hollyburn Mountain, four blocks above the water. It was a small house with a view across the bay to downtown. A steep, dark forest ravine with a creek, which I also spent a lot of time exploring, ran along the north side of the house. A stream came off the mountain behind us and, at the time, the wilderness started only a block above us. Now the area is smothered in housing developments and even the ravine hosts a house.

When I began kindergarten I fell madly in love with Dafne, another five-year-old. Alas, I was rebuffed and was so inconsolably bewildered and lost without my mother that I was sent home until I entered the first grade the following year. By then, I had made a successful transition from home to school, but it was not a happy time. I carry few memories of those early grades. I was not a good student, so when we left suddenly while I was in fifth grade, neither my classmates nor I lamented my departure.

When we fled, my mother and I headed for downtown Vancouver to the Canadian Pacific Railway station and probably passed my father who would have been driving home from work. It must have been a wrenching and heroic act on my mother's part to flee like that, but all I was aware of was the adventure of a winter train trip across the mountains and the promise of a new bicycle awaiting me.

There was no direct paved road across British Columbia then, just the railroad to the rest of Canada. We had taken the same train to Calgary every summer but this was the first trip during the winter. I remember waking up in our sleeping compartment, looking out the window at the lights of small-mountain-village train stations, deep snow banks, steam rising from under the carriages, and then pulling out into the darkness of the mountains of central British Columbia. We were in Calgary the next day, but after Christmas we had to flee further east to escape a court order to return filed by my father. My mother and I continued by train to Minneapolis, then further into the wilds of central Wisconsin, where there were distant relatives who owned a summer lodge on a frozen lake in the forest where they lived year round.

For me, it was more adventure. I had occasionally skied above our house at Hollyburn Mountain, but now I was in real snow country. I was plunked into the sixth grade and, for the first time, became a star student. I knew the answer to everything because I was repeating the equivalent of the fifth grade that I had finished the year before in Vancouver. It was a wonderful two or three months. I was foreign and exotic; I skied every weekend and lived with relatives who had a beautiful daughter my age. School was a few miles away on a bus ride through high snow banks and forest.

Some accord must have occurred between my parents because in the spring we returned on the train to Calgary. I was deposited back into the fifth grade along with my cousin Sheila. For the first time in my life I made good friends, which was like coming into the sunshine after social darkness. In Calgary I had my mother, my grandmother, *and* my new bike. My grandfather, a gray stern figure who left the house in the early morning, would return just in time for dinner and a cigar before retiring to bed. He and I seldom crossed paths. He died in Chicago the following winter and in the spring my mother and I moved to a small house on the Elbow River.

I completed the year with my friends but I was now in a different district, so I started with a clean slate and quickly made more friends at middle school, which was just downstream and across a small pedestrian swinging bridge. In the three years I went to school there I tried every mode of transportation—kayak, ice skates, and riding ice floes in the spring

—but I mainly went by bike and foot. School sports were limited to a soccer field with one soccer ball; neither the Canadian school system nor I were oriented toward sports.

At middle school I discovered girls and all the wonderful horrors that hormones could offer. My classmate Kay came to class one spring morning and shrugged off her winter coat. I suddenly discovered breasts, minimally covered by a white T-shirt. Kay was a dark-complexioned Texan, one of several Americans who had come to Canada with their parents for the oil boom. Like spring daffodils, several other girls, as if in competition with Kay, suddenly appeared in class with spring T-shirts and breasts. My male hormones were triggered with a roar.

I was now in the ninth grade and faced with improving my abysmal grades in time for the academic separation exams. I was also the class clown, a witty fuck-up and least likely to make it to prep school. I was trade school bound, but that would mean separation from my friends. Toward the end of the academic year I pounced on changing my academic record and studied for the upcoming exams, which I interspersed with relatively innocent frolics with a couple of girlfriends. Back then, a sexual encounter with neighborhood girls was limited to the challenge of unharnessing breasts from bras. The grail was cupping a bare breast in a movie theater. I became the neighborhood's hormone-fueled, breast-directed terrorist.

I was also relatively well traveled. After the first winter of separation my father picked me up to drive east and visit his family. We never made it past Yellowstone Park because of the summer heat. The next spring vacation Mom and I drove all the way to the Grand Canyon and Phoenix through Great Falls and Salt Lake City. In Phoenix I saw cactus and palm trees, and at the Grand Canyon I rode a mule to the bottom. Not to be outdone, the next spring my father had me flown to Vancouver in a primitive four-engine passenger plane, and from there we drove all the way to Ensenada, Mexico. I saw Hollywood and Laguna Beach along the way. I came back with a large sombrero, a bull's horn, and more assorted souvenirs. I was the class hero for a day.

During Easter-week vacation I was given a job at one of the family-owned lumber yards in Calgary. My only task during that week was packing the parts to lawn chairs in a cohesive bundle wrapped by cardboard. I later heard that most of the chairs sold that spring were returned by angry customers because of critical missing parts. I was never invited to work for the family company again.

Instead, I started an entrepreneurial enterprise of stealing cars. On one of my joy rides I drove through a stop sign and nailed a Pontiac coming through the intersection. No one was hurt but it must have been costly and messy and my doom was sealed. A family council was convened and it was decided that I would finish high school at the Shattuck Military Academy in Minnesota. My two uncles on my mother's side had gone to school there and had left outstanding records. I went but didn't follow in their footsteps.

That summer, 1953, I went to the mountains to work as a busboy in Jasper National Park, a twenty-two mile hike into the Hooker Ice Field. The Canadian Mountain Association maintained a base camp for serious mountaineers there and I bussed dishes. At the end of my stint, I hitched a ride to Vancouver to visit my father and my new stepmother for the few remaining weeks of summer. My dad had a small sailboat and we spent our time sailing up the British Columbia coast and my wonderfully endowed stepmother spent the whole time in a bathing suit. It was an Oedipal experience. She was understanding of the father/son tension and a loving arbitrator.

My final summer adventure was being dropped on the Trans-Canada Highway by my stepmother and thumbing my way back to Calgary. It was a watershed moment, standing alone on the side of the highway. I was on my own and ready, I hoped, for whatever the road would bring me. The first night I ended up breaking into a car in a used car lot with a road bum who had befriended me late in the day. That was cool. We woke up early and walked into a hotel in a small town in southern British Columbia to clean up. Before he left he plied me with all the information I would ever need to get laid, something about *Once you get your hands in their pants, they're yours.* Unfortunately he didn't supply me with the moves on how to get to that point.

Later the second day, again traveling alone, I got picked up by a gay traveling salesman who started a tentative grope which I rebuffed. He bought me lunch anyway and left me on the side of the highway. My final ride took me all the way to Calgary without further road-related misadventures.

A few days later, my worldly possessions packed in a trunk, Mom and I drove east to Minnesota. I was excited and looking forward to the new experience. Three days after that I entered Shattuck Military School's campus, leaving my childhood behind.

SHATTUCK

I was remanded to Shattuck in 1953 at almost seventeen for a variety of reasons, but the most significant was the car accident I had caused that previous spring. I had borrowed someone's automobile under my usual guise of washing it: "Hi Sir, I'll wash your car for a dollar and have it back in an hour." The trusting owner would hand over the keys and I would pick up my friends and we would cruise around town, then throw in a five-minute group car wash before returning the vehicle. One Sunday afternoon I cruised through a busy intersection and broadsided another car. No one was hurt, but both cars were substantially damaged.

Besides being the class fuck-up I was obsessed with the two girls who lived down the street and who, that spring, had magically developed into gloriously endowed young women. Being sent to Shattuck became inevitable.

Shattuck turned 97 years old the year I arrived. As my mother and I entered the lovely campus, we were both close to tears. Mom was leaving behind her only child and I was forever leaving the comfortable nest she had provided. I was now to reside at Shumway Hall, Shattuck's main building with a stern façade that housed the dining hall, classrooms, theater, administration for 200 students, and a dormitory for twelve new boys.

The dorm head, a friendly senior classman, came out to greet us and help me with my trunk. I said good-bye to my mother and followed him up to my tiny single room on the top floor. My room was fitted with a small single steel-framed bed and a set of drawers with a small desk. There was a bathroom down the hall, affectionately known as *the can*, which I would get to know all too soon. The dorm quickly filled up with new arrivals, all of them as nervous as I was.

Four seniors, who would act as our counselors, had two rooms at the entrance. The senior who helped me with my trunk was Bob Williams, captain of the football team and a company commander. We new boys mingled together in the dorm trying to establish some social order or hierarchy of coolness.

At 6:30 p.m. we assembled, dressed in slacks and blazers, in the refectory or dining room, which was large enough to seat the entire student body, the military contingent of about ten regular army personnel, and all the teachers and their families. On an alcove six feet above sat the rector and headmaster, Sydney W. Goldsmith. Sydney was an Episcopalian cleric, handsome and smooth; he would also become my nemesis for the next three years.

We were officially welcomed and rules were promulgated. We ate, still trying to recognize clues as to how to fit in. Each dining table seated eight and at the end of each table sat a senior class man or a teacher. Each setting held a napkin rolled into a napkin ring. It was replaced weekly, but halfway through the week it was filthy. The privileged received new linen daily.

After the meal more rules and scheduling were pronounced, such as *lights out at 10 p.m.* The following day was full of further rules and organizing. Classes would begin the following week. In the meantime we would be turned into malleable clean slates by the senior class. The cleansing and hazing began for me that night.

I was safely tucked into my trundle by ten o'clock sharp and not a peep was heard in our dorm. My emotions ran from homesickness to exhilaration. I was eager for the new day and new adventures. At 10:15 my door was thrown open as Williams, the previously friendly senior, entered my room dressed in full military regalia, saber in hand. I was informed that a new world was in place and that he was the head of it. I was ordered to the floor and told to start doing push-ups while he whacked me across the butt with the flat of his saber.

From that moment, my life took a sudden dramatic turn. I was dirt, the bottom of the social pecking order. Everything I had known before was gone. I was now to be controlled through a strict military hierarchy ruled by the senior class. These men, still teenagers, were the elite, sponsored personally by Headmaster Sydney. After demonstrating my prowess at push-ups, I was told to come to the can for a meeting. As in boot camp, the once-friendly dorm seniors were going to break us. We filed into the can in our pajamas and braced at attention, chins tucked onto our chests, eyes staring straight ahead. Any infraction brought screaming abuse or a basketball in the belly. The can meeting went on for several hours and we left terrified.

We arrived for breakfast the next morning exhausted and haunted. As word of our ordeal spread throughout the rest of the new boy dorms, we found out that we were the only group that had been given that kind of abuse. We spent the rest of the week getting organized into military units, fitted for uniforms, and trying to avoid any contact with our dorm leaders, especially Williams.

By the end of that first week it seemed as if my prior life had been a dream and that military school had been going on forever. We wore uniform pants and shirts with a tie and black spit-shined shoes we had spent endless hours polishing to a sheen. Our brass collar buttons and belt buckles were also burnished with enthusiasm. All of this had to be done or we were left open to punishment details by the senior class.

We quickly recognized who the main brutes were and gave them plenty of room. Fortunately, they were few. Many were even friendly and helpful and recognized what we were going through. Williams was the exception.

Classes started and the weeks rolled by. The caliber of the teaching was excellent, and I became interested in the subject matter and grades. Years later I can still remember the teachers who opened doors for me to intellectual excitement. I thrived academically for the first time in my life.

Not long after classes started we were given IQ and aptitude tests. I sincerely wanted to find out what I might be suited for, so I took them seriously. A month later I was invited into an administration office to meet several testers from the University of Minnesota. I had scored so low that my highest score was below the baseline on their graphs. They gave me more tests and finally concluded that I had a barely measurable aptitude for mechanics, which I had never demonstrated before and haven't since.

Because I was Canadian it was assumed that I would be on the hockey team, despite the fact that I had hardly ever played hockey. I weighed 180 pounds and I was fast—so fast that when late fall came, I was put on the team. After some scrimmages I was included in the first string. Hockey was the big winter sport at Shattuck and throughout Minnesota. My status as underclass scum changed after I joined the team. It changed again after my final run-in with Williams.

Shortly before the end of the football season, Williams was at the height of his Shattuck career. One night he was in my room after lights out, casually whacking me with the flat of his saber while I did push-ups. Coach Trigger, both the football and hockey coach, was prowling the dorm that evening after looking for infractions. When he spotted the light under my door, he was intrigued by the whacking sound. He opened the door and there I was on the floor and there was Williams taking aim at my pajama-clad bottom. Williams was caught red handed in mid-whack.

Like a worm, I turned on him. Hazing or physical abuse such as I was receiving was, even at Shattuck, a capital offense. It happened all the time but seldom so blatantly. Williams was sent to his room and I was taken to Trigger's office where I was briefly interrogated. Trigger offered me a couple of chances to recant, but I knew I had Williams and this was my chance to rid myself of his abuse. I squealed like a rat. I left Trigger's office after 11:00 and walked down a dark flight of stairs to the main entrance hall where I met a delegation of seniors waiting for me. I was a squealer but I had Williams nailed and I was going to see him expelled. I was pretty inured to verbal abuse by then, but these seniors went a step further and proceeded to rough me up a bit.

Williams was gone by the weekend. I was given special standing after that. I was untouchable and I was happy. Coach Trigger never referred to the incident again, although he must have been deeply disappointed to lose the captain of the football team to a new boy, a Canadian at that.

We Canadians were occasionally segregated during certain crucial military moments, such as during films portraying secrets of American dental hygiene. We were armed, however, with standard army M1 Garand rifles. The armory had some weapons other than our personal rifles and I probably could have smuggled out some equipment, but not the secrets of flossing.

One winter Sunday afternoon during inspection, a portly major strutted by me, his saber cocked against his right shoulder, and said something snide about my country. After the Williams incident I was empowered. National pride required instant reaction, so without thought, I stepped out of rank and whacked the major across his back with the shoulder stock of my M1. He fell forward in mid-step and landed with a crash of saber, scabbard, and brass on the hardwood gym floor. I stepped immediately back into rank realizing, too late, there would be retribution. All through chapel and dinner I was filled with dread. The senior class would really close ranks on me now. No one gets away with striking an officer.

But nothing happened. Although everyone had heard the noise, only four or five in my platoon witnessed the event. None were officers so I went unpunished. That night I blocked my door with my steel framed bed just in case.

Our hockey team traveled a lot, mainly up to Minneapolis to play the other private schools in our league. Our entire first line was Canadian. I don't remember getting into fights, getting hurt, or scoring a goal during the entire three years I played, but I remained either right wing or right defense. I was a lackluster performer so possibly my grandmother paid the athletic department to keep me on the team.

That Thanksgiving I was invited to go to Vinton, Iowa, with two of my dorm mates, both nascent alcoholics and, like me, at Shattuck for disciplinary reasons. All I remember about the long weekend was their heavy drinking. One night my host fell dead drunk into a large urinal trough at a road house out in the country. I was loathe to save him from drowning in piss, but I think I helped drag him to the car and back to his parents' home.

On Sundays we would walk across campus to our sister school, St. Marie's. The girls, dressed in Sunday afternoon tea dance regalia, came down an imposing staircase and were formally announced. We wore our class A uniforms, buttoned down so tight that nothing could extrude. We were allowed to walk our dates into a well-lit area for some polite dancing, all the while minutely inspected by several dowager chaperones.

I had a wealthy girlfriend from Mexico at St. Marie's but, even when I met her in Switzerland the winter after we graduated, we never progressed past alpine walks and hand holding. When I went back to Calgary for that first Christmas, however, Deanne, my hometown true love, seduced me in the back seat of my mother's two-door Chevy. It was very cold, scary, and uncomfortable. I despaired of ever partaking in sex again.

During my senior year the school organized a flying club, which I joined. I soloed that fall with seven hours of flight instruction. My three solo landings ended further flight training until I bought my first airplane five years later.

My mother drove down at the end of the school term that first year and gave me her car to drive back to Calgary on my own, which was a big rite of passage. I drove a friend to Arkansas, then I went to the top of Pike's Peak, followed by a trip to Yellowstone to camp. I made it back to Calgary unscathed.

The next two years passed uneventfully. Sydney used me as an example of how not to act or survive at Shattuck. Since Williams's expulsion I must have been a burr in his side. I was not one of his chosen few.

Early into my senior year I came to grips with not making it to the gentlemanly status of an officer, which I secretly craved. Half the senior class had made the grade, while the rest of us were consigned to the ranks. In my case, it was clear I didn't deserve officer rank.

At spring break I went to Hawaii with my grandmother and my cousin Sheila while the majority of the class went to Havana and came back with the clap, another rite of passage I mercifully missed. My mom came down for graduation ceremonies. It was also the school's 100th anniversary. Some of us were disappointed that Marlon Brando, once a Shattuck cadet, didn't give the commencement address. Some general showed up instead and made pithy comments. After a final battalion parade, we threw our hats in the air and it was over. A friend and fellow classmate and I shot and burned our uniforms. Nursing a hangover, I drove back to Calgary with my mother.

I have visited Shattuck several times in the intervening years, regretfully missing class reunions. The campus is far prettier than I remembered from my student days. From the perspective of many years, I have learned I actually did benefit, ironically, from my sudden and thorough introduction to the real world.

EMPLOYMENT

I was never a good employee. My first menial job was during the summer of 1950, when I was thirteen years old, delivering newspapers in Vancouver, where I was visiting my father. I don't remember any negative repercussions and I recall experiencing some slight bonding with the other paperboys.

In 1956 I graduated from Shattuck Military School without any further work experience. But that summer I threw myself into the job market with great enthusiasm. I bought an old pickup truck with a friend and we drove to Alaska to sell it. We succeeded, but then I was deported after two days working as a sweeper in a hangar at the nearby airbase.

At the start of the second day the American authorities came and transported me to the nearest Canadian border point, Prince Rupert on the B.C. coast. I was, apparently, an enemy alien armed with a push broom. That was an expensive trip for the U.S. government. The last leg of my deportation was a charter flight from the southernmost Alaskan town of Ketchikan to Prince Rupert in a small seaplane. The pilot and I made the most of the flight and landed in several small coves to fish for rock cod from the plane's pontoons.

I hitched back to Calgary to team up with another pal who, like me, was back from school with no contacts. We placed an ad in the local paper: "Strong backs, weak minds, will work hard." We were soon employed at the bottom of the home building trade.

When all my friends went off to college that fall, I worked as a grade man building roads. I never really figured out what I was supposed to do, but I went where I was told, stuck stakes in the ground, and shoveled a lot of dirt back and forth. I was paid $1.25 an hour and had a lunch bucket like everyone else. But that employment was also short-lived and replaced by driving new cars from Windsor, Ontario, to Calgary for a dealership.

EARLY TRAVELS

TANGIERS

I arrived in Tangiers in early December of 1956 by crossing the Atlantic to Gibraltar on *The Count Biacamano,* an Italian passenger liner that had spent the war years underwater after having been sunk by the British. I had five days to wait for a ship going to Naples, so after exploring The Rock and a night of pub crawling, I took the morning ferry across the straits to Tangiers with my traveling buddy Don, who was also from Calgary. We were both recent high school graduates bound for Innsbruck, Austria, for a winter of skiing. Although we were innocents I had, I thought, having read Laurence Durrel and Paul Bowles, a rudimentary understanding of the culture of our destination.

Even before we got off the dock in Tangiers, I was accosted by a ten-year-old street hustler who promised me his virgin sister and some drugs. The virgin turned out to be my mother's age but I accepted the drugs, which I quickly consumed following his uncle's instructions. The uncle ran a small pharmacy in the Medina, a section of town by the docks which was mysterious and wonderful. The uncle's instructions were to take an opium pipe packed with kief and a tiny bead of opium to my room, which was to be provided by another uncle in the hotel business, draw a hot bath, order hot mint tea, soak in the tub of hot water, light the long-stemmed pipe and...

I followed his instructions to the letter and awoke some hours later in a bath of cold water. I retired what was left of me to the bed to recover from the delightful fugue-like state of semiconsciousness.

In the early spring of the following year, having spent the winter skiing and traveling around Europe, I ended up in Zermatt, Switzerland, where Chet, another friend from Calgary, was going to a school for children of the wealthy. One of his friends, the son of a well-placed politico in Franco's Spain, invited us to Madrid for the *Semana Santa* bullfights. We would stay in the family estate and have use of Franco's box at the main bullring when it wasn't in use.

Chet and I and another Canadian rented a modest two-door Opel in Geneva and drove to Madrid via Barcelona. We were derailed by the night life in Barcelona but finally arrived in Madrid in time to catch an afternoon bullfight. The ballet of death was lost on me; it was time to move on.

Chet was, as I found out, a practicing alcoholic but I hoped to wean him off booze by introducing him to kief and opium. He was on a tight budget which hardly allowed him the luxury of his excesses so I suggested that we enter the drug trade through my Tangiers contact.

Once again, I was on the ferry to Tangiers but now with my two friends. We had pooled our limited funds to buy a couple pounds of Moroccan hashish and our plan was to bring it back to Spain and then enter France from the coast road from Barcelona. It would be tough getting the hash into France but we had friends in Barcelona who promised to put us in contact with someone who would re-engineer the exhaust system of the Opel to smuggle it in.

As expected, we had no problem getting the hash into Spain and up the coast to Barcelona. There we had an exhaust cut-out installed on the now sadly beaten-up Opel. The idea was to stuff the hash into aluminum cigar tubes and pack them in the exhaust pipe behind the muffler, thermodynamics be damned. After a few more days of wretched excess in Barcelona we left for the border and I was elected to be the border-crossing driver.

Just before we reached the checkpoint, I pulled over at a Spanish railway station to check our stash. We were suddenly enveloped in a greenish cloud of smoke which caused us immediate concern for our future. I looked for a side road to make some hasty adjustments. We drove through some olive groves, which screened us as I turned off the engine and where we discovered smoke coming from underneath the car and a trickle of dripping sludge, our hash, melting inside the exhaust pipe.

After cooling the pipe down, we tried to collect the goo. We tore the exhaust off the end of the muffler and returned to Barcelona to complain to the welding shop. Alas, our dreams of riches were dashed. The bulk of the hash was now a thick tar coating the inside of the pipe.

Our friends found our story hilarious but agreed to buy the remains of our hash at a price that didn't cover its cost or the welding fee plus the cost of the toilet deodorant we used to cover up the smell that had penetrated the interior of the Opel. We then drove nonstop to Geneva and ended our short, brilliant careers as smugglers.

I spent the winter traveling through Europe and working for room and board as an assistant coach for the Zermatt hockey team in the Swiss Alps. I skied whenever I could. In the spring I drove my graduation present, a brand-new MGA, from Europe toward the Middle East.

ISTANBUL

I have a photo of myself at 19 in 1957 standing beside my glacier-blue sports car outside the western wall of Istanbul with Horst, my German traveling companion. I had met Horst several days before in southern Yugoslavia after passing an old bus on a muddy mountain road. Looking out the bus window was a blond-haired passenger—an unusual sight because that spring there weren't many westerners traveling in Macedonia heading for the Greek border.

At the next village, I stopped to wait for the arrival of the bus and to see if the blond guy was continuing south. I was looking for company on my journey east to however far or long my car would last, after which I would continue on foot. I had a fantasy of emulating the explorer Richard Burton. Horst was indeed going my way, bound for Baghdad. We hit it off right away.

That night we made it to Thessaloniki, a port town in northern Greece. The next morning, while we were having coffee at an outdoor cafe, some young Greek guys tried to pick a fight with us. My car had GB plates, which indicated the car was British therefore we must be too. At the time, the Brits were hanging Greek Cypriot terrorists so there was no love lost between the two countries. Horst picked up an empty wine bottle and hurled it at them.

Then Horst threw both Greeks to the floor. I peeled him off and we ran to my car and sped out of town, followed by a volley of stones and more bottles. It was only eight o'clock in the morning. The day had barely begun.

By the next day, we were at the Greek/Turkish border trying to exit Greece, but we were being given a hard time by a Greek border official. As a recent graduate of a three-year stint in military school, I had developed a bad attitude about people in uniform. As a result, the soldier clubbed me with the side of his rifle. As I lay bleeding on the ground, the official evidently reconsidered his actions, since we were hurriedly sent on our way. Horst and I drove across a no-man's-land to the Turkish frontier. My shoulder and neck were numb from the blow, but at least the bleeding from my scalp wound had stopped.

The Turks were a great change from the Greeks. After all, I was British or at least the owner of a British-licensed car, and thus a supposed friend of the Turkish Cypriots. Within minutes we were on the road to Istanbul. By evening we were 100 miles down a deserted road, driving along the Sea of Marmara. We pulled onto an empty beach and with just enough light left, we set up a tent.

A half-mile farther away was a small village, so we walked down the beach in hopes of finding some food. We must have appeared as apparitions to the villagers. For some reason, in honor of our arrival, we were both hosted to a shave and a haircut in the local barbershop, as well as shots of the local, but lethal, *raki* liquor. A crowd grew around us. Someone had a relative in New Jersey, did we know him? Another had friends working in Düsseldorf, and so on. German was our common language. Dinner was served to us from someone's kitchen while we were still sitting in the barber chairs.

After several toasts to our respective glorious countries, someone asked where we were staying. We told them we were camped on the beach. "But you can't," they said. "Bandits! You'll be robbed!"

That was sobering. Had we already been robbed? Horst and I started walking down the highway to get back to our camp. It was extremely dark. About a hundred yards from the edge of the village we started hearing voices behind us and the sound of someone walking in the brush between the beach and us. We were being flanked. Were *they* the bandits? The village had few electric lights that were still visible. I thought we should try and get back to the village. Horst thought the same. By now we were quite sober and frightened.

I was carrying a German paratrooper knife, the kind where the blade drops out of the handle and locks in place. For me, it was a camping/utility tool. We whispered our plan to each other. We would run wildly through the people following us, knock them down, stab them, and get back inside the village to safety.

We had taken off our sandals and started running barefoot toward whoever was following us. I had the knife in my right hand, my sandals in my left. We ran quietly on the pavement and passed through a line of people.

Shouting broke out behind us, but we continued running. Inside the village, the lights turned out to be globes on pedestals on either side of an official building that turned out to be the jail. We ran up the steps and pounded on the closed doors. By the time people started appearing from the direction we had run from, the door opened and the village mayor let us in.

The people on the road were apparently just out to give us a scare. It was a *joke?* We ended up riding back to our site in an old dump truck to pick up our gear and drive the MGA back to the jail. I parked right in front of the two lights and we spent the night camped inside a vacant cell. The next morning the mayor took a photo of me and Horst and we gave him a ride to Istanbul.

My first stay in the walled city of Istanbul was for only two days. There was a paved road of sorts to Ankara, the capital, and it then went south a couple hundred miles to the Mediterranean coast. A few days earlier there had been an earthquake somewhere between Istanbul and Ankara. We came upon a village beside the road where the adobe brick minarets had fallen into the surrounding houses. Many people had died in the destruction and you could smell decaying bodies. Every minaret in the village had fallen, leaving swaths of devastation.

The road south from Ankara dwindled to nothing more than a camel track across dry salt lakes. In the late afternoon, the MGA's fuel pump gave out. We were driving across salt pans, heading south following tire tracks in the salt. Camel caravans could be seen in the distance. The only way I could keep the engine running was by tapping the electric fuel pump, conveniently located just under the door on my side, with a tire iron. I would hit it and the pump would start clicking away.

We drove about 50 miles this way until we came to another village at the south end of the dry lakes. There we found a blacksmith who disassembled the pump, cleaned the points, then led us to a local restaurant and fed us a delicious lamb stew out of a huge earthenware cooking pot.

Even under the most primitive conditions, the food in Turkey was great. We never got sick and I never ate anything I didn't want seconds of, especially pudding. We ate all kinds of puddings, even those from street vendors where you had to peel off the congealed skin that protected the rest from street dirt, exhaust gases, and insects. Then you could scoop into the pristine interior to discover what flavor it was.

I drove the blue MGA across central Turkey and around the northeast corner of the Mediterranean Sea and down the coast to Beirut. I was planning on driving east, possibly to Baghdad, where I would arrange to have the car "disappeared." Then I'd be able to go on with the insurance proceeds. But right after we arrived in Beirut, I discovered I could get deck passage on a small steamer going to Alexandria that very night. I left the MGA with Horst, promising him we'd rendezvous in maybe a month, and got on the steamer.

EGYPT

The next morning I awoke with the ship pulling into Port Said. The harbor and entrance to the Suez Canal were choked with sunken ships from the Canal War, which had ended six months earlier. I discovered to my delight that I was at that time one of the few tourists entering Egypt. Later in the morning the steamer continued along the Egyptian coast to Alexandria where I arrived in the early evening. I spent a couple days there as a guest in one of the recently converted palaces once owned by King Farouk, who had just been ousted.

While tea-dancing with the young ladies in Zermatt, Switzerland, I had the opportunity to meet King Farouk, who was visiting his daughter at the time. When he learned that I was heading to the Middle East, he insisted that his attaché write a letter of introduction for me. This *To Whom It May Concern* note gave me access to everyone in Egypt. Some of Farouk's palaces had been converted to youth hostels and they were at my disposal. The one in Alexandria was right on the beach and I basked in isolated splendor.

After a couple of days, I caught a late bus up to Cairo. I had the address of another youth hostel in Giza, just across the Nile, where I wanted to spend some time exploring the pyramids. I took the late bus to avoid the oppressive daytime heat and arrived in Giza at midnight. There was a full moon, the temperature was over a hundred degrees, but there was still some activity on the street. It centered primarily on relieving me of my pack, initially under the pretext of helping me carry it to a waiting horse taxi: a heat-stupefied nag attached to an open carriage near where I had been dropped. A driver sat on a seat at the front of the rig watching me as I dragged at least three guys over to his coach. I had written directions to the youth hostel that I wanted to give him but I had a more important problem at hand, and that was to keep my pack.

Ownership was being hotly contested and the guys were doing their best to rob me. I got to the carriage, put my back against it, and holding my pack with one hand, pulled a knife out of my pocket, the same one I had used in the last escapade. It was a modest knife but very effective for cutting bread and cheese. I was told it was a German paratrooper's knife and it had a blade in the handle. To get it out, one pressed a catch that allowed all four inches of steel to drop and lock securely in place. It was much sturdier than a switchblade and very sharp. I had never thought of using it for defense, but to maintain possession of my bag I had to do something. I hoped by pulling the knife out my problems on the other side of my pack would end.

I released the catch and shook the blade free of its handle where it locked with a sturdy German metallic click. Suddenly there was only one guy still holding on with grim determination. I remember he was wearing a thirties-style ragged pinstripe suit with wide lapels. He studied me intensely, then reached into his coat pocket and pulled out a switchblade. He flicked the blade open.

We were now both armed with a common interest in my pack. No one had spoken except for me yelling "No!" to the hustlers. Everything was calm; it was just the two of us with our knives and my pack under the full moon, a classic standoff. Without thinking, I reached across and stabbed the arm that was holding my pack. I remember that as I struck, I gave fury and strength to the blow. The knife entered his arm just below his elbow and with all my anger, I pulled the blade down the length of his arm. There was no scream or cry, he just suddenly wasn't there anymore. He disappeared and I was left with my pack, my fear, and surging adrenaline.

I was now pumped up and I turned to the horse taxi driver, an older guy, who could have done something earlier to defuse the situation. I put the knife against his side just hard enough to let him know I had every intention of pushing harder. I pulled the directions from my pocket and handed them to him.

He was now extremely attentive to my wish to be taken to my destination. I stood behind him in the carriage with my knife still against his side while he hissed the old horse into a trot and we rattled down cobbled streets to a two-story building behind a gated entry. I got the driver off his seat and walked him to the gate. He rang the bell and after a few moments a door opened and out came a German guy who spoke English.

I quickly told him the story while standing there ludicrously with my knife still pressing against the taxi driver. The guy told me we should go to the police station and report the incident so once again I boarded the taxi and the three of us clomped off down the road. It was a short ride and at the station the German went inside and quickly brought out two uniformed policemen who began questioning the driver and me in our respective languages.

I presented my Canadian passport and was instructed to return to the hostel with my host to spend the night, but that I should leave for Cairo the next morning where it would be safer. I should not be seen on the streets of Giza again. The policeman then turned to the driver and told him if we were bothered again that night he would be to blame.

The next morning my host drove me across the bridge over the Nile River to the Cairo youth hostel, a multi-storied building in a great location on the river. As in Alexandria, I was the only person staying there so I had an entire floor to myself with a room overlooking the Nile.

I spent a few days visiting the pyramids with the luxury again of being one of few tourists. I clambered over and through the massive structures with a guide who claimed me the first morning when I got off the bus at the park. Cairo was not an attraction and I took the Nile train down to Karnak/ Luxor where I spent a week in another of Farouk's palaces. My private bedroom was suspended right over the Nile. The toilet and shower flushed vertically twenty feet into the river that gurgled by under my window. Again, I was the only resident. But it was hot, 110 degrees even after dark.

One early morning in full Burton-the-explorer mode I arranged to be rowed across the Nile in a little boat. From the west bank of the river, I walked a half mile across the flood plain via the huge Colossus of Memnon to the palace of Der al Bahari. The sun was coming up as I left and by the time I got to the palace the day was turning into a furnace. The palace rose in steps and tiers above the flat plain against red-walled cliffs. I found a small steep track still in the shade to ascend. On the other side was the Valley of the Kings. There was a formal entrance further down the Nile Valley where one could enter from tour buses, but it was closed for lack of tourists. My short-cut got me right into the valley and the ornate tombs. There was absolutely no one around.

I spent the day in the cool of the ruins enjoying the royal blue and gold-leaf frescoes that decorated the walls. In the late afternoon, I climbed out of the valley and descended back down to the plain and began my long walk, in the early evening heat, back to the Nile. Along the way I hired a guy with a donkey to take me back to where I was to be picked up at sunset by the boatman who had taken me across earlier that morning.

That night I bought several watermelons and spent the evening sitting in a bathtub eating them while a cold shower beat down upon me; I was trying to stay cool and rehydrate while the hot night desert wind blew in from the Sahara.

After several days spent in luxury, touring the ruins in the early morning and evening, reading and eating melons during the midday heat, I continued my train journey south. I was still planning on reaching the Sudan despite the early July heat.

At Aswan I left the train. It had pulled into the small station and its roof almost met the side of the rail car but for a five-foot gap. It was noon and probably 120 degrees. As I crossed the gap, the sun slammed down on me like a physical blow. I realized that the Burton in me was defeated. I couldn't take the heat anymore.

The train I came down on from Luxor was returning to Cairo that evening. It was a twenty-four-hour journey and I was going back. The Sudan and Kenya be damned; the heat had done in my wanderlust. I would go to school and work in a tall air-conditioned office in a large American city. My future life had been determined by a five-foot gap on a mid-July day on a railroad station in the upper Nile Valley.

But before I got back on the train and started the rest of my life, I would make one more daring move. I would swim the first Cataract of the Nile that was conveniently just down the track from the station. I left my pack with the station clerk and hoofed it to the narrowest part of the river. At that point, the Nile flowed through a rock defile, a couple hundred feet wide. Red cliffs formed the far side where hieroglyphics were carved. I would swim across the Nile at that point.

The current was slow; the Aswan Dam was in the process of drowning out the cataract and dissolving the rock carvings on the wall of the gorge. Sailing dhows were moving up and down the river so if I had trouble I would merely hail one for assistance. I plunged in and swam across to the far cliffs and pulled myself out of the river via the incisions carved in the walls of the gorge. I climbed up ten feet above the river and, standing in the relative cool of the shade, looked back across the Nile. I had achieved my Burton epiphany at last. Had a large fat deadly water serpent not surfaced and started undulating its way upstream just below my perch, I would have probably continued south into the Sudan. Years later, I still can't believe it was real.

I couldn't climb further up and I certainly didn't want to re-enter the river. I clung to the cliff, barely hanging from the rock carvings, calling to passing dhows for assistance. All I got in return were waves and laughter.

One finally came downstream on my side of the river, and I dove in and swam like a water bug, knowing the snake was right behind me. No one threw me a rope or showed any sign of assistance.

The boat was moving several knots faster than the current, with help from an afternoon valley wind. As it passed, I swam under its extended stern, then grabbed on to the top of the wooden rudder. I could jam the rudder hard over against the pressure of the guy holding its wheel above me. Several of the crew were trying to lash at me with ropes to force me to let go but they couldn't reach me. The dhow was forced across the river to the edge despite loud, profuse, and no doubt colorful invectives hurled against me.

A hundred feet from the shore I let go and again, like a water bug, swam to the bank thinking, *Oh God, if you let me out of this river, I will work happily as an insurance guy in a large office for the rest of my life.* I walked the long way back to the station in the withering heat.

As the fear and adrenaline left, it was replaced by a sudden onset of nausea. By the time I reached the shade of the station I was feeling quite ill. Shortly after dark the train left and during the night I entered a coma of sorts. The people on the train, the *fedayeen* of the Nile Valley, mercifully took care of me, gave me water, and kept me and my pack together during the journey north.

The next afternoon, I regained consciousness when the train pulled into Cairo, where I spent several days recovering enough to travel and return to Beirut by plane. I was broke and still very weak when I got to Beirut but I was hoping to get mail, general delivery, at the central post office. With the very last of my money I got a cab from the airport into town.

I walked out of the post office clutching a wad of $100 American Express checks from my mother, along with my acceptance letter from Whitman College. My experiences in Egypt had evaporated all thoughts about college. Then, magically, Horst pulled up in front of the post office in my MGA. I surprised him by opening the passenger door and jumping in. I was the last person he expected to see. I had told him if I wasn't back within a month, the car was his. I was to report it stolen and he could do with it what he wanted.

We were delighted to see each other. We drove over to the nearby American Express office where I cashed my checks and I was funded for my return to London. It was late July and I knew I could get a job teaching at a private school in Istanbul. But I was still too weak to go anywhere.

Horst had made arrangements to sleep on the rooftop of a four-story apartment building in the Armenian enclave, two or three square blocks of semi-fortified buildings. Within moments they could shutter all the windows and doors of their buildings and create a relative fortress. Each building had its own armory of weapons, food, and water to withstand a siege.

I ended up spending a couple weeks with Horst, sleeping on the roof and sweeping the yard of a nearby convent for $1 US and breakfast. After that I would buy the morning International Herald Tribune and drive to Pigeon Beach, where I had made a deal to park the MGA outside the beach concession stand in exchange for lunch, a chair, a mat, and beach umbrella. The little sports car attracted business.

I was getting stronger so Horst and I started exploring the rest of Lebanon: the Druze mountains behind the city, Baalbek, and the beaches and archeological sites south to the Israeli border. Two weeks later I left Beirut and dropped Horst in Damascus from where he would go on to seek his future in Baghdad.

I drove the MGA back across Turkey to Istanbul and got a job teaching English to Kurdish girls in the resort town of Kadikoy, across the Bosporus. The pay was room and board in the school building, an old mansion, plus an American dollar bill per day. The rest of the teachers were dissolute college-aged Brits hired to come over for the summer from Cambridge. A guy named David, an earl's son, was one of the Brits. Together, he and I skated through several bizarre drug and drinking weeks. Because of the car, we could hang out at an elegant opium den after school getting stoned on hash and opium. I ran up an impressive bill. Unlike strict Istanbul, Kadikoy was a town where you could let your hair down.

My final night started with David and I heading off to the local opium emporium. We had both sold a pint of blood for five American dollars, and although we were slightly anemic, we planned on getting stoned again. Five dollars could go a long way in Turkey then.

I was leaving for college in a few days so I wanted to say a poignant goodbye to my new girlfriend, a lovely German whore my age who plied her trade at the most elegant of the Kadikoy clubs. It had a roof garden for dining and dancing and where I had another bar bill. The management knew I would try to flee the tab as summer was ending and the school was closing. When David and I showed up, they set a couple of bill collectors on us. I had just enough time to give my German true love a necklace as a token of my esteem and then we made a quick departure off the rooftop and onto the lawn.

David and I were stoned on hash and slightly tipsy from the ubiquitous *raki* so we felt invincible. We hopped in the car and took off down the street heading for the center of Kadikoy. There was a full moon and it was late but the Turks love their evening coffee houses. I passed through the old center of town following the shining rails of a streetcar line.

All I was aware of were the rails in the moonlight and the buildings passing by on the narrow road when suddenly I was driving into a crowded outdoor cafe. I crossed the curb, smashed my way through the wicker furniture and came to a stop with a mass of twisted wicker crumpled in front of the

MGA. No one was hurt but I took down an awning. It fell on top of us so we were covered by heavy canvas.

I couldn't see what was happening but there were a lot of angry noises. People were trying to pull the canvas off so they could extract and kill us. Turks have a reputation for retribution. I suddenly became very sober and very scared. It was then that I *really* decided to return home, go to school and never venture offshore again. *Oh, please God, if you'll just get me out of this one, I'll be good forever! Really!*

David had been thrown forward and was hiding in the space under the dash. When the awning was hauled off I was the only person they could wreak havoc on, but just as that got underway, a tiny cop appeared waving a tiny pistol. Even with all that I had done, destroying the front of a coffeehouse, the cop knew the MGA was probably the only sports car in that part of Asia, ergo I was someone important despite being young and fucked up.

The little cop held the angry crowd at bay. In the ensuing argument, I told him I wanted to be taken immediately to his supervisor, that everything would soon be straightened out. By this time, David had reappeared from under the dash and was sitting quietly in the passenger seat. I was still in my seat and the cop was holding me by my collar, trying to yank me out of the car. I kept telling him in my bad Turkish and German that I wouldn't leave the car, that I would go to his superior and that he could ride on the top right behind the seats. He finally agreed.

Debris was cleared until we could be rolled out of the cafe. The engine had stalled but thankfully started again. I had no idea how or if the front end had survived, but I knew that if I could get rolling there would be no stopping me until I was curled up in my mother's lap in London.

Now I was driving back in the street in low gear. When I revved the engine and popped the clutch, the cop with the little gun was gone. The MGA roared away. David and I headed back up the same hill we had recently come down, keeping our heads low in case the cop decided to shoot at us. There were no shots, and soon we were heading back to the school on the other side of Kadikoy.

I parked the car inside the walled compound out of sight from the street. We slept on the third floor of the old mansion until banging on the gate awakened us. It was barely light. We could see what we thought were the people from the nightclub who had chased us the previous evening. They were trying to get the attention of the school's night watchman but failed.

I decided then and there to immediately depart for Europe via a short ferry ride across the Bosporus. A week earlier, David and I had gotten Bulgarian transit visas so I could avoid again traveling across Greece and southern Yugoslavia. If I could get across the Bosporus, through the Western Gate and across western Turkey to the Bulgarian border, I would be able to leave the problems of the night behind.

My MGA would be an easy target. It wouldn't be easy getting aboard the ferry to Istanbul on the European side of the Bosporus undetected. David and I tossed our gear out the window down into the schoolyard and quickly followed. In the daylight, my MGA showed no signs of damage from the night before. The light grill in front had already been dented beyond recognition from previous minor collisions and now there were pieces of wicker sticking out of it like whiskers.

David opened the gate, I drove out onto the street, and we drove down to the ferry. It was early and we could immediately board without being apprehended. A half hour later we were driving through Istanbul, heading for the gate where I had entered the city from Greece four months earlier.

After the gate, we drove across the dry farming fields of western Turkey to Edirne and the Bulgarian border. The border posts were fortified towers a mile apart. Leaving Turkey, we entered the paranoid police state of Bulgaria. There were checkpoints along the road which passed through rich farmland and endless apple orchards with luscious, ripe fruit hanging almost within reach. Somewhere between checkpoints we left the highway and headed toward a small village beside a river, where some kind of celebration was going on. We were immediately incorporated into a Bulgarian peasant bachelor party, which will remain undescribed. Suffice to say that it was very primitive.

The next morning, after a night of too much *slivovitz*, we continued to the capital, Sophia, where we sought asylum in the British Legation. We had become lost to the authorities, so the Brits arranged for our departure to the Yugoslavian border the next day. Due to a series of flat tires, we barely made it across but we ended up in a student dormitory at the university in Belgrade at three in the morning. When I awoke and went down to retrieve my car, I found it occupied by a lovely young brunette. She was sitting on the fender waiting for me. She had fallen in love with my car and soon expanded her affections to include me.

Three days later she and I tearfully separated and David and I headed to the Adriatic coast. The beaches were filled with German vacationers who, a short twelve years before, were our mortal enemies. We had again overstayed our transit visas but crossed into Trieste with no problem. I drove to Innsbruck to pick up my belongings I'd left there in the spring, dropped

David off, and then headed for London for a short visit with my mother.

She paid the princely sum of $199 to book me and my car on a Canadian Pacific steamship to Montreal. I left London for South Hampton and the boat and later that afternoon we docked at Le Havre to pick up more passengers. I had a two-bed cabin above the water line in a brand-new ship carrying students back to Canada and, compared to my crossing from America in steerage the year before, it was first class.

My roommate appeared at Le Havre. He was tall and had a long scar across his cheek. During the previous winter a Canadian friend had told me about his friend, another David, who had been in a car accident in Spain. I asked him if he was the one. He was.

We were instant companions, both of us returning from a year in Europe. The boat was filled with girls returning from supervised summer tours so he and I became romantic interests for the crossing. For the next five nights we held court, fabricating our adventures to our advantages. David's facial disfigurement became a Heidelberg dueling scar. I was, I thought, incredibly mysterious and romantic, telling stories about my time in the Middle East. I enjoyed a classic shipboard romance.

We docked in Montreal early one morning and I drove west to Calgary. I made one rest stop for a brief sleep at an abandoned blueberry stand on the shores of Lake Superior and arrived, stained blue from the rotting blueberries I had bedded down on.

I then went to Whitman College for three semesters where I met, impregnated, and married Judy, my first wife.

AL'S RUN

The historic manner of arriving in Taos, New Mexico, has been by horse and hardship; many have been forced to stop here because of a broken wheel or flat tire. In my case, I arrived in town, having driven from Mexico City, in my green Volvo on an early January day in 1959.

I was traveling to Calgary to see my family and had planned on visiting several Rocky Mountain ski resorts along the way. The first one I came to was Santa Fe Ski Basin. I had arrived that morning, my eyes eager for something to break the endless flat horizon of west Texas. Then a bump appeared ahead, and for the next two hours it grew into the southern tip of the Sangre de Cristo Mountains. By noon, I had passed through Santa Fe and driven 2,000 feet up to the town's small ski area overlooking the Rio Grand Valley. Unfortunately, that view was denied me by a heavy winter storm. Having always imagined northern New Mexico as a wind-swept desert, I was delighted to find fresh powder snow that I trashed for the next day and a half.

The next evening I arrived in Taos where I ordered a Baked Alaska in a mud-walled restaurant on Taos Plaza. I was quite taken with the flaming pile served in rustic New Mexican ambiance. When I finished my meal, I drove up to Taos Ski Valley, twenty miles beyond the village, on an increasingly challenging gravel road. It had started to snow in town, so I decided to drive up before the road became impassable. I climbed 2,400 vertical feet, the last eight miles through the bottom of a tight canyon that the road shares with the Hondo River.

When I arrived at the ski valley parking lot it was snowing heavily. There were no lights to indicate anything was open. The road just stopped at a steep embankment where a couple of other cars were parked below a log building. As I couldn't see any signs of activity, I spent the night in my car. The seats folded down and I had a sleeping bag, so I curled up and slept soundly until daylight started showing through the snow on the windshield. It was still snowing, and the car was so smothered that the doors wouldn't open. I crawled out a window and struggled up an embankment to a lodge where I found a French guy cooking crepes on a hot plate by a large stone fireplace. There were one or two guests staying there in the Hondo Lodge and the crepe-maker was Jean Mayer, recently of the U.S. Army Ski Patrol in Garmisch, Germany.

At that time, a powerful Poma lift pulled skiers up the left side of a very steep and narrow cut through heavy forest. Built in 1958, Al's Run is still the signature run of Taos Ski Valley. It's an intimidating, 1,700-foot vertical strip cut down a north-facing, 30+ degree slope. The five-minute trip up on the high-speed Poma was good preparation for the daunting trip back down. The first and last pitches on Al's are the steepest, making skiing in between seem deceptively easy. But miss a turn on any part of Al's, and you're fighting for control before the dense trees on the sides of the narrow run eat you. In fresh powder, it's a delight. Al's is steep enough to give you a free-fall sensation in the turns but in chop, it's very, very fast. When it's hard-packed and bumpy, no one but a masochist would ski it.

In stormy conditions, Al's vertical aspect is reduced to hundred feet or less and one's concentration is focused solely on the next turn. But in sunshine, you can see the bottom of the run far beneath your skis. Hyperventilating from fear and exertion, skiers are left standing at different points, trying to look nonchalant to those above riding the two lifts. I have often been unable to even speak while riding up the lift, knowing that within minutes, I, too, will be on my way down, exposed to the ridicule of my peers. But it's impossible to ignore Al's in good conditions. When it starts snowing, we appear like lemmings and head directly to the top of Al's. The older I get, the easier it is to satisfy my craving for adrenaline from skiing Al's. From the first turn at the top, where the inner voice of age and reason tells me to stop and enjoy the cerulean sky above, or perhaps indulge in a conversation with a good friend, I am overcome by my airhead, brainless ego. Now a senior, I watch, appalled, as my body moves across the top of Al's, looking for the groove of the first turn. Then my two selves, the airhead and the horrified geriatric, converse in some sort of interior banter, *You fool, why?* with a quick reply, *OK, if I get to the bottom, I'll never do this again. Really!*

That morning in 1959 when I skied with my new friend, Jean, I was wearing 215 cm wood skis with no side cut and bindings that were called bear traps. The heel was locked down with long thongs, three feet of leather strapping artfully wrapped around leather boots which were then tied to the skis. There was so much snow that we had to pick up speed down the Poma track. We wallowed out into the thigh-deep powder for a couple turns, occasionally suffocating from face shots of cold dry snow. We were finally able to chop up the snow pack and by late morning we were skiing down effortlessly. There were no other skiers on Al's that morning. By the end of the day, I was exhausted. I departed for Aspen, wondering why

I was leaving. Skiing would never be better and I was right; I never skied Al's again in such superb conditions.

The next time I came to Taos was in 1963. I was in graduate school in Arizona and had driven over from Phoenix in the early spring and I hit perfect skiing conditions again. A big storm had dropped thirty inches of snow two days before I arrived. Again, I had the run almost to myself for the weekend. I didn't bother to ski any of the other four runs that descended from the top of the mountain. I was in love with Al's.

Six months later, I wrote Ernie Blake, the autocratic owner of Taos Ski Valley, offering my services as a ski instructor. I was in New York City, trying to rekindle my Ocean Marine Insurance underwriter career. I was bored and couldn't help thinking of ditching my job and spending a winter teaching at TSV. I was an ex-ski patrolman from Aspen and an ex-ski instructor from several other resorts.

I quickly got a reply from Ernie. Not only could I teach, but because I spoke what I thought was Spanish, I could direct the bilingual ski school. I soon learned that Ernie liked to hook people with job titles. Only later, they discovered they were assigned to parking lot patrol or shoveling snow. I was able to skip that step because I owned a plane. Ernie thought my aging Piper Super Cruiser could be an easy way to offer access to the ski valley from the rest of the world. He treated me more kindly than he did most new arrivals. At first.

That first winter of 1963-64, there were seven ski instructors, including Ernie's icy, but beautiful, German secretary, Elizabeth, who could teach on crowded weekends. We all patrolled sweep at the end of the day, and several of us lived in a little bunkhouse under the lift cable at the bottom of Al's. By then, both the Poma and a new chair lift both serviced Al's.

Jean, whom I had skied with that memorable powder day three years earlier, had, in the meantime, built his own lodge, the St. Bernard. Fifty years later, the St. Bernard still exists as it did back then, a charming medieval inn, with Jean serving iconic cuisine from a kitchen designed to fit in a French submarine.

I skied Al's whenever there was fresh snow. I would even try to take intermediate classes down it just to get onto Al's. I would often leave the class stranded halfway down. Somehow, I found it impossible to stop skiing to teach. After all, I figured, I could coach them from the lift as I rode back up.

One Saturday, with my class left halfway down Al's, I was getting on the chairlift and leaving the platform when I felt a heavy tug on my feet. I looked down and there was Ernie hanging from my boots. Realizing that I had again abandoned my class, he had dashed out of his nearby office and launched off the platform just as I was leaving. He was swinging five feet off the ground, glaring up at me from between my skis.

The operator stopped the lift and there he hung in front of twenty other weekend skiers. Dignity hung by a thread, so to speak. I was gripping the chair with one arm and beating him with my poles so he couldn't dislodge me and send both of us down in a tangle. Ernie finally let go and dropped to the snow. He picked himself up and stomped off in a rage toward his office.

I knew he kept a rifle there and would probably enjoy shooting me out of the chair. I hopped off and skied over to the office door. I thought that if he came out with his Mauser, I would defend myself with my poles. There was a group of skiers hanging around, waiting to see the results of our altercation. Ernie burst out of the door with a check in his hand, shouting, "Von now on you *pay!*" He handed me my paycheck, which I exchanged for a ticket. I continued skiing without the burden of my class.

A week later, Ernie hired me back to teach private powder lessons. On my first day in the new position, Ernie introduced me to two of his friends. Up we went with his admonition, "Don't break their legs, ha ha!" There was a blizzard and visibility was poor. On the first pitch, one of Ernie's friends fell and twisted his ankle but continued sliding down the steep face. All I could see was a moaning lump moving through deep powder.

I stopped the lump and was bending over to attend to him when Ernie showed up. He had been overhead on the chair when his friend, my student, had fallen. By the time Ernie got to me, he had worked himself up into one of his great rages. He skied up, yelling, "Get off my mountain and when you get down, tell the patrol." I was truly horrified and fled.

A week later, I was told that I could ski free if I wore an instructor's jacket and skied sweep at the end of the day. That, along with starting a flying business, was how I survived my first Taos Ski Valley winter.

The last night of the season, I invited Elizabeth to dinner at Casa Cordova, a restaurant twelve miles away in the village of Arroyo Seco. We drove down the canyon in a borrowed Studebaker station wagon, had a romantic candlelit evening, and then I returned her to her abode in the infamous bunkhouse under the lift cable. I had long since moved out and was living just beyond Arroyo Seco. I received a chaste kiss and a promise to meet me at the Phoenix bus station in three weeks. I had invited her to join me on a trip to Mexico in my plane.

It was snowing heavily when I left and all my ski equipment was in the back of the station wagon. Halfway down the canyon road to Taos, with a song in my heart, the headlights suddenly blinked off and I found myself trying to negotiate a right turn in pitch darkness. I held the steering wheel in what I hoped would take me through the arc of the curve, and was almost thinking that I was going to make it when the nose of the car dropped off the top of the stream bank. The wagon plunged vertically into a huge billowy pile of snow.

I was thrown over the steering wheel and ended up curled in a fetal position on top of the dash, pressed against the windshield. The bank had been used by a plow to shove snow off the road and I had managed to bury myself in an enormous soft pillow. I crawled back through the shambles of ski gear and general detritus and found the interior latch that opened the upper section of the Studebaker's tailgate. I was gratified to feel fresh snowflakes falling on my face. I wasn't entombed and I wasn't even slightly injured. I had my skis and boots, but I was wearing only a sports coat, shirt, and slacks.

I found my boots and put them on, collected my skis and poles, threw them out of the open hatch, and then floundered off the back of the vehicle to the bank and adjacent road. I proceeded to pole myself, in the inky darkness, down to the mouth of the canyon. By then the snow had turned to rain so I walked, in my ski boots, three miles to my rental house.

Fifty years later, I am still attracted to the fear and horror of Al's. If it's storming and there's more than two feet of fresh powder, I am incapable of ignoring its siren call. The bumps are awful, it's too steep to groom, and there are two lifts providing an inexhaustible supply of critics overhead. But there I am again, crossing the top pitch and looking for that first turn next to the tree line, the bottom far away, visible beneath my skis.

MEXICO TO ASPEN

Judy and I arrived in Mexico City in the late winter of 1959. We had driven down from Canada to attend school at the English-speaking Mexico City College that catered to Americans on the G.I. Bill. As we came over the western ridge from Toluca, I could clearly see two snow-capped volcanoes, Iztaccíhuatl and Popocatépctl. For the rest of that year, we lived in a small two-room casita above the campus in a eucalyptus forest. From my morning walk to the tiny *collegio,* I could clearly see both volcanoes across the valley, fifty miles away. Popo was the dominant of the two with its classic snow-capped peak at almost 18,000 feet.

On a Friday afternoon in July, and without much advanced planning, I arranged to climb Popo the next day with a school friend. We left after classes to rent crampons and ice axes. At the rental outlet, we met another young guy who hitched a ride with us to the volcano. He was also a student, but at the main university. We drove to the town of Amecameca, below Izta and Popo. There we bought chocolate and some apples and oranges for the climb.

That evening, we had dinner at a rustic restaurant. Afterward, we drove up a rough road in the dark to a saddle between the two volcanoes and a primitive climbing hut, at 12,000 feet. A foot trail started from there, which wound gently across the northeast side of the peak, then ascended 5,000 feet to an open and semi-active crater.

Several groups of climbers were already resting in the shelter. Like us, they were waiting to begin their ascent before dawn. The weather was forecast to remain clear but sudden changes could happen due to the proximity of the Gulf and Pacific coasts. It was late in the year to be climbing Popo; weather that would start off clear might turn into a blizzard within hours.

By 4 a.m. we were on the trail, walking by starlight. The other groups had departed earlier. All I had was a pair of loose fitting jodhpurs without laces that rose to mid-calf. I wore several pairs of socks and managed to stuff the cuffs of my jeans into my boots. I was wearing a nifty red Tyrolean hat that had seen better days, a down ski jacket, jeans, and my dubious footwear. The pockets of my jacket were filled with chocolate and I had a small waist pack for a water bottle and the fruit.

Two hours later we were at snowline with the first light. Pico Orizaba, the tallest mountain in Mexico eighty miles to the east, was backlit by the rising sun. Popo's summit, 5,000 feet above us, looked to be a boring trudge.

We put on our crampons and started up the wind-blasted, snowy slope. No skill was needed, just chocolate to sustain us. At 17,000 feet, I found myself the sole climber. My companions were out of sight, well ahead of me. I had eaten all my chocolate, and I was running on empty. My ascent continued step by exhausted step and I was frequently bent over my ice axe gasping for air.

This continued until, finally, I could see my friends outlined by clear blue sky, sitting on the edge of the crater above me. They were peeling oranges and sliding slices down to me that I grabbed and gobbled. With their aid, I trudged on the remaining fifty vertical feet to the crater's rim. Within minutes

I was feeling wonderful. One of my companions took a photo of me standing on the rim with Iztaccíhuatl behind me.

Right in front of us was a vertical 1,700-foot crater. Vents at the bottom roared like jet engines, steam and sulfur plumes rose out of its center. Five hundred years earlier, Cortez's soldiers had climbed up, then gone into the crater to bring up sulfur deposits to make gunpowder. From our perch, I realized that the crater ring was elliptical. We were at a false summit and the actual summit was still a couple hundred feet above us. I could see several of the earlier climbers coming down. When we met up with them, we had taken off our crampons and were just starting to climb the snowless rim of the crater to the top. They suggested that we turn back and get off the mountain immediately. Thousands of feet below us, clouds were forming on the saddle stretching across to Izta. Toward Orizaba, more clouds were growing vertical as moisture moved in from the Gulf of Mexico. In a very short time convective mist would turn to fog and rise toward us. We had to get off the volcano now.

Several other climbers passed us hurriedly going down and we joined them. When we got back to a low point on the crater rim we all took out our ice axes and started glissading down the slope. We did not attempt to put on our crampons. I had practiced the simple art of glissading before but never on snow that was as hard as concrete. The surface was fluted and runnels had carved shallow channels down the slope and into the rising mist. It was a bumpy ride.

What kills climbers on Popo was exactly what was happening to us. Sudden weather changes bring ice fog causing everything to become opaque. You lose the horizon, and without nearby trees to indicate up and down, vertigo can be so disorienting that just standing still is a challenge. An unarrested fall can lead to a fast slide into the rocks below. The three of us stayed within sight of each other and quickly descended several thousand feet to meet the rising clouds. I was leaning on my ax with the pick digging into the icy snow. My feet, without crampons, acted like outriggers for stability. We met the ascending mist and ice fog and lost all sense of direction.

At this point we put our crampons back on and continued slowly down through the fog. Although we couldn't see each other we could talk back and forth but couldn't tell how far apart we were or who was below or above. Fortunately, after a short but slow descent, mostly on my ass for stability, I started seeing black rocks in the snow. We were almost through the opaque part of our descent. Visibility came back as we arrived at snow line and off to our left were the other climbers who had started down before us, eating their lunch.

Several hours later we were back at the shelter and by late afternoon we were back in the city. Popo remained buried in clouds for the rest of that summer. I lived in Mexico City for another year without the slightest interest in completing my climb to the real summit, or for that matter, any summit, anywhere. Although I have traveled in many countries, I stand in wonder of the world's majestic mountains, all unclimbed by me.

ASPEN

In the fall of 1960, I graduated from Mexico City College. By then, Judy and I had a two-year-old son, Michael, and we were waiting in Acapulco for the ski season in Aspen to begin. I packed up my little family and headed north in our station wagon filled with handmade Toluca sweaters that I planned to sell at Colorado ski resorts. I had a job lined up at an expensive Aspen restaurant, Le Rendezvous, which would start right before Christmas. A friend from college had worked there the winter before, and his recommendation guaranteed me the job.

We arrived in town on Thanksgiving Day and feasted on frozen TV turkey dinners in a shabby motel. The next day we found an old log cabin to rent. Heating it was twice as expensive as the rent, but both Judy and I shortly got jobs. I became a ski patrolman, a made man in Aspen. I would have *paid* to wear a ski patrol jacket in Aspen. At the same time Judy worked waiting tables at both the Red Onion and the Crystal Palace. Within a few days of arriving in Aspen, we had money flowing in.

The Highlands Patrol was not to be confused with the Aspen Mountain Patrol. Highlands Patrolmen were alcoholic animals, or at least my co-workers were. Chuck Bolty, a local character and big-time Red Onion bar habitué, was the head of patrol. He must have had something on Whip Jones, the owner of Highlands, otherwise why would anyone hire Chuck for anything? And more to the point, why did Chuck hire me? I was given a trial run with a couple old patrol guys. The first test was to see how I could boot pack a steep slope littered with stumps and rocks and other debris. The next morning, when everything I had packed was still frozen into icy, horizontal ridges with the debris and bushes sticking through, I was invited to ski the slope. I survived the test, which earned me the coveted red jacket.

Every morning at 7 a.m., Chuck would pick me up for the drive to work in his topless Cadillac convertible. It was often filled with snow from the previous night's snowfall. How Chuck worked at all was the big question. He would put the Red Onion to bed every night and somehow stay on his feet all day running patrol. Each day ended with a sweep of the mountain's ski trails looking for laggards or injuries. I instituted the custom of getting the entire team stoned at the top patrol shack just before sweep. I liberally applied some Mexican hash to a red hot iron and we hyperventilated at 11,000 feet. I watched some unique sunsets as I skied down the mountain those early December evenings. Just before Christmas, I skied sweep while dragging a Christmas tree I had cut for my family. Could life get any better?

I was fired in January for leaving my station on powder days to ski. Chuck was apologetic, but I was devastated. I had crested and fallen from the heights of the skiing world all within a few weeks. To walk into Aspen without my patrol jacket was the ultimate humiliation. No more complimentary drinks at the Aspen bars; I would be just another skier.

This setback was preceded by my job waiting tables right before Christmas. Work started Thursday, the day before the holiday crowds arrived. I had assured the manager that I was a qualified waiter and I figured I would pick up all the skills I needed on the first night. Instead, I was a disaster. The next evening, dressed in a tuxedo, I was also a disaster. I was finally saved when the large Hungarian manager, realizing what a dolt I was, grabbed me and hurled me out of the restaurant.

It was snowing lightly that night and Aspen's streets were crowded with happy vacationers, so I joined the throngs with a song in my heart, still dressed in my smart tuxedo. I walked down to the Red Onion, ordered the "Skiers Special" and thanked the gods I was no longer a waiter. With two employment failures within three months of college graduation, I was forced to reassess my future. I saw that the patrol fiasco was somewhat political and the waiter fiasco was due to overstepping my skill level.

Next, I became a Highlands lift operator. I spent part of a snowless January sitting in a pit at the top of Thunder Bowl lift reading *The Rise and Fall of the Third Reich*. Meanwhile, the mountain turned to ice. Next, I became the evening bartender/manager at the Highlands Bar at the bottom of the lifts. This brought me another coveted job of running the torchlight procession down the lower half of the mountain three nights a week. This job required split-second timing in getting to the Red Onion in time to recruit five or six of the local drunks before they were too shit-faced to ski, but shit-faced enough to agree to carry sulfur-burning railway flares down the face of Highlands to the delight of the Hindquarter's guests.

By now I was a Chuck Bolty clone with my own convertible, an old Plymouth. With the promise of a gallon of cheap red wine plus dinner, I would pile the drunks into my car and drive back out to Highlands. I'd fire up the lift and get them on it. We would get off at mid-mountain, which sometimes proved to be difficult as some of my team would forget to exit and would ride on into the dark, to be left swinging. I would shout out that they had two choices—either stay there, ten feet above the ground until morning, or jump. They jumped.

When we were finally all together, I would light their flares and we would take off down the mountain. At the best of times it's difficult to ski carrying a flare. From down below the diners would see a flare swoop and snuff as a skier would plunge head-first into irregular terrain. I followed the procession, standing the drunks back up on their skis and relighting their torches. By the time we made it to the bottom, most of the diners had gone back inside to finish dinner.

One night we were caught in a small avalanche. No one was carried into the trees but it took an hour to dislodge the merry band from chest-deep snow. I did the torch procession for a per-trip fee of $50, plus food and wine for the crew. That alone paid all our family's living expenses in Aspen. Bartending was equally lucrative. The operator of the bar where I worked had an enlightened attitude toward bookkeeping. He expected a certain amount of cash from each bottle he inventoried; everything after that ended up in my pocket.

At the end of the season Highlands closed with a toga party. I made a punch from all the weird leftover liqueurs. I poured the nasty brew into a large bowl along with vodka and chunks of sherbet to modify the taste and color. I charged a dollar a cup. A lot of happy participants vomited in the bar that night. The owner of the resort threw a case of empties at me. I left with a record amount of cash but had to walk to town because my ride had passed out and lost his car keys.

My last night in Aspen was clear and starry at two in the morning. When I got to the old bridge across Castle Creek that was being torn down, I decided to walk across the chasm on a 2-inch by 14-inch plank nailed on the top of one piling to the next. I walked across with no problem until I found, just short of the Aspen side, the last couple of planks had been removed to discourage just what I was doing. I stood there frustrated, then turned to walk back. It was bright enough to see my footprints in the snow. Gazing at them while being suspended 60 feet above the canyon floor brought on vertigo. I couldn't move for fear of falling. I finally straddled the plank and humped my way back.

The next day, Judy and I loaded up the Chevy with Michael and the dog and a few belongings. We left our landlady the unsold Toluca sweaters in exchange for back rent and struck out for Seattle. I had decided to bless either Canada or America with my business acumen.

The first opportunity came while we were in Seattle. An ad in the Seattle Times read: "Young, upward bound, international opportunities in sales, no experience. Training provided." I answered the ad and was picked up that night at my home and ushered into the world of high-pressure encyclopedia sales. I lasted two nights.

A month after leaving Aspen, no other opportunities had appeared on either side of the border and our cash reserve had dwindled. I went to an executive hiring agency that was advertising for a "Junior Executive Trainee." An old gentleman asked me if I liked the smell of salt water, foreign ports, exotic adventure. When I nodded he gave me an address in the city for an interview, and I was hired to train as an Ocean Marine underwriter for Fireman's Fund Insurance.

Instead of enjoying salt water and adventure, I spent fifteen months trying to look busy after attending a one-month training school at the San Francisco headquarters. I was bound for the top of the corporate ladder. After all, I had received the best grades in my class because I had nothing else to do with my time but study. I hated the work but loved the paternal corporate attitude. We were family.

The apogee of that career came when I turned to Marge, my secretary who was lodged at a large steel desk directly behind me. I commented pleasantly on the day's weather, which was, as usual, rainy. Marge was a career secretary who had been working in our department for twenty years. Her work was her life. I was an unfortunate but temporary blip in her world, but she adored our department head, Warren, whom I liked as well. All he asked of me was to get the best grades in the class and to look busy because if I didn't, it would reflect negatively on him.

I was always cheery and busy, doing totally unnecessary loss reports on an old hand-cranked calculator that produced long spools of figures no one read. Marge was correct in thinking I was an unnecessary addition to the department. Sitting directly in front of her, I separated her from Warren, who sat directly in front of me at the front of a long line of steel desks. Each row had twelve desks and there were six identical rows in the office. No one but the head of the Seattle office had any privacy.

That morning I turned to Marge and, with fake camaraderie, cheerily mentioned the weather again. Marge had a large electric stapler on her desk and on this day, the power cord to her calculator had snaked between the business end of the stapler. As I swiveled around, I put my arm down on her stapler, which then stapled the power cord to her metal desk, which shorted out the entire office. There was a big electrical discharge under my elbow. The stapler, the calculator, and the desk were welded together into one smoking unit. Marge was blown back in her swivel chair and I was blown off my chair by the electrical jolt and the entire office went dark.

I had already been thinking along other lines for employment. Of course there was always graduate school, for which I was then ideally suited, what with practical and career-level experience as a professional Ocean Marine underwriter.

A year and another degree later, I arrived in New York City alone. Judy and I had separated during the previous year. I was hired, as all my classmates were, before graduation. I would continue working as a marine underwriter in Latin America for the American Foreign Insurance Association, but first I would spend six month at their headquarters in midtown Manhattan. I was to orient myself at the home office, which entailed doing exactly what I had been doing in Seattle the year before: nothing.

The pay was good, more than triple that in Seattle, and I was provided with an uptown apartment. The future looked rosy, but for the office boredom. I lasted two months. My final day with AFIA ended with lunch. I had been assigned a secretary, but neither she nor I had had any real contact, professionally or otherwise. She was a Sophia Loren look-alike, gum-chewing Brooklynite. I was spellbound by her beauty until she opened her mouth. Her native language was, I think, English, but she spoke it with an accent and syntax foreign to me. I owed her a lunch as she too would be released from employment when I departed.

We went to one of those ubiquitous financial district joints that specialized in drinking lunches. I ordered a carafe of Manhattans to take care of our cultural and language differences and we then proceeded to fall into lust. Two carafes later we staggered out onto the street and wove to our office, which just happened to be adjacent to the Maiden Lane entrance to the IRT subway station. I told my beauty that her services would not require her to work that afternoon and escorted her to the subway entrance, down the stairs to the old wooden turnstiles where my hazy memory seems to recall that we consummated a special moment with her ass supported by the crotch of the subway's turnstile. Every few minutes our passion was interrupted by a rush of hot fetid September air, followed by another rush of mid-afternoon workers as the inbound train came to a screeching stop below us. When the loving moment was over, I spun her around for the local to Brooklyn.

I spent another month hanging out in the city in a state of shock from having abandoned my career. I interviewed with some companies, but there was an undeniable siren song of entrepreneurship in my ear. One of my friends from graduate school was joining a small company in Mexico City to grow bananas in Belize. There was a position for me and a chance to return to Mexico. A month later, in November, 1963, I was employed as a ski instructor in Taos, New Mexico, waiting for spring and another career opportunity to begin as a banana plantation manager in British Honduras.

LUNCH WITH THE PRIME MINISTER

In the spring of 1959, when I was still a college student living in Mexico City, I was invited to lunch with the Canadian prime minister and the Mexican president. At the time the Canadian Embassy kept a list of Canadians living in town who could talk coherently, and occasionally I would be invited to minor state functions. I eagerly attended them because they served good liquor and fancy food.

I had a week's notice for a gala luncheon for Lopez Mateos, the Mexican presidential host, and Prime Minister John Diefenbaker, the Canadian guest. About the time I received the invitation, a minor toothache erupted into full fury. Since I was terrified of dentists, I asked around and learned of a Chinese herbalist in Mexico City's Chinatown.

Five days before the luncheon I made my first visit to his office, up a narrow flight of stairs in a dingy old building. I arrived without an appointment. The waiting room, which was the stairway and corridor, was full of other sufferers sitting and standing against the wall. I was the only Anglo; everyone else was either Mexican or Chinese.

I joined the group with the expectation of a long wait, but I was ushered quickly into an inner office. Word had obviously spread that someone with a chance of paying his bill had arrived and I was seated in a chair looking at an array of tiny pots filled with colored ointments. *Tengo mucho dolor en un diente,*" I explained while pointing to the offending side of my mouth. The little Chinese doctor gave me a look of great compassion and assured me I would be fine within minutes.

He swabbed a Q-Tip with a mixture of unguents and proceeded to paint the tooth. Then, with a dab of cotton, he packed the cratered cavity with more mixtures from the pots and sent me on my way with immediate relief. No needles, no pain. Alternative dentistry!

By morning the pain was back, and I was in his office the next afternoon receiving the same procedure and assurances. Two days later, with increasing pain, I gave up and made an appointment with a Mexican dentist. It was only after explaining that I was having lunch with his president and my Canadian prime minister that he promised to see me the next morning, Saturday, the day of the event.

My dental appointment was set for 10 a.m. The lunch was at 2 p.m. No problem. I was on time. The dentist was solicitous. The procedure started with both of us taking a shot of Scotch whiskey as a toast to our two great nations. He was determined to get me to the lunch in presentable shape. After an injection of Novocain, we each had another shot. Then he went to work with tongs trying to rip the offending molar out of my lower jaw. After a short struggle in which the tooth stubbornly remained in place, we each took another shot of his dwindling whiskey supply. This rhythm of extraction went on through several more efforts until the tooth was suddenly jerked free.

By this time, we were both exhausted and inebriated. He stuffed my mouth with cotton packing. My jaw was numb and I couldn't talk. Somehow, I assured my new friend the dentist that he had saved me for important affairs of state and that I would pass on his regards to both his president and my PM.

Instead, I left his office and slunk home to bleed and drool the afternoon away.

Years later, in 1975, when I was living in Taos, my friend Graham called from Aspen to invite me to dine with Canada's new PM, Pierre Trudeau, for a casual lunch on Aspen Mountain and dinner later at Graham's house. Graham, knowing of my nationality and earlier non-luncheon in Mexico, said he was giving me a second chance.

I hopped in my plane and flew to Aspen in time to get to the top of Ajax Mountain by noon. The picnic location was in a glade of trees off the main trail and access was controlled by security details from both countries. I gave my name as an invitee to the humorless guards and was admitted. There were probably ten guests with Trudeau and Graham, and there were at least ten more people who were security or from the Aspen Ski Patrol, my erstwhile compatriots.

Everyone stood around eating dainties. I was introduced to Trudeau who, I knew, had recently been heli-skiing in British Columbia. I brought that up and lamented that we were sadly not enjoying the same quality of skiing on top of Ajax that day. When he agreed, I suggested that we break away from the lunch and ski out of bounds on Walsh's Gulch, a closed avalanche chute that was guaranteed to have deep powder snow. I jokingly said we would make some great headlines if we got caught by the ski patrol.

Just as I was basking in the warmth of being the PM's new best friend and ski confidante, a burly factotum in ski garb rudely stepped between us and proceeded to belly me away. As soon as he had bumped me out of earshot, another guy, a ski patrolman, whispered that I was no longer an invited guest and it would be best that I leave immediately. The PM's security must have had a listening device and heard my remarks. I put my skis on slowly, thinking that someone would surely notice my absence and come to my rescue. No one did, so I left. My invitation to dinner that night was canceled as well.

FLYING STORIES

BEACH LANDING

I bought my first airplane, a 1937 Porterfield, when I was 25 years old and living in Seattle during the early summer of 1961. The plane and I were the same age. (I had received seven hours of flight instruction five years earlier at military school.) As an Ocean Marine underwriter trainee making $380 a month, I couldn't afford the luxury of a plane. But after a short introductory flight and much illogical justification, I made the seller an optimistic offer of the family car. The next morning I was the owner of the Porterfield and found myself riding my Lambretta motor scooter back to Renton Field for my second solo flight, this time as the owner of an $800 plane.

For much of that summer I spent my free time flying. The Porterfield was a basic fabric-covered cub powered by a 65 hp engine with an altimeter and an airspeed indicator. The sole altitude instrument was a slightly curved glass tube glued horizontally to the panel with a ball bearing inside. At one time the tube was filled with liquid to dampen the oscillations of the steel ball. If I banked the airplane, the ball would just clang against the lower side of the tube. The fuel gauge was a wire attached to a cork that floated on the fuel, so when the gas tank was empty the wire all but disappeared inside the tank. The plane had no radio, no starter, and no generator. I had no experience, no license, and no clue about flight regulations. The Porterfield and I were a perfect match.

By midsummer I was a proficient pilot. I dazzled my fellow office workers with my flying stories. Seattle in the summer is a pilot's paradise as there are many islands and mountain valleys with airstrips. In addition, my father lived right across the border in Canada on a mountain lake with an airstrip nearby. I could fly there in an hour without bothering to clear customs.

Aviation was so convenient. I thought nothing of flying through the glacier-covered Olympics and Cascades. The passes were all low enough so that even my anemic craft could make it safely through the mountains. My abiding flying philosophy became *If you can see it, you won't hit it.*

One Saturday morning in July, Judy and three-year-old Michael and I decided to go on a beach picnic to Dungeness Spit on the northeast side of the Olympic Peninsula. The spit stuck out into the Strait of Juan de Fuca and offered several miles of packed sand at water's edge where I could land. After a short thirty-mile flight across the sound, I spotted what looked like another landing spot that was half the distance to our destination.

The Hood Canal is a natural channel just off the eastern side of the Olympic Peninsula. At the north end of the canal, where the floating bridge connects Bainbridge Island to the peninsula, I found another spit of sand that looked perfect for our picnic. The tide was low and I landed on hard-packed sand next to the water. But as soon as we got out of the plane, I knew that my family would have to take the ferry home because the strip was too short to take off with them aboard. By myself, I'd be able to get the plane airborne.

Nevertheless, we were there. So we walked to the other side of the spit by the lagoon and ate lunch. There were other picnickers who appeared to be undecided as to whether or not

I was a fool or a flying bon vivant. I chose to believe the latter while trying not to think of the upcoming takeoff.

Meanwhile, the tide was coming in. An hour later, when I finally got around to facing my departure, I discovered that the plane's wheels were underwater. I arranged with others on the beach to give Michael and Judy a ride to the ferry, then I strode over to my partly submerged Porterfield, fired it up, and started to taxi out of the water and up the angled beach to dry sand. This required, as it turned out, more skill than I possessed.

To get the plane to move, even at full power, I had to raise the tail wheel out of the water. Then, balanced on the plane's two main tires, I moved precariously forward. I slowly edged the little craft to higher ground. But as I continued, I traded water resistance for soft sand. Suddenly, the wheels rolled into a small depression, and the plane pitched over onto its nose. The propeller smashed to splinters, and I was thrown forward against the windshield. The plane, its engine dead, remained perched on its nose. I climbed out unhurt.

People rushed to help, and we were able to right the craft and push it through the sand to the tree line. Someone lent me a wrench and I unbolted the remains of the propeller from the crankshaft. Except for my ego, the propeller and the dented engine cowling, everything seemed fine. We left the plane and hitched a ride to the ferry.

All week long I agonized over the price of a new propeller —a week's wages. I also worried about takeoff the following weekend. Reality was not on my side. I would be forced to take off from soft dry sand instead of a tidal-packed hard surface. If I had a favorable wind, I thought I might have a chance.

The next Saturday, with my new propeller and a good weather forecast, we retraced our path back to the beach via the Bremerton Ferry. So did everyone else who had witnessed the earlier incident, along with their extended families. The beach was crowded, as if for an air show. Even the other sand spit at the far end of my takeoff path was filled with picnickers. Between the two sand spits was a hundred foot channel of water to cross. My hope was to become airborne before I sank or smashed into the heavy driftwood atop the opposing spit.

The scene was festive and expectant. Most of the viewers were placing bets that were not in my favor. The viewers on the far spit were right in line with my takeoff and they were pretty sure I would be underwater before I got to their log bleachers.

I maintained a facade of confidence as I walked to the plane carrying my new propeller and attached it to the engine's crankshaft. In reality, of course, I was frightened, although I felt that the combination of distance, temperature, and a slight headwind was favorable. I was also equipped with a puffy life jacket should my optimism be unwarranted. I wouldn't wear it but keep it on my lap to cushion my head and chest against any potential impact.

There was no lack of helpers to push the plane back as far into the tree line as it would go. The first hundred feet of takeoff roll were relatively compacted with a slight covering of sand grass. Then there was 200 feet of soft dry sand to the high water mark. The tide was out, so I had another hundred feet of descending compacted sand to the water where, with a slight headwind, I hoped to get airborne.

In final preparation, I removed every unnecessary thing from the plane. Although most of the fuel had drained out of the tank while it had been perched on its nose, the floating cork on a wire indicated I had enough fuel to cross to Seattle. I hand-propped the engine to life and told Judy I would meet her back at the house for dinner. I asked several of the onlookers to push on the wing struts to help me get up enough speed to lift the tail wheel from the sand. I hopped in, belted down, but kept the door unlatched in case I had to vacate if I sank in the channel.

I gave the Porterfield full power and released the brakes. With four guys pushing on the wing struts, I quickly lifted the tail wheel free and started accelerating. Then I hit the soft sand atop the spit. All I could do was maintain my speed, maybe twenty mph, but I needed forty to get airborne. Then I was on an incline of tidal-packed sand accelerating rapidly to the water. Just before the water I eased the elevator control back, felt the wings taking the weight of the plane, and, according to viewers, the main wheels brushed the water and left a slight wake and prop wash spray across the channel. Ahead I could see the log-covered spit and the people who had been betting on my immersion running for cover. I could feel the wings coming alive with lift, but I feared raising the nose and hooking the tail wheel in the water. So I held the plane down until the last moment. Then I applied back pressure on the elevators and soared over the spit while the spectators pulled themselves from behind their logs. I continued my climb and had an uneventful flight across the sound to Seattle and dinner with my family.

STEVEN'S PASS

On a Saturday morning in late May, 1962, I was enjoying a splendid flight in and out of a tight canyon with a waterfall at its terminal end. I was sitting in the back seat of my antique Porterfield while my friend Milt did most of the flying from the front seat of the dual-control plane.

Like me, Milt was a marine insurance underwriter in Seattle. We were stoned and focusing on the brilliant colors in front of us as we repeatedly flew toward a cascade of sunlit water, surrounded on two sides by emerald green fir trees, and topped by a blinding white band of snow with a dark cerulean blue sky above.

After the third flyby I suggested we continue over Steven's Pass, which began only a couple of miles up the Skykomish River Valley. There the road turned and climbed five miles into the Cascade Mountains to cross the 4,000-foot pass.

Milt turned the plane up the valley and I, for reasons I blame on being high, continued reading an article in a magazine I had started before we encountered the waterfall.

Sitting in the back seat of the Porterfield gave me a view ahead that was not unlike peering through the wrong end of a telescope. When I finally looked up over Milt's head and shoulders I saw a solid wall of greenery. Then I saw a road rising from the bottom to the top of the windshield—it was the one to the pass, now only two miles ahead.

Absorbed in my magazine, I hadn't noticed that Milt had left the broad Skykomish Valley for a much tighter climb. The closer the road got to the pass the tighter the sides of the steep valley became until an image of the saddle, which will forever be preserved in my memory, appeared ahead, 500 or 600 feet above us. I instantly recognized that we were going to make headlines for our imminent encounter with Steven's Pass. It was too late to turn away, so our only option was to keep the plane flying until it contacted the two-lane road.

After notifying Milt in my pilot-in-command voice that I was taking the controls, I trimmed the nose up to what is called best rate of climb, or just above stall speed. Even with the nose angled up I couldn't see the top of the pass, but I could see where the road disappeared as it started over the crest.

The road was just off to the left, hugging the mountain-side, so I could keep an eye on uphill traffic. Fortunately, there was very little in either direction, but I knew that anybody driving faster than fifty mph could overtake us from behind. The Porterfield was small enough to take up only one lane but I didn't want to compound our problems when it came time for a landing. The downhill traffic would, I hoped, be able to avoid us altogether. Even with the view closing in on him, Milt was strangely unresponsive. There was little to do but keep the plane flying until we hit the road.

The first indication that the summit wasn't the road crest-ing was the sight of multiple hydroelectric power lines sag-ging down across the actual top of the mountain. My next view, from less than twenty feet above the road, was a concrete divider between the two lanes but there was thankfully no traf-fic in either lane. That gave me the idea to just keep rolling until I was on the downhill side of the pass and fly off under the power lines.

A rest area on the left side of the pass provided the next threat—a semi-truck was coming out of it to enter the west-bound downhill lane. When he saw me at eye level he swung his rig away and disappeared in a cloud of gravel dust. By then I was past him and still in the air. Would that I could say I land-ed on the top of Steven's Pass, but no, I flew across it without contact, safely under the power lines and smoothly down the other side. Neither Milt nor I expressed any real emotion about our survival. My body and mind expressed their relief by an involuntary, uncontrolled spastic jerking of my left leg, which lasted until we were clear of the mountains.

I never learned Milt's thoughts about the crossing. After we safely landed back in Seattle, we never talked again.

TSUNAMI

On Easter weekend, 1964, I headed to Mexico with two Taos friends, Rachel and Malcolm Brown, and my true love at the time, Helen. We flew down in my Cessna 182 on Thursday, the day before Good Friday, and crossed the Sea of Cortez to Mulegé, in Baja, California. The one hotel was packed with pilots and fishing buffs who had flown in from Los Angeles; there were no rooms to be had in Mulegé that night. As we had arrived in the late afternoon and had no option to continue further down the coast before dark, we sat in the bar, determined to work out accommodations for the night.

Helen was a tall, good-looking Pan Am stewardess who caught the eye of the owner of the hotel. He soon joined us at the bar with a tray of complimentary snacks and margaritas. This gesture was repeated several times, and as he continued to play the role of genial host, Helen became more and more seductive. I didn't hear their conversations but I imagine she intimated to him that although she was traveling with us, she felt no attachment and found him interesting and attractive. There was an unspoken promise of delights awaiting him if he would just find some modest lodging for the rest of us.

By dinnertime, we had graciously accepted the owner's offer of his own apartment in the hotel and dinner in the dining room as well. As the evening progressed, so did the nascent affair between Helen and the owner. His consumption of alcohol increased as well. After dinner, we returned to the bar for drinks. By then, Helen had acquired a key to the owner's suite and had assured us that our host and her lover-to-be would be trashed long before he tried to collect his due. By midnight, we were all asleep in the owner's quarters, and he was probably propped up in a closet somewhere.

The next morning, we had a leisurely breakfast but could not find our host to thank him for his hospitality and generosity. We flew on down to Cabo, and then went back across to the mainland.

On the return flight across the Sea of Cortez, Malcolm began to experience the acute intestinal distress so commonly acquired in Mexico. By the time the coastline came into view, we were all on the edge of our seats with trepidation. I hate flying over an endless expanse of water but when a seatmate is about ready to vent in a plane's tight confines, you can imagine the urgency I felt to land. When we reached the coast, I put down on an open beach, and even before we stopped rolling on the sand, Malcolm was out the door, waddling around behind the airplane.

The Belmar was then the grand old hotel of Mazatlán and it fronts on the little bay just before the old downtown. It had an opulent lobby with ornate woodwork carved around the front desk. It was rumored that some of the upright timbers in the lobby had boa constrictors, live ones, wrapped around them, and in the evening they prowled the interior walls looking for rats.

Helen and I got a room in the back on the second floor, off the courtyard garden. Malcolm and Rachel found other accommodations at the Olas Altas, up the hill from where we were staying. We had eaten dinner and retired early as we were still recovering from the previous evening's bacchanal.

Sometime in the early hours of the morning, through my sleep-fogged brain, I started to hear sirens and horns. I could hear running footsteps on the sidewalk but nothing really got my attention until someone cried out, "*Ya viene, las ollas!*" from the street. I worked on that for a couple of minutes in my half sleep until my brain decoded it as *tidal waves*. I untwined from Helen and screamed, "Tidal wave—run, run!"

Helen woke in a flash; as a stewardess, she was trained for emergencies. In an instant, we were both in our clothes. We grabbed our money and passports and darted out the door and down the outdoor stairs to the garden. The hotel was empty, since everyone else had already fled. When I entered the lobby, Helen screamed, "Wait for me!" as she turned and ran back up to the room. I stood there in desperation, fully expecting a huge wave to rear up from the beach, cross the road and smash into the hotel. Through the large open carriage entrance of the Belmar, I could see an almost-full moon hanging above a placid seascape horizon.

I heard Helen running back down the stairs and into the lobby where I was waiting. I grabbed her and we ran through the front, expecting a giant wave to meet us. I asked her why she had gone back to the room, risking her life and mine? She clutched the current *Time Magazine,* which she hadn't finished reading.

As we ran up the hill, we passed Malcolm and Rachel's appropriately named hotel, the Olas Altas. I ran inside to see if they were still there and, like us, they had missed the evacuation sirens that had been going on for hours. They were still in their room, sound asleep. It was a small two-story hotel and also totally deserted. My call down their hallway got their attention and I kindly passed on the information that they were going to be washed away by a tidal wave at any moment. They popped out of their room dragging clothing behind them and exited the hotel in a state of semi-dress.

The four of us continued up the hill to an old lighthouse that was choked with cars and people. These earlier evacuees had chosen to watch the tidal wave's approach from the safe height of the hill rather than drive inland to yet higher ground. We spent what little remained of the night on someone's porch, drinking tea and staring at the moonlit horizon, looking for a tell-tale ripple. At dawn, a loudspeaker truck came through the deserted streets announcing that the tidal wave had missed Mazatlán. The emergency was over.

That night, there had indeed been a tidal wave that swept down the west coast from an Alaskan earthquake, but the Baja Peninsula deflected it away from Mazatlán. I later heard that a few people had been washed off the beaches on the Pacific coast.

Easter Sunday morning was anticlimactic. The city was dead, as most of the occupants had not yet returned from fleeing inland. The four of us were exhausted but couldn't sleep, so we had breakfast and returned to Taos.

BELIZE

Later in 1964 I had a bizarre airplane accident in British Honduras, now known as Belize. I was the on-site managing partner of a banana plantation ten miles from Belize City. My most recent trips down from Mexico City were spectacular. I passed 18,000-foot volcanoes and wove through cumulus build-ups over the jungle as the hours went by. Mayan ruins and large rivers like the Usumacinta would orient me to the otherwise featureless jungle of the Yucatan Peninsula.

On one trip, I was flying a small single-engine, low-wing Mooney that I'd parked at an old military strip right next to town, since I'd agreed to fly a friend out to Ambergris Cay, a short hop out to the reef. Due to a weak battery, I had to hand-prop the engine to life. This meant getting out of the plane and spinning the propeller while my passenger sat in the plane to keep the brakes locked with her feet. The throttle was set to idle and my instructions were to not touch a thing.

On the first swing of the prop, the engine suddenly erupt-ed to full power. The plane leapt at me. I barely managed to dodge it, but the left wing scooped me up and I slid over it head first and off the trailing edge to the ground. I watched, horrified, as my plane and passenger were quickly approach-ing takeoff speed down the gravel runway. Fortunately, the torque from the propeller veered the plane to the left into a marshy area, where the nose and right landing gear collapsed and the plane slid to a stop in the mud.

The propeller had been broken and there was more serious damage to the airframe and right wing. I had no insurance south of Mexico and my major asset was now a wreck lying in a swamp. The British Honduran government impounded the plane pending an investigation into my quasi-legal status in the country. It was September, extremely hot and humid, and I became very depressed.

The damage turned out to be greater than it looked. There was a long gash from the bottom of the right wing all the way back to the flap. Only one landing gear was unscathed. Both the nose and right gear needed temporary welding to hold them in place so we could move it from the swamp. I sent the prop to the states for repairs. The accident may have been caused when my passenger got back in the plane to apply the brakes and inadvertently shoved the throttle in while moving across the seats.

Although the plane was impounded by the government and guarded by an elderly Belizean cop with an old rifle, I managed to fuel it by filling the plane's tanks, night by night, with auto gas carried by taxi from town in five-gallon cans. When the repaired prop finally arrived weeks after the accident, I was there to guide it smoothly through customs, out the door, into a taxi, and off to be reunited with my plane. I had already put the few things I owned into the airplane's baggage compartment.

Whenever I came out to the strip to do repair work I always brought a few bottles of beer for the guard. When I arrived with the prop, I came with the usual supply. He had been helpful with some of the crude repairs and that afternoon he helped me bolt the prop back on the engine. With the prop on, I asked him if it would be all right to start the engine to test the propeller. He was sleepy and unconcerned. I walked back to the plane, carefully set the throttle to idle and, because the battery was still dead, hand-propped the engine to life. It magically ignited and sounded fine although the earlier prop strike could have ruined the engine.

It was now late afternoon and my intention was to depart British Honduras for Mexico. I still had to worry about the sorry state of the landing gear, the potential for the engine to come apart in flight, and the old gentleman with his ancient rifle. I had only one brake that worked and the nose wheel wouldn't steer. Nevertheless, I had planned ahead. I had earlier moved the plane under some shade by a tree and it was aligned with the runway. I hoped that by the time I needed to steer, I'd have enough speed to be able to use the rudder.

The old guy was still sitting in the shade with his rifle. The engine had been running for a couple of minutes and I had cycled the prop. It all seemed to work so I gently shoved the throttle to full power, released the one working brake and bumped along the grass to the gravel strip then tore off down the runway. I held my breath and prayed that if I got the plane off the ground I would never, ever leave home again.

The airplane staggered into the air. There was so much drag from the wing and gear repairs that I could barely make it over hundred miles per hour. But I was in the air.

The nearest Mexican airport was Chetumal, just up the coast, but I didn't want to land there as it was too close to the border. As bad as communication was out of British Honduras, I was afraid I might get stopped. I hadn't turned in my legal papers because I'd never checked out, but once I was back inside Mexico, my plane would be insured if the landing gear collapsed or if we just fell out of the sky in pieces.

I set a course for Villahermosa, 400 miles west across the jungle, at a hundred mph. Hours later I landed, after dark. It was a world-class soft landing and the gear held up. The next day I added enough fuel to get to Mexico City and continued my slow, but happy, journey. In Mexico City, the landing gear was repaired and the wing was patched. I filed my insurance claim with some made-up story about a forced landing, but I had to get the airplane to the states for further repairs.

Two friends in Mexico City, Mark and Susan, wanted to go north so early one morning we found ourselves at the end of one of the two long runways at the airport, taking off toward Lake Texcoco. At the far end of the runway were the ubiquitous slums stretching along the lake. The other direction took off right over the heart of Mexico City.

Off we lumbered down the 14,000-foot runway. At sixty mph I rotated the nose but nothing happened, except the airplane danced lightly on its main wheels. It wouldn't fly. At eighty mph it barely raised off the ground. The plane wouldn't climb out of ground effect without collapsing back onto the runway. On we roared. I flashed over the numbers at the far end of the runway and miraculously over the slums of Texcoco. I was trying hard to raise the gear without hitting laundry lines or shanties. I desperately needed to reduce drag so I could climb higher.

I was finally able to muscle the gear up and I inched my way above the rooflines. There was still no power in that part of the slums so I didn't have to worry about electrical lines. Soon I was over the lake and away from any buildings. The plane slowly hauled itself up until we had enough altitude to relax and enjoy the calm early morning flight to Brownsville. It flew perfectly and a couple hours later we were clearing customs.

The wing patches had attracted the attention of a mechanic and before we could leave, the FAA came by for an inspection and grounded the plane pending further inspection of the airframe. I left it there and continued my travels. Three days later the insurance company called to inform me that my airplane was considered a total loss because of extensive damage to the tail, landing gear, and the wing. The tail on the Mooney pivoted on a couple of hinged joints for trim. It turned out that several of those joints had been bent or broken during the accident, and the entire tail section was being held to the fuselage solely by the control rods to the elevator and rudder. Any significant turbulence in the 1,300-mile flight from Belize could have knocked the entire tail from the fuselage and turned the plane into a lawn dart.

I returned to Taos. The banana operation failed that winter. I decided to seek my fortune with something safe, such as becoming a ski instructor and flying people around in small planes.

INTO A TREE

In 1965, I bought and sold small private airplanes to supplement whatever income I could eke out of my struggling air taxi business in Taos. I flew a variety of aircraft as test flights. One extremely cold January morning, I took a single-engine Bonanza out from 7 Bar, a small satellite airport beside the Rio Grande River in Albuquerque. The plane had just been refurbished with a new paint job and interior.

Before takeoff, I did a thorough check of the engine and flight controls. Everything worked. I took off and climbed 300 feet and turned right to depart the traffic pattern when the engine quit. I quickly reversed the turn to the left and flew back toward an irrigated pasture along the river. The landing gear was retracting when the engine had stopped, so I immediately put it back down and changed fuel tanks.

I had taken off on a full left tank so I switched to the full right one. When I switched, the engine roared to life for a few seconds, then died again. I was still at a climb angle so I shoved the nose down. As it dropped, my field of vision was filled with a large cottonwood. My glide was taking me right through the top of the tree and I had no time to avoid it. The plane was jarred but stayed upright as I crashed through the branches and the main landing gear took the full impact.

The landing was smooth, but now I was rolling at an angle across shallow irrigation ditches. I hit the brakes and the plane skidded toward a fence and a much larger ditch. I released the right brake and went into a tight arc to a stop beside the fence. I stepped out of the plane, grateful to be alive and uninjured. Less than a couple of minutes had passed from takeoff to landing.

Except for scratches from the tree branches under the wings, belly, and the leading edge of both wings, the plane was intact. I walked back down my landing track. I had rolled across three ditches, any one of which could have knocked out the plane's nose gear if I'd been going any slower. The main landing gear had knocked the bigger branches off the old cottonwood. If it hadn't been so cold, the branches wouldn't have snapped so easily and I would have been derailed from my glide and crashed.

Meanwhile, the 7 Bar staff had seen my sudden descent and they were out in trucks trying to find me. I walked back to the terminal in a state of disbelief. Twenty minutes later the plane was towed back to the airport. Apparently, the upholsterer had re-installed the four-position fuel tank switch ninety degrees off.

Although the switch indicated I had a full left tank at takeoff, it was on the almost-empty auxiliary tank. When the engine stopped, I had switched to the full right tank and passed through the full left tank to the shut-off position. The electric fuel pump was on as the switch passed through the full left tank, so fuel went into the engine which caused it to run for those few seconds. That little burst of power gave me just enough altitude to pass through the top of the tree instead of into its four-foot thick trunk, with a very different outcome.

I was in such a state of relief at surviving that I forgave the incompetent upholsterer and allowed the owner of 7 Bar to take me out for lunch.

DENVER DEPARTURE

The leaves on the cottonwood trees were just starting to cover their limbs on 32nd Street in Denver. It was early morning, May 5th, 1965, and I could already tell it would be a hot and humid day.

My plane wouldn't start because of a weak battery and, as it was already loaded, I asked the fuel guys who had just topped off the tanks to give me a boost since we had 1,800 miles to go for dinner that evening in New York City. Hitching a ride were two friends, Larry and Fred from Taos, who were heading for Europe. Sitting beside me was Hueri, my brand-new girlfriend from Montana, who was supposed to be visiting her mother in Albuquerque for the weekend, not en route with me to the Big Apple.

We were at the end of runway 26R at Denver Airport, waiting for tower clearance to start rolling. I was flying my single engine Bonanza, which I knew was loaded to performance limits. It was still cool at that hour and I knew I would be safely airborne and into even cooler air after climbing to cruising altitude. As I had instructed the back seaters to put as much luggage on their laps as they could so the tail wouldn't drag during takeoff, they were behind a wall of gear, including four one-gallon jugs of Mexican rum, the kind wrapped in wicker. Once in flight, with the landing gear and flaps up, they could move the stuff behind their seats to the luggage area.

Cleared for takeoff, we started rolling down the runway.

At sixty mph, I lifted the nose slightly and at seventy the plane waddled into the air. I reached across to the panel with my right hand, fingered the safety on the landing gear switch to bring the wheels up. We were almost at the threshold of the western end of the runway heading toward downtown Denver and not even hundred feet above the ground. The switch clicked into the up position, and I heard the gear motor running beneath my seat. With the gear up, I would accelerate and increase my rate of climb.

Then the gear motor stopped. The propeller, which had been turning at 2000 rpm, surged to 2700 rpm, way beyond its limits. The original plastic/wood propeller that came with the plane sixteen years before was now turning so fast it was bound to throw one of its blades. If it went into asymmetrical rotation, it would cause the engine to tear loose from the plane. The sudden loss of 400 pounds from the nose would cause the plane to pitch up from all the weight at the wrong end of the fuselage and initiate a fatal stall. And willy-nilly, aft-loaded, we would fall to the ground, with an ignominious, painful, most-likely fatal end to our flight.

I had lost all electrical power. Compounding this, which always happens when something goes wrong in the air, the landing gear doors were hanging open with the wheels only partially retracted, creating more drag. The electric propeller controls had failed. I couldn't control the excessive rpm except by reducing power, which would cause us to descend. *Should I hang on to full power and risk losing a propeller blade? Or should I bring the power back and descend through the electrical bus cables on 32nd Street into Denver's heavy morning traffic with the resulting crash and fuel explosion engulfing innocent vehicles?* I weighed the options.

By now I'd already descended below the tops of the cottonwoods lining 32nd Street. There ahead was the Platte River and downtown. I hastily gave my backseat passengers instructions about turning the emergency gear handle to get the wheels up and the gear doors closed. But the gear handle wouldn't turn.

On the plus side, 32nd Street was descending gently into the Platte River Valley. Its slope was just about the same as my rate of descent even when I eased the power back to bring the prop to 2400 rpm. Maybe the blades would stay on long enough for me to find a street where I could put the plane down.

Everywhere I looked there was heavy morning traffic. Until I could clear the cottonwood trees, I could barely stay above the bus wires, which were just twenty feet beneath the plane's belly. Down 32nd Street we staggered, getting closer and closer to the tall buildings of downtown.

I was starting to hold my altitude. Soon I could see over the tree tops toward the northwest. I picked a large intersection and made a gentle turn away from 32nd Street. Now I had a chance at putting down on less-trafficked streets. Anything would do if I could just squeeze between the trees and get to the pavement without stalling or hitting wires. My airspeed was still around sixty mph, barely above stall speed, but the Bonanza was starting to climb. I now had at least fifty feet between the plane's belly and the treetops. Up ahead I could see the right-of-way for the new I-70 Freeway. If I could get there and make another ninety-degree turn to the east, I would put down on the construction site.

I gently banked the plane while trying not to lose any precious altitude. With the turn completed, I was right over a wide section of I-70 construction. But it was filled with large construction vehicles, so there was no chance of putting down there. By then, though, I had the luxury of one hundred feet of altitude, enough to start thinking of continuing east to set up an approach for the same runway we'd just departed from. By then I was coming up north of the airport control tower. Only two more gentle turns and I would be on final for the runway. If only the prop blades would stay on. I further reduced power as I didn't need any more altitude and continued flying just above stall speed.

I could only assume the tower had declared us an emergency. I was hoping they had picked me up visually as I climbed above the treetops and that runway 26R would be open as I turned for final. There were no other options; I would be bellying the old plane in a few seconds. As I came out of the last turn right on top of the numbers of 26R, I exhaled. Several large crash trucks were already waiting on the adjacent taxiway. I pulled the mixture control out to stop the engine, reached across Hueri to unlock the door, and held the nose back. The tail rumbled as it scraped down the runway, the prop blades shattered as they hit the concrete and the fuselage skidded down the center line. The impact was as gentle as a regular landing on wheels.

Even before we had stopped skidding, Hueri was pushed forward by Fred and Larry exiting the plane. A large yellow crash vehicle was rolling right beside us. On top was a guy in a yellow fire suit with a large nozzle pointed directly at us; he was ready to let us have a blast in case of fire. Fortunately, there was none, but smoke was coming into the cabin where friction from the skid had ignited residual oil on the plane's belly. Hueri and I climbed out with a degree of dignity that was sadly lacking in the earlier evacuees. As soon as we were off the wing, the guy on top of the truck gave the belly area a huge squirt that immediately stopped the smoke.

Just behind the crash truck was a van with a TV cameraman standing on its top. He shot the entire landing sequence with the four of us departing the plane. He got a particularly good one of Hueri, which her friends back in Red Lodge easily recognized on the evening news.

I was pretty puffed up. It was good to be alive. One of the crash crew came over to congratulate me on making it back on the ground in one piece. Afterward the FAA functionaries showed up along with news reporters and I was interrogated by the former and interviewed by the latter.

Meanwhile, a winch truck came out and lifted the plane off the ground with its boom. Someone hopped in the cockpit and got the landing gear down and the airplane was towed off the runway. Except for the shattered blades and scuffs down the belly, the Bonanza was undamaged.

A weak battery and faulty circuit breakers were to blame for lost electrical power and the ensuing chain of events. When I had attempted to raise the wheels, the generator wasn't able to handle the load. The master relay had blown, shutting down all electrical power. The gear motor had also bound on the manual gear extension device so it couldn't be turned by the hand crank.

The FAA weighed all the plane's contents and estimated we were 300 pounds overweight. They gave me grief over not being able to crank the gear up or down manually but I guess they finally decided to lay off, in that I had managed to get back on the ground safely without causing harm to anyone. I was instructed to take my commercial flight exam again but no violations were filed.

Cady, a friend, pilot, and aircraft mechanic, flew up from Albuquerque that morning with my twin engine Piper Apache and an extra propeller. He quickly attached it and flew back to Albuquerque in the Bonanza that afternoon. The rest of us had a celebratory dinner, basking in the TV coverage of our emergency landing. The next day we flew on to New York City in the twin.

RAFTING STORIES

THE BOX

In the late spring of 1965, I bought a small rubber surplus raft to float a seventeen-mile section of the Rio Grande known as The Box. Two friends, fellow employees from Taos Ski Valley, joined me in the adventure. We had no prior experience in river rafting and no knowledge of what to expect from the river as it flowed through 600-foot vertical canyon walls.

The old John Dunn Bridge at Arroyo Hondo marked the beginning of the raftable portion of The Box and was where we planned to launch. At the lower end of the Box was Taos Junction Bridge and a precipitous road that led up out of the gorge to town. Between the two bridges there was no access to or from the river except for a couple of rough trails that fishermen, mountain goats, and rattlesnakes used.

On the way to the launching point, we stopped at a gas station to inflate our raft. Either it was defective or we were careless, because it blew apart even before we left the air pump. This ended our first attempt at rafting.

The next weekend, we arrived with a new raft at the bridge where it was successfully inflated. We were equipped with paddles, old kapok life jackets, a six-pack of beer, and great enthusiasm for adventure. Starting 150 miles north of us, from snowmelt off the Continental Divide, the Rio Grande was running full and cold. Small mountain streams and tributaries added to the river as it flowed south. The Rio Hondo, coming in at the John Dunn Bridge, was contributing a significant quantity of water from the winter's snowpack above 10,000 feet in the Sangre de Cristos. In the words of James Joyce, the water was "scrotum-tightening" cold. But it was a warm and sunny day, and as we were soon to learn, fear trumps frigid water.

Being the self-appointed captain, I sat in back while my crew of two sat forward on either side of the air tubes. The raft was nothing more than a slightly elongated inner tube with a flimsy rubberized sheet for a floor. We handled the first half of The Box without memorable incident, but shortly after entering a rough stretch, we found ourselves without a floor. This happened somewhere right before what is known as Rock Garden, in a quarter mile of serious whitewater.

My friends now straddled the forward tubes as we tumbled through the first set of heavy rapids. I remember doing a recovery from a backward exit of one set only to find a rock, like the prow of a speedboat, coming at us from only ten feet away. "It's a ripper!" I yelled, as our bow impacted straight on the rock's upstream point. The stern buckled from the impact and threw me over my crew, both of whom had lost their paddles. I landed in the river alongside one of the paddles and managed to grab it, still holding mine in my other hand. I somehow got to the east bank below the boat.

The raft was impaled on the rock like a donut with my two partners still perched on top of the inflated tubes. We were screaming and laughing with excitement. I walked back up to them, threw them the two paddles, and jumped into the river to swim to the raft. Together, we yanked our slightly elongated inner tube off the rock and continued our descent, unscathed, to the confluence with the Rio Pueblo and Taos Junction Bridge.

MAROON CREEK

Four years later, I decided to resume river running with a small inflatable kayak. By that time, in 1970, I was flying commercially in and out of Aspen. I thought I would start an adventurous trip from Maroon Creek to the Roaring Fork River to the Colorado River and through the Grand Canyon.

My Taos friend Tony and I drove up Maroon Creek on a lovely sunny June morning to look for a suitable place to put in. The current was ripping along as fast as we could run. We found an eddy I thought would give me a chance to get positioned in the boat before getting out into the current. I pumped up the kayak and placed it in the water, then I carefully climbed in with my double-bladed paddle. The floor of the tiny boat was nothing more than an air mattress.

I pushed out into the flow. As the bow poked into the stream it was grabbed and twisted under water. The rest of the kayak followed. Soon it was completely submerged, and I was being swept down the creek at tremendous speed. Moments later, my left knee hit a rock with such impact that I still have a crease on my patella. If I hadn't been so scared, I would have collapsed in pain to the bottom of the craft. But I remained in the paddling position, trying to survive.

The current swept me around a sharp bend in the creek to confront a log straddling the stream. Short, spiky branches stuck off from it at menacing angles. There was no way to avoid the log, so I threw myself flat on the bottom of my submerged boat. Fortunately, I was wearing an old life jacket, and it took the full impact of the log's spikes. The jacket was ripped to pieces as I passed under, but one especially sharp spike hooked a shoulder strap and pulled me from my rubber submarine.

What had seemed like a good idea moments earlier now created another life-threatening dilemma. I had wrapped the boat's bowline around my wrist in a loose slipknot so it would be handy when needed. The spike had pulled me free but now the water-filled boat, probably weighing 400 pounds and lurching along at twelve miles an hour, gave me a tremendous yank on my left arm and shoulder. That broke off the spike. The line attached from the bow to my left wrist was now towing me along horizontally. Compounding all this, I was being bounced across the rocks in the stream. For a moment, the boat slowed in an eddy. I jumped to my feet to get back into it to at least undo the slipknot from my wrist. But before I could do either, the kayak took off again.

Tony had seen what was happening from the moment I had put in. He ran across to the downstream side of the turn just in time to catch the boat as it floated by. He leapt off the bank and into the water beside me, where he held the kayak still long enough for me to undo the line. The two of us managed to hold the boat against the current and swing it to shore. I wouldn't have survived without Tony's help.

The boat was saved but the paddle and life jacket were lost. I was bruised from head to toe and felt sick from the pain in my knee. I just wanted to get home to Taos. I was sure my knee was broken and wanted to see my local doctor and be at home when I received his diagnosis. We drove to the Aspen Airport and loaded the equipment into my plane. With increasing decrepitude, I crawled into the seat for the flight home.

During the next hour, I stiffened to complete immobility. Tony had to drag me from the pilot seat and load me into the passenger seat of my car. He drove me to the clinic, where my compassionate friend Dr. Cetrulo gleefully told me that I was a medical first. I had no broken bones but would have a permanent scar on my kneecap. He told me to take an aspirin and go home and to bed.

THE UPPER BOX

The next year, in the spring of 1971, I joined a group of beginning rafters from Aspen who had decided to buy some real rafts and float the Grand Canyon. I ordered my own state-of-the-art thirteen-footer with glued-on rubber oarlocks and two tiny jointed oars.

As I had already paddled the Lower Box of the Rio Grande a couple of years earlier, I decided I wouldn't waste my new equipment and expertise on that section. Instead, I would do the Upper Box, which was, back then, a truly undone section of the river.

I contacted two friends, Nate and Reynolds, and told them we would spend the afternoon rafting a pretty canyon on a warm river with cold beer. They had a critical softball game to play that evening back in Taos. I assured them we would be back in town in time for the game. At the last minute, I decided to bring along my twelve-year-old son, Michael.

My girlfriend, Linda, drove us north to the Black Bridge on the Colorado border where the Rio Grande begins to enter a canyon. On the drive up, we left another car on the canyon rim at the mid-point of the float. In case we were running late, I could let the ball players out early and they, in turn, would notify Linda as to when Michael and I would arrive at the John Dunn Bridge for pickup.

We drove another twenty miles across a barren sage-brush-covered mesa where Linda dropped us off and we set about inflating the raft and getting it onto the river for its maiden voyage. I knew then that we weren't going to be back for the baseball game; the river's current in this section was no more than a leisurely walking pace.

The only tip I had received about running the upper portion of The Box was that we shouldn't float past a solitary rock in mid-river with a sign painted on it saying, *Sheep Crossing*. We had, I thought, put the car at the top of the Sheep Crossing Trail.

We each had life jackets of some sort and Nate and Reynolds even brought along old football helmets. I had a cooler full of beer plus some picnic items and an old ratty sleeping bag for an emergency. We put in and started a gentle afternoon float through the deepening canyon. Within a couple of miles, we were locked into the gorge. We were less than a hundred feet down in the canyon but the walls blocked out all sight of the mountains and any reference point we might have had for discerning distance.

All afternoon, we floated through the canyon. In the early evening, Reynolds ran up a faint trail to the rim to see where we were. When he came back, he had no information other than that the mountains down by Questa were too far away to get to before dark. We were now committed to an overnight in the gorge. Ugly comments were made about my planning and provisioning skills.

At dark, we came to where the Rio Costilla flows into the Rio Grande. There was a sandbar there, so we set up camp for the night and we all slept. There was no breakfast, so we simply got up and resumed floating. The current became marginally swifter. We passed through some riffles, which became gradually more significant as the morning unfolded. At some point, we started seeing some of the mountaintops on the east side of the gorge, indicating that we were getting closer to the mythical Sheep Crossing rock.

Because of the increasing current, we could hear the river hissing against its rocky banks, but by midday there was still no whitewater.

The gorge was now 500 feet deep and we came around a bend to find the rock in the river with *Sheep Crossing* painted on its upstream side. Reynolds again got out and ran up to the rim on a barely detectable path. When he came back, he reported that we were still miles north of where we had parked the car, and he couldn't see any serious whitewater ahead. We decided to float on rather than climb out there and walk across the interminable sagebrush mesa carrying the raft to where the car was parked.

A half mile on, we came to a straight stretch of the river. At the far end, I could hear the rumble of heavy water as the river dropped out of sight, replaced by mist and spray. So that was why they had painted a sign on the mid-river boulder. A warning!

There weren't many options at that point; we could evacuate the river and boulder-hop back to Sheep Crossing, leaving our equipment behind, or we could continue floating downstream. We decided to continue. After all, how bad could it get? The whitewater we had seen from the rim where we left the car wasn't all that bad, and I now had equipment suitable for the Grand Canyon. I was rowing a real river raft.

We stopped just above the angle change of the river to scout and tie down what gear we had. From where I stood, the river turned from a relatively friendly current into a maelstrom. It was spring, and the river was running at full flood. At the time, it looked like an exciting ride. We loaded up and shoved off into the current. Nate and Reynolds were sitting side-by-side on the forward cross tube. They put on their helmets. I was sitting on the back cross tube in the rowing position. The cooler was behind me on the floor, wedged between the cross tube and the rear of the boat. Michael was sitting on the cooler and holding onto my life jacket.

We passed into the wild rapids and were immediately swamped. This saved our lives because with the added weight, the boat became relatively stable and didn't flip. Rowing became a joke. Every time I pulled hard on the little oars they would pop out of the rubber oarlocks. Finally, they both broke at their joints and we were left at the mercy of the river. I was terrified, but I still had the paddle half to one of the oars so I used it to try to keep the bow pointed downstream. The current was too fast to make the shore. If we were swept out of the boat, we would be killed. If we flipped, we would be killed.

My hope was that luck would sweep us through, right side up, and that nobody would get ejected. Michael, still sitting behind me, transferred his grasp from my life jacket to a stranglehold around my neck. I had no further control of the boat. Down we plunged. The current was foaming off both boulder-lined sides of the river. There was a rooster tail of spray where the two off-bank currents collided and, in the center of the river, rocks were visible through the raging water. Whenever we hit them, the boat spun violently off sideways or backward. There was seemingly no end to the rapid.

A quarter mile from where we had entered the maelstrom, we fell over a small waterfall between two large boulders. The boat was pointed downstream with both Nate and Reynolds in front, still seeming as though they were enjoying themselves. They were oblivious to the dangerous straits we were in. Then we came up on a large boulder sitting just off the west bank. Below the boulder was an eddy, which was our chance to escape. I screamed at the two in front.

Reynolds, who was sitting on the right side of the cross tube, turned and looked at me. The expression on my face must have told him the whole story. I pointed at the boulder and as we came abreast he jumped, bow line in hand, for the rock. He had just enough time to brace himself for the impact of the surging raft. But the weight of the raft and the current dragged him over the top of the boulder. At the same time, his resistance helped slow the boat down. It swung like a pendulum into the eddy and for a moment, we were out of the current.

When I felt the boat slow down, I turned to Michael and told him to jump and swim for shore. We both plunged into the river below the boulder, where an eddy kept us from the current. In two or three strokes, we could grab some rocks on the bank and pull ourselves up out of the water. Reynolds had been dragged off the rock but was still in the eddy, trying to make it to shore. He still held the bowline, which he threw to me. I looped it over a rock. Nate was still in the raft, somehow still unaware of the whole deadly drama. Once he saw us straining to hold the raft by the rope, he finally got the message and daintily stepped ashore.

Reynolds was on shore by now, and we lowered the boat around a couple more boulders until it finally found its own eddy. With the boat secured to rocks, we crept up onto warm boulders above the river to dry out. Below us, the river raged on. Some distance downstream, I could see calm water. But for luck, we would have ended there, drowned or dead from multiple injuries.

We spent the next hour slowly lining the boat through rough water until, suddenly, the river became a placid pond. How was that previous brute energy manacled so quickly? From the west bank, I could see a sketchy trail coming down from the east rim. We still had to cross to the east bank of the now-benign river. I feared the River Gods would try to claim us again. I still had the half paddle and I used it to get us across the seventy feet of calm water. We packed up the gear and lugged everything up 500 vertical feet to the car. It was the end of our second day on the river and we were very happy to be alive.

A FLIP

Many trips later through The Box, my passengers and I were eddied out in mid-Rock Garden, smoking dope and enjoying the sun. By then, in 1974, I had run other western rivers and had excellent equipment. Commercial rafting had begun on The Box and I noted one of the sixteen-footers entering Rock Garden, a quarter mile upstream. That raft flipped in the first hole and four of its occupants were floating down the rapids in their orange life jackets like a string of brightly colored dots.

We had just bailed my fourteen-footer so we were light and maneuverable. I waited for the first floater to come abreast and then pulled out into the current to try and pluck her from the river. Her head cradled by her orange life jacket, she was unconscious. My timing was off and she was swept out of reach. Right behind her was another person in the same state. My two forward passengers grabbed him and hauled him over the side, where he lay, crumpled and unconscious, on the bottom of our raft. We were back in heavy whitewater and further attention to rescue would have to wait until we were beyond that section of the river.

The guy we hauled aboard started spluttering and he was soon fully aware, inquiring as to where his wife was. She had been in the full current, and without any of the wind resistance that we faced, floated much faster than we did. One of my passengers said that he thought he had seen her in an eddy off the east bank; hopefully she was alive and would be picked up later. A half hour later we were at the Junction Bridge. We left the worried husband waiting for the survivors to arrive while we trucked back to Taos and our post-trip margaritas. We never did find out what happened to her.

FIRE ON THE WATER

Through the '70s, commercial rafting continued to increase on The Box. Good snowpack runoff always provided plenty of water, sometimes well into July. By Memorial Day weekend, The Box would be flowing as high as 6,000 cubic feet per second. Ernie Blake, owner of Taos Ski Valley, would sometimes open the bottom lift for a few of us to ski Al's Run in the morning. We would then run The Box in the afternoon. During a couple of good snow years, water on the Rio made it into August with at least 1,000 cfs water. Below that, the river became too boulder-choked for anything but kayaks.

In early June 1979, I was parked at Power Line Falls, named for the electric cables that cross the gorge 600 feet above. We were scouting a route through a dam of large boulders and ingesting marijuana (and probably a little cocaine) for the heavy whitewater that began a quarter mile below and lasted until the Junction Bridge.

We pushed off, made our way through the falls and floated in the last of the easy water to a slight left turn, the beginning of Rock Garden. The river was running at an ideal 2,000 cfs and twenty mph spring winds were blowing upstream. After the turn, it would be a wild and wet ride to the bridge. I was sitting in the rowing frame with three friends, high but relaxed and enjoying a rush of adrenalin while waiting for the plunge. No one was talking and the current was ponding before tipping over into the maelstrom.

Without warning, we were surrounded by flickering blue flames on top of the water. No one spoke and we continued floating calmly through the fire. *Was I having a (dope-induced) religious experience?* I wondered. But then we were into the tumultuous rapids.

An hour later, we arrived at the bridge. A fire truck and an ambulance were parked nearby. Someone called out, "Is anyone alive?" I was stunned. What was he talking about? The preceding hour of rafting excitement had washed away any memory of the incongruous phenomenon we had passed through. I responded that I hadn't seen anyone, alive or otherwise. We pulled ashore below the bridge and waded into a crowd of would-be rescuers.

We were told that a military fighter had flown into the power lines over our heads while we were down below. Two single-seat fighters had been flying south at rim level, one behind the other. The first jet went into the lines, lost most of a wing and spun into the river just below us. The pilot ejected but his chute had no time to deploy. My "religious experience" was floating over the top of the crashed jet and the blue flames were from burning jet fuel. Later that afternoon, I flew my plane down the gorge to inspect the impact area and I was amazed to see the amount of aircraft aluminum clearly visible on the boulders of the west bank of the gorge. We had been too mesmerized by the flaming river to notice anything else.

TWIN ENGINE PLANES

The first twin-engine airplane I owned was a Piper Apache, vintage late fifties, powered by two 150 hp Lycoming engines that gave me a sense of invincibility. By January 1965, I had already logged several hundred hours of single-engine flight time, so after some instruction in preparation for my multi-engine-check ride, I hopped in the Apache to fly to a nearby airport to pick up the FAA examiner.

I taxied out to the end of the runway, and just as I shoved the two throttles to full power, I noted with appreciation that my instructor was waving to me from a single-engine plane beside me. I deduced that it was his "bon voyage" gesture. Off I went down the runway when I noticed him flying by on my left side still waving. I was still on the ground but just about rotation speed. What a fellow! But then it was time to rotate. I pulled back on the yoke to begin lifting off the runway but nothing happened. The nose didn't rise, the plane didn't fly. Instead the end of the runway was getting closer at ninety mph. I tried rotating again; the yoke pulled back but nothing happened. Then it hit me. The instructor wasn't waving, he was pointing, but at what? Rather than continue my internal dialogue, I killed the power and slammed on the brakes just in time to skid to a stop several hundred feet beyond the end of the runway. Neither the plane nor I were physically damaged.

It turned out that while I had left the plane for a few moments to phone the examiner I was on my way to meet, the line boy had put gust locks on my elevator/rudder controls because of the windy ramp conditions. If the nose had been trimmed up any more the plane might have taken off and I would have been in the air without rudder or elevator controls. In theory, I might have gotten it back on the ground if I'd had enough time to think things through. Undaunted, I continued for the test and hours later I was a legal twin pilot.

Shortly afterward, in mid-January, I headed to New York on business. I was giving some friends a ride back whose payment for the flight was to provide me with an elegant dinner. We took off in the late afternoon. The weather was forecast to be perfect for the entire flight and I was planning on arriving in NYC at dawn. We refueled in Wichita just after dark. From Wichita, I engaged the autopilot and at a cruising altitude of 7,500 feet, locked to an easterly heading and turned on the interior cabin lights.

Dinner was broken out with wine, linen, and relaxing evening music from the ADF receiver. Two hour later, my attention turned to determining our cross-country status. I turned off the interior light and after my eyes recovered, I examined the pattern of city lights ahead of us. Everything was where it should be. We droned along for the next three hours, watching the lights of Indianapolis and Columbus come over the horizon and pass under the nose in predictable procession. We refueled in Pittsburgh, napped in the pilots' lounge for a couple hours, and finished the two-hour hop to NYC with a lovely sunrise from over the Atlantic Ocean.

While staying in New York, I made a quick trip to the Bahamas with other friends, but on the way back we encountered increasingly marginal weather. There was little traffic so I just flew up the coast at 1500 feet and kept track of our route again by the cities we flew over. The weather continued deteriorating, and by the time we were off the Maryland and Jersey shores we were down to 500 feet to keep from getting into the clouds. We needed the lights to give definition to the coastline.

Atlantic City went by and shortly I could see the glow of New York through light snow showers. It was three in the morning with no air traffic, so I flew by the Statue of Liberty to the Battery and up the Hudson River to the George Washington Bridge. The navigation lights on top of the bridge towers were just a glow in the clouds, but it was clear and unrestricted between the clouds and the ground. If it had been daylight it would have looked unflyable, but at night and in my little twin I felt secure.

Just before the bridge I swung to the east, picked up the airport beacon for White Plains Airport, and lined up for final approach. With the flaps and gear down, I did a quick scan of the engine instruments and was startled to note that the left engine had lost oil pressure but the engine temperature was still good and it sounded fine. When I felt confident I had the runway made, with or without power, I shut down the left engine and feathered the propeller to horizontal for an uneventful landing. Later that morning I found that an external oil line had ruptured and had pumped all the oil out of the engine somewhere after the turn at the George Washington Bridge, during the last five minutes of an eight-hour trip.

On the return to Taos three days later, I ended up at the wrong end of an approaching cold front in the Ohio River Valley area. I got a hurried weather briefing in Columbus where I had stopped to refuel. I was told that If I didn't get out of the Ohio River Basin area we would be sitting for days waiting for the weather to clear out. But I was now a twin pilot! I loaded up my passengers and took off. The weather quickly deteriorated as we headed west. I wasn't yet instrument rated, but I had a great autopilot and what I didn't know didn't bother me.

I quickly became flooded with self-doubt. I was flying on solid instruments with ice building on the airframe and windshield. It was so bad that if I had been in a car I would have parked on the shoulder of the road, if I could have found it. The next best thing was to find the nearest airport and land. Burlington, Iowa, on the west bank of the Mississippi River, was the nearest haven. The VOR (Very High-Frequency Omnidirectional Range) station emitting an electronic navigational signal, was about eight miles to the east on the other side of the river.

When I got over the VOR, I was down to 300 feet and could barely maintain altitude with the load of ice the plane was carrying. I was in contact with the tower and cleared to land. Nobody else was crowding my airspace that day. I continued toward the airport with help from the VOR beacon, but other than identifying the Mississippi as I flew over it, I saw nothing. I had passed over the airport shrouded in fog and turned back to the river for another approach. The tower told me, helpfully, that if I headed upriver I would be able to pick up a railway bridge as a landmark. My altitude now was just above the high banks of the river and I was under a layer of fog. Ahead and at my level was the black railway bridge.

The tower said the airport was several miles west of the bridge and on the north side of the tracks. To avoid a head-on with the bridge, I had to climb just enough to clear its girders but not so high as to lose precious sight of the ground. As I cleared the bridge, I swung southwest, paralleling the tracks, and swept over the western bank of the river. I lowered the landing gear, knowing that it was irreversibly downhill until I hit the runway, or at least open pasture. The tower told me to look for blinking runway lights in the deep snow ahead and added, "Good luck." I saw the lights and without them I would never have seen the runway buried in snow. Seconds later I thumped down, a very relieved, new Twin pilot.

I kept the Apache for a couple of years and used it to receive my instrument rating. The plane finally came to rest in an arroyo just north of Albuquerque one summer when a flight instructor had shut down one engine for practice. He couldn't get it started again and panicked. He declared an emergency, and tried to make a landing at Coronado Airport. He touched down mid-runway and instead of applying brakes and blowing out the tires, he elected to make another pass. He almost made it; he cleared the power lines and freeway on the north end of the runway before doing his second landing. This time he landed on open sagebrush which sloped to the irrigated pastures of the Rio Grande Valley. It was a good landing, and if he had been in the left seat where the brakes were, all would have ended well. The student, however, was not listening to his screaming order to apply the brakes. The student was hiding his head between his legs and bracing his feet against the instrument panel. My poor old twin rolled gracefully through the sagebrush until it finally stumbled down an arroyo and ended up on its back. Student and instructor were found at each other's throats, but uninjured.

A couple of years passed and I gravitated to a Baron with twin 260 hp engines. I had accumulated a thousand hours of twin engine time and, with it, some flight wisdom. I had, however, lost whatever common sense I had and become the owner and pilot of a charter aircraft operation that flew through the southern Rocky Mountains, delivering well-heeled skiers to and from ski resorts.

One early morning in August of 1970, having just finished a family holiday in Aspen, I was climbing out of the Aspen Valley toward Taylor Pass with my two sons aboard. At 12,000 feet, the pass is one of the two southern routes through the mountains away from Aspen. It's only about fifteen miles from the airport but 4,000 feet above it. It's a dramatic route with towering 14,000-foot mountains in every direction. I'd flown this departure from Aspen many times, in both singles and twins.

That day the weather was perfect—cool, clear, with no wind for the hour flight to Taos. The Baron climbed up the valley following the road to Ashcroft doing 130 knots. It initially climbed at 1,000 feet per minute which, as I gained altitude, bled down to half that at 12,000 feet. At 11,000 I was flying alongside Ajax Mountain with the pass just beyond, but still tucked out of sight behind a bulge in the ridge. The bulge was the same height as Taylor Pass and marked the entrance to a well-defined gully that climbed steeply from Ashcroft over the saddle. At one time, it was an old wagon road to Gunnison but was now a sporting challenge for jeeps and motorcycles. Once in the slot, it was too narrow to turn out, especially in a twin. A prudent pilot would have been above 13,000 feet, but because of the beautiful morning, my experience, and my rate of climb, I continued flying just below the bulge.

I could see the saddle of the pass a mile ahead, and to my surprise and horror, I was still just below it and entering the narrowing slot. By then I was doing less than 100 mph and rather than make an immediate turn I elected to raise the nose for altitude. I only had to gain 100 feet to clear the saddle so I continued into the slot hoping to trade airspeed for altitude.

Within seconds I could see the trade hadn't worked. I was still below the saddle with no rate of climb and approaching a stall. The left wing was almost in the trees of the tightening gully and the right shoulder of the angling gully was way too close.

Out of options, with only a few seconds before becoming a mountain flying statistic, I flicked the flap switch control down, jammed the elevator control yoke forward, turned the aileron control wheel over, and kicked the right rudder. We instantly felt a full stall. The elevator control yoke bucked back and forth, indicating a loss of control, and as we nosed over we were lofted into our seat belts as we challenged gravity. The nose continued to drop and the plane started to roll to the right, plunging us into the center axis of the gully. My forward vision was filled with trees. Both engines were running at full power, but I had no control as the plane continued to dive in a complete stall. I was completely useless as a pilot, only awaiting impact.

Then feeling came back to the controls and I started easing back on the elevator. By then the flaps were fully extended and in those five or ten seconds the plane had miraculously fallen right down the axis of the gully. From being weightless moments before we were once again in the loving grip of gravity. I gently added back pressure on the elevator and at over 200 mph, pulled the power back and retracted the flaps. We came out of the gully right over Ashcroft where I circled until I gained an altitude of 13,000 feet and made another try at Taylor Pass, which was successful. Both boys agreed that free-falling 1,500 feet down the gully was wonderfully exciting and they hoped we would do it again.

Since that event, I have flown many different types of twins, mostly on deliveries. One typical flight was from Fresno to Phoenix on a winter day in February of 1997. My partner

Don and I had flown commercially into Fresno from Los Angeles. Fresno weather was foggy. At noon cars were driving with their headlights on. The airplane we were to retrieve was an old 680 Aero Commander. I had never flown one before, and this Commander hadn't flown in years. We found it sitting in a puddle of its own oil with flat tires. We remedied those issues and did an inspection of the more critical aspects of the plane. I read the manual while sitting in the cockpit trying to memorize the location of the important switches, the fuel system, and the specified airspeeds.

The airport was a satellite of the main Fresno terminal so I was cleared to take off from their tower via radio relay. With the ceiling less than fifty feet, I would soon be airborne in solid IFR (Instrument Flight Rules) fog as soon as we lifted off the ground. Lined up at the end of the runway, I set the gyro compass to runway heading while waiting for clearance to take off. When it came, I gave the Commander power and we roared down the runway and were quickly in the air. Even before the gear was up we were in solid fog; clear sky was 5,000 feet above us. I had been cleared to the Fresno VOR with a thirty-degree turn after takeoff. When things settled down in the cockpit, I looked to check the magnetic compass with the gyro compass and discovered that our primary navigational instrument, the old magnetic compass, was *entirely missing* from its windshield mount. It was the one instrument we had overlooked in our supposedly thorough preflight exam.

I was a 6,000-hour pilot and my partner Don was an A&E mechanic. Here we were blindly groping for a heading without verification that the gyro compass was accurate.

However, unknown to either of us, the gyro compass had a forty-five-year old black box magnetic slaving device that was working. This, combined with the old fashioned timed turn technique, where you fly at a known rate per second, allowed me to turn toward the VOR and again turn outbound to our departure heading without being screamed at by radar control. We climbed uneventfully to clear, cold weather and flew on to Phoenix, occasionally checking our heading by confirming the gyro's accuracy by runway alignments we passed over. We didn't turn the heaters on for fear of carbon monoxide leaks in the old system.

On another departure out of Long Beach in an old Twin Comanche, I ended up bellying the airplane on my first landing. It had been an uneventful flight back to Taos until I lowered the gear for landing and nothing happened. I read the manual to verify the emergency procedure. Don was again aboard so we reconfirmed protocol and even tried brute force. Don got in the back seat to leverage his full weight against the emergency handle for lowering the gear. He bent the aluminum lever with his feet but the gear still wouldn't come down. It was getting dark so I flew the plane north to Monte Vista where there was a mechanic. That way I could save the expense of having to disassemble the plane to ship it to a repair shop.

The end of the month had been the deadline and it was now February 2; my flight medical was overdue making our trip illegal and voiding my insurance. We flew north to the airport and I notified the mechanic, asking him to please come out on the runway with a fire extinguisher. I didn't want to declare an emergency in case someone notified the FAA. Aeronautics had become so paperwork-intensive there wasn't a possibility of flying anywhere without breaking some regulation. Given that I would be bellying the plane without benefit of insurance, I decided to land with both engines off and both propellers feathered horizontally so they wouldn't strike the ground. A good belly landing would result in just some scuffed fuselage skin.

It was dark by the time we touched down within 1,000 feet of the start of the runway.

This was my second belly landing so I was prepared for the sound—like an empty beer can blowing down a road at eighty miles an hour. It was as smooth as any ordinary landing but the deceleration on white ice was dramatic. The airplane skidded 700 feet down the center line to a stop and we were quickly out in the cold night air. The mechanic joined us and, with the help of two others, we lifted the plane, one wing at a time, and dropped the landing gear by unlocking the gear struts. Some old paint had jammed in a housing, locking the extender rod. We towed it into the hangar and then went off for a congratulatory steak dinner in nearby Alamosa.

The next day the FAA drove all the way down from Denver but amazingly, nothing happened. They might even have been impressed that the plane was still air worthy. Even the insurance company agreed to pay for the minimal damage, and my overdue medical wasn't even mentioned.

My ten-year career of buying and selling planes with Don ended with the purchase of a twin-engine Cessna 421 that I quickly sold. I had no reason to fly that kind of expensive equipment and, as oil prices continued to climb, fuel became the major expense in flying. From then until 2015, I flew small and simple; a Cessna 150 and a 182. Both were ideal for flights to Bear Paw, my ranch two hours east of Taos where I pumped auto gas at half the price of aviation fuel into my wing tanks with a smile. Now my life is simpler still as I have sold them both and I drive back and forth to the ranch.

TAMAZULA

A Mexican village called Tamazula lies east of Culiacan in the rugged foothills of the Sierras in the state of Sinaloa. During the Second World War, the U.S. developed an opium-growing operation there to have a steady supply of morphine nearby for the war effort. When the war came to an end, the Mexican farmers realized that they could continue production while finding markets in the United States. for their black tar heroin.

At the end of the 1967 Taos ski season, I had arranged to take two planeloads of tourists down to Puerto Vallarta. My friend Jerry would pilot the second plane. Jerry was widely known in the pilot community of the Rio Grande as the person who ran the State of New Mexico Aeronautical Institute where he trained would-be mechanics in the fine art of aircraft maintenance. Coincidentally, another pilot had asked him to ferry his airplane back from Sinaloa. It had been damaged when landing at a mining strip in the Sierras of western Mexico, a couple hundred miles north of Puerto Vallarta.

When I first met Jerry in 1964 he was a flight instructor and head of maintenance at 7-Bar, a private airport on the west side of Albuquerque. I was a beginning pilot getting my ratings under his tutelage.

Having deposited our passengers in PV, Jerry and I flew on to Tamazula in my Cessna 205 with the repaired propeller for the damaged plane under the seats. We headed north toward the village just inside the western ridges of the Sierra

Madres. We'd been told by the owner that the landing strip was a short distance up a narrow canyon from the town and that we should locate the town but never get below the steep ridge lines surrounding it. He told us to fly up the canyon, identify the strip, turn around and fly back past the village, then make a U-turn and descend to 200 hundred feet with full flaps and creep back up the one-way canyon, committed to landing no matter what.

Indeed, once we passed over the town and into the gorge we had to land; there was no way to out-climb the canyon ahead of us.

On the flyover we could see, off to the side of the dirt strip, the plane we were going to take back to the U.S. I was flying and I turned back over the town, dropped full flaps, then turned again and descended to pass over the town at 200 feet. The total commitment strip was only 1,500 feet ahead, but it couldn't be seen until I was less than 500 feet from touchdown. The canyon turned hard to the left, so when the strip came into view, from my perspective at seventy miles an hour, it was like flying into a wall of granite. I descended to the downhill end of the strip, flared, and thumped down while we coasted past the damaged Cessna. Even before we stopped, we realized it was a total loss. It was still on its landing gear but the wheels were gone as was the engine and the pilot's door. It had been plundered.

I shut down the engine, blocked the wheels with rocks, and we walked down the strip to take pictures of the derelict plane. Everything inside the cockpit had been removed, including the seats, radios, and instruments in the panel. We were being paid by the plane's owner to bring it back, but since he had bellied it, the locals had gutted it.

We took a couple of pictures, but before we could leave, we heard the rumble of a vehicle coming up the dry riverbed. Suddenly a dump truck lurched onto the bottom of the strip and proceeded in low gear toward us. The truck, with a couple guys sitting in the cab, pulled up alongside us. From the bed of the dump truck three other guys popped into view with rifles pointed at us. We must have been a sight. The guys in the cab started laughing along with the guys in the truck bed. Jerry and I looked like frightened rabbits staring into the barrels of those guns.

They quickly realized that we weren't the law or anyone to worry about. It was a Sunday afternoon and these gentlemen had been drinking at the Tamazula bar. When we passed over the second time they had piled into the truck to come up and welcome us or kill us. And, what the hell, they had probably thought, we'll take them back to the bar for rounds of drinks and then maybe we'll kill them. We were ushered into the cab and bounced down the dry riverbed to the bar.

I remember thinking that the bar and its clientele were right out of a "Star Wars" movie. There were about fifteen men plus our new friends from the dump truck, all wearing the ubiquitous Mexican straw cowboy hats. Some had big pistols, mostly 1911 autos, tucked under their belts. We had been invited to a Sunday afternoon get-together of poppy growers.

The bar was made of wooden planks and had some rustic tables and chairs. We quickly realized we were expected to buy drinks for the house from the menu of beer, unlabeled tequila, mescal, and an earthen pot of *pulque*. Jerry and I agreed that the only way out of this social gathering was to keep an unending stream of alcohol flowing for our new friends. When the time was appropriate, we would bid a fond farewell with a flurry of

American twenties. As the shadows lengthened in the canyon, we did exactly that. I gave the bar owner a handful of bills and explained that we had to get back home to our wives and children in the states: "*Esposas y ninos esperandonos en los Estados.*"

There was talk about giving us a ride back to the plane, but we demurred politely, telling them that we needed the exercise. I remember our terror as we ran up the riverbed, expecting to hear the noise of the dump truck behind us. We dashed up the steep strip to the plane, threw the rocks away from the wheels, and jumped into our seats. I turned the starter switch, praying the engine would fire on the first turn of the prop. Then we were in the air, climbing steeply and safely out of that one-way canyon.

* * *

Tamazula is still there and from 5,000 feet still looks the same. In 2008 Antonio, an architect friend from Puerto Vallarta, was driving down the toll road from the border, towing a sporty new speedboat with his shiny new truck. He had friends in Culiacan and although he knew better than to leave the toll road, he decided to get lunch and gas in town where he was promptly pulled over by two motorcycle cops. They asked for the papers for his truck.

The cops walked back to their cycles, talked on their cell phones and a Chevy Suburban with darkened windows soon pulled up. The new guys talked with the cops and then beckoned to my friend to come to the window of their vehicle. The driver offered him a deal: "We'll give you a ride to the bus station or a ride to *el campo.*" The second choice was a euphemism for "We'll shoot you and leave you to die." Antonio wisely agreed to the first and was driven to the bus station minus his boat and truck.

Two days later, back in PV, he was telling his story of having made the almost lethal mistake of leaving the toll road. Maybe the insurance would pay for his losses? Upon hearing his tale, the girlfriend of another friend offered to make a phone call. She was from Sinaloa and she had connections. The next morning Antonio received a call from the Sinaloa governor's office in Culiacan. He was to go to the PV airport at noon where the governor's plane would be waiting. Antonio was flown to Culiacan, given back his car and boat as well as a police escort to the toll road. Who you know in Mexico is *muy importante*.

HONEYMOON

In the spring of 1967, Hueri became my second wife and we took off for a Caribbean honeymoon in my single-engine Beech Bonanza. The first leg of our journey from Taos was to New Orleans, with a stop in Austin for fuel that was extended to include a delightful drinking lunch at the famed Driscoll Hotel. Two hours later, in the late afternoon, we returned to the plane for the remaining two-hour flight to New Orleans where we had hotel and dinner reservations. Somehow, fueled by lust, drink, and autopilot, I found myself flying into the lowering sun and, after some reflection, realized we'd been heading southwesterly instead of southeasterly and were nearing the Mexican border.

So much for reservations; we had run out of daylight. As the shadows lengthened and the little puffy clouds turned pink we headed for Georgetown in the Bahamas where we landed for the night. The taxi driver mentioned that Tom, the owner of the Green Turtle Inn, was also a pilot and the owner of the only other plane parked at the airport. Our arrival was perfectly timed for dinner and we were the only guests. As pilots are wont to do, Tom and I began trading our best flying stories; each one had to be better than the last. With the benefit of our host's good food, good drinks, and dope, he and I were both entertained. Hueri, like any intelligent wife, went to bed while Tom and I spent the evening recounting tales of flying disasters.

I remember Tom's stories to this day. Two years before we dropped in on him, he had been flying back from Florida in his Cessna 205 after making a meat run for the inn. He had a hundred pounds of steak aboard for an upcoming fishing tournament and as he was descending for his approach, his engine quit. The plane splashed into shallow Bahamian waters a half mile from shore, tipped on its nose, and settled down in ten feet of water. Tom extricated himself from the half-submerged plane and climbed onto the exposed tail portion of the fuselage just above water. He had survival gear aboard but with the immediacy of the crash he could only grab his life jacket, which he used as a pillow during impact to keep his head out of the instrument panel. He had no time to declare an emergency on the radio, not that anyone would be listening.

Tom was now sitting, wet and shaken, on the tail feathers of his plane with his life jacket as a cushion, thinking how to get to shore. While he was pondering his dilemma, he noted a flurry in the water below him. Fins! Shark fins! The fresh meat he was carrying wasn't frozen and was now under water. The bloody steaks had telegraphed their presence to the reef sharks and he was perched on the tail of his airplane with a feeding frenzy just below his ass. He spent the night propped up on the stabilizer trying to stay awake and out of reach of the melee. The next day at dawn he was rescued by local fishermen coming out from the village in a skiff.

By this time I, too, had a couple crashes under my belt that I traded to keep the dope, drinks, and more of his stories flowing. Tom's next one was from when he was in college and flying as a part-time spray pilot. He was offered a job to ferry a prewar biplane from Atlanta to a museum in Tampa. The old military biplane had been in a farmer's barn since the

118

thirties. Tom was delighted at the opportunity and spent a lot of time making the antique ready for flight. At the last minute, he invited one of his new fraternity brothers along as a passenger. The new frat boy was the antithesis of Tom: fat, lonely, and lost, but Tom had decided to bring a little adventure into his life. The biplane was a two-seater where the pilot sits in front and the passenger is in the seat behind. The seat cushions were old military parachutes. Due to the noise of the engine, once the flight began there was no communication between the two except through silent gesticulations.

The first leg of their trip was uneventful. They landed to refuel and Tom asked his friend if he was enjoying the flight. The friend was ecstatic, so Tom asked him if he'd like to do some maneuvers. They flew for a while at ground level then climbed up for some minor acrobatics. First Tom did a barrel roll; to see the earth rotate in front of you is quite thrilling. Tom turned to see his friend and was greeted with a big grin. By now Tom was confident in the plane and as they were approaching their destination, he decided that the next trick would be a loop starting at 4,000 feet. He turned to his friend and indicated with hand gestures that he would be doing a loop. He was given another big smile and thumbs up.

Tom nosed the plane into a dive to pick up speed, hauled back on the stick and up and over the old plane went. He recovered from the loop and once level again, looked back at his passenger. No passenger! Gone! Tom quickly reversed course but he was now a mile away from where he did the loop. Maybe his friend could survive the fall? Could he be saved? Maybe he could spot him in the shallow swamp below? Tom flew back and forth, horrified. No, there would only be a body to find. No one could have survived falling 4,000 feet.

Tom landed and reported the incident. Both air and ground searches were organized. Airboats scoured the marsh while an air search flew patterns over the drop zone. That went on throughout the afternoon without success while Tom sat, glumly, waiting. There was finally a telephone call from the police saying a guy, wet and muddy, had made it to a road where he had been picked up and taken to a service station to use the phone. He was all right and, except for spending three hours tromping through the swamp to the highway, he was jubilant. He was alive, he'd had his first flight in a small plane, done a loop and made an unplanned parachute jump. When he had tied himself into the back seat after refueling, he'd inadvertently attached himself to the parachute straps instead of to the seat belt.

During the barrel roll, although upside down for a moment, he was held in place by gravity. At the top of the loop, he had fallen free of the plane. As disoriented as he was, he quickly realized what had happened, and rather than falling like a rock, he reached for the D ring. He pulled it and the chute, which had been packed thirty years earlier, responded as designed. It opened and he floated into waist-deep water.

What a story. Nothing could beat that. It had a happy ending although Tom was stripped of his pilot's license for a year. Multiple infractions were filed: flying a plane out of license, without a ferry permit, illegal this and that. Tom's story ended our evening since I had nothing better. I went to bed, defeated.

The next day Hueri and I flew down the Bahamian chain and stayed for two nights on South Caicos, which back then was endless reefs and miles of lobster beds and lagoons, where Morton Salt mined table salt. The only place to stay was the converted governor's mansion with meals of fresh lobster, conch, and crab.

As we continued our honeymoon, we were required to cross 120 miles of open water from Grand Turk to the north coast of the Dominican Republic followed by the Mona Passage, a modest seventy miles to Puerto Rico for a three-day stop. I am perfectly comfortable flying in high mountains, but phobic when crossing large bodies of water. I was grateful when we landed. We rented a car and drove to a new resort at the east end of the Dominican and stayed, courtesy of the owner, in a luxury suite for a few days. The owner, a recent import from Las Vegas, had spotted Hueri in her white sundress at dinner the first night. He was not the first to be smitten by her and he comped us our room and board.

In the rainforest park above San Juan we celebrated our departure with libations at lunch and again, as in Austin, were soon airborne in the late afternoon, headed for the island of Antigua. We saw pink puffy clouds and then, once out of the Caribbean, ahead of us rose a fairytale vision: Saba, the pinnacle of an underwater mountain that juts up over a thousand feet from the sea, surrounded with a rosy halo of clouds.

We landed in Antigua after dark, checked into a proper tourist resort, but were gone late the next afternoon for something less British and yachty. We flew on to Martinique. We rented a car and headed inland to the old town of St. Helens on the side of a volcano. The town had once been the capital of the French West Indies but had been wiped out by an eruption in the 18th century. It was now all but deserted. The luxury of Antigua and the poverty of St. Helens made quite a contrast. The few inhabitants of the ruins spoke no English and we spoke hardly a word of French. We found an unused bed in a whorehouse and the next morning fled to beach hotel to recover from our cultural juxtaposition.

Several days and islands later we found our perfect honeymoon destination at Young's Island, a tiny resort just a hundred yards off the larger island of St. Vincent. A hotel had just opened with six elegant *palapa* huts scattered around a small outdoor dining room and bar. The food was exceptional and the hotel was empty. Our unplanned four-day stay was delightful.

With regret, we adventured further south to the north shore of South America via Grenada and Trinidad, and then an extended flight along the coast to Caracas. We stopped only to refuel and rejected staying at either island because they didn't meet our new standards for elegance discovered at Young's Island. We ended the day at the Caracas Airport down on the coast.

When we got there a South American potentate was also arriving and I was told we couldn't land. They relented when I said my only other option was to put down in the water or on an adjoining beach as I was out of fuel. Uniformed thugs with guns in a military jeep met us. I was ordered to empty the plane of everything on the ramp. We were tired from a long day of flying so I very slowly and deliberately placed all our luggage lovingly on the concrete. One of the thugs shoved me away and proceeded to dump our stuff on the ground, breaking a bottle of good rum I had just bought. I flew into a rage, seemingly about the rum but really because I remembered I had stashed a carbine under the seats and I feared what they would do when it was discovered. My outburst turned the tables and now they were my servants, carefully reloading our luggage and escorting us politely through immigration.

Caracas turned out to be a non-event and two days later we flew over to Curacao, another non-event but one with casinos and beaches. We should have returned home after Young's Island.

We continued west to refuel at Cartagena, Columbia, and then made an over-water crossing to Panama City via the Darien Rainforest. It was not enough to be flying a hundred miles over open water with no land in sight but, in the middle of that stretch, oil started spreading over the windshield. It was late afternoon and the trade winds were howling below and the ocean was a white froth. I held my breath while waiting for the engine to start overheating and seize with a horrible squeal, forcing us into the maelstrom below.

The jungle of southern Panama finally came into view and we traded the dangers of the ocean for those of the jungle where we would disappear into the canopy and rot to death if we survived. Sixty miles later we cleared the isthmus and there was Panama City, with the sun setting over the Pacific Ocean. After clearing Panamanian customs we went directly to one of the waterfront glass towers where we celebrated our survival.

The next day I looked out from our oceanfront room to the bay thinking there was something wrong with the window. Although it was sunny, visibility was down to less than half a mile. The glass was fine but the temperature was over a hundred and there was 100% humidity outside.

Back at the airport the mechanic told us that the oil on the windshield had been caused by a leaking prop gasket, but that he had fixed it by forcing a bit of toilet paper into the seal. We then headed northwest for a refueling stop in Nicaragua. Our route took us over the canal to the Caribbean and then back to the Pacific and over to Managua.

Later in the afternoon, somewhere over the Gulf of Fonseca, we were weaving between towering nimbus clouds. The combination of a hangover and flying fatigue finally escalated a minor complaint into an explosion of marital discord which, in the cramped cockpit, was like two cats fighting in a sack. My darling bride attacked me. To protect myself, I slammed the elevator control forward and the plane tried to somersault. An hour later we coasted out of the evening skies into Guatemala City, all fight gone.

The next day we awoke with slightly improved accord. I knew this part of the world from previous visits so we rented a car and traveled up to Antigua and Lake Atitlán where we stayed at a hotel built over the water where I could dive into the lake twenty feet below. Guatemala was still in a low-grade civil war and we had the entire hotel to ourselves.

Our next stop, after a long haul up the Mexican coast, was in Acapulco for the night. We then flew over the hills to Mexico City to visit family and friends. After several days in El D.F. we completed the loop home. We had been gone one month, stayed in seventeen different resorts, flown 10,000 miles in 54 flight hours, and were severely over-honeymooned.

SEX IN THE AIR

In the fall of 1968 I was again flying up the west coast of Mexico north of Puerto Vallarta, with Hueri, in a single engine Cessna T-210. There was a long crescent beach fringed with coconut palms a few miles south of San Blas where I had been before. The firm sand next to the water was ideal for landing, and with the midday ocean breeze the beach would be bug-free and ideal for a swim. We landed and rolled to a stop beside the water. The entire two miles of beach was ours so we shed our bathing suits and made love in the shade of the wing. Surfacing back to reality, I opened my eyes to see bare feet attached to legs only thirty feet away on the other side of the plane. Hueri was lying face down in the sand dozing until I gently suggested that we should move on, that there was a crowd of people quietly observing us. Looking under the plane and through the legs I could see a small *palapa* village inside the palm trees hidden in the shade. I had rolled to a stop right in front of a small community recently built for workers of a coconut plantation.

With little dignity but great speed, Hueri and I quickly donned our bathing attire and without apologizing for our intrusion into the voyeurs' bucolic life, fled that part of the beach for a swim.

That winter, several months later, Hueri and I had just dropped off friends at the Salt Lake City Airport and were heading back to Taos in my twin engine Cessna T-337. We were flying on instrument in opaque ice crystal clouds at 15,000 feet with the autopilot in control when we were suddenly overcome with primal lust. We were instantly on each other with clothes flying. I discarded my seat belt and lowered her seat back to horizontal and joined her on her side.

The autopilot worked admirably and no one was trying to talk to me on the radio. God was in his heaven until a dramatic jolt from sudden turbulence uncoupled us along with the autopilot. We were flattened against the ceiling of the cabin. The autopilot clicked off with an electrical *bong* as if to say, "You're on your own, stupid!" and the plane went rolling into a diving turn. We ended up lying against the right-hand door with gravity pinning us down. My pants were tangled around my ankles.

Picture the confusion—we were transported instantly from blissful passion to stark *I'm-going-to-die-soon* fear. Looking up from the chaos I could only see opaque windows that had been frosted over from our heavy breathing. I was trying to roll back into my seat, but as the plane began to pull out of its dive, I was pressed back down onto my once-passionate wife who now was staring into my face with her own *I'm-going-to-die-soon* expression.

The plane's inherently stable design brought it out of its dive but only for a moment. Gravity's downward pull was increasing but now the nose was pitching up from excess speed. Soon the nose would be pointing nearly vertical and then there would be a stall, another wing-over and a dive that would plunge us into the mountains below. I struggled back onto my seat, my pants still around my ankles. I pulled the power back and shoved the elevator control forward to bring the nose down. Moisture had fogged all the flight instruments, including the all-important airspeed indicator; the gyros had tumbled from being inverted so they were useless and the compass would require help before it ever settled down again. I was flying by the seat of my undone pants.

The plane was stable for the moment. I switched on the auto-pilot and was relieved to feel it take over. I then opened the small pilot side window and looked out. We were between cloud layers and I could see snow-covered peaks below us. We had crossed the mountains and were somewhere north of Moab, Utah. We had lost several thousand feet in the rolling dive and I hated to think what the airspeed had gone to as it must have been beyond the plane's structural capability. I called center to check in and see if they had anything to say. Everything was normal. They hadn't noticed my descent but by then I was back up to 15,000 feet.

Hueri and I both dressed, still in shock. The windows were cleared of frost and the instruments were again visible and working, but I needed therapy to treat my ensuing impotence.

BECOMING A HELICOPTER PILOT

In the late winter of 1968 my employer, Sid Cutter, offered to sell me a small two-seat Hughes 269A helicopter with a 180 hp Lycoming engine that had been in an accident in Alaska. The machine was in crates sitting in the back of his large hangar in Albuquerque. We worked out a deal in which his mechanics would put it back together and he would throw in flight instruction, so I bought it.

A month later in March, when the machine was reassembled, I started flight training with Sid. Learning to fly a chopper is basically trying to keep it in one spot while hovering three feet off the ground. Sid and I spent the first three hours skidding all over a two-acre concrete pad next to his facility at the airport. The first lesson lasted only a few horror-filled minutes in which I was humbled by hand, eye, and mind overload.

One controls a helicopter by subtle touch and coordination between hands and feet. Each hand is doing something different from the other. If you need to think about what you're supposed to be doing, you've fallen behind the curve of control. The learning phase is mostly exploring the limits of your own overload frontier; eye to hands and feet reactions must be instantaneous.

Clutched in a death grip in the right hand is the cyclic, the control stick. Move it in any rotary motion and the entire machine responds accordingly. Tilt the stick forward and the machine tips forward then moves forward. Tilt the stick right and the machine tilts right and moves sideways and so on. The cyclic is supposed to be gripped gently between thumb and forefinger instead of crushed. Picture yourself standing on top of a large beach ball.

Meanwhile, the left hand holds the collective and the throttle, a twist device at the end of the collective lever. The way to stationary hover is to pull up on the lever while twisting the throttle for power while watching the rotor and engine rpm, which are conveniently overlaid on each other so you only need to read one gauge. As you do all this, your senses are besieged by noise and vibration and, if your feet are inattentive, your world starts revolving briskly. The feet control the direction of the tail rotor, which is there to counter the torque from the main rotor. Without the tail rotor, the machine starts spinning wildly, which severely limits one's ability to survive.

After three hours of ground hovering interspersed with some flight time, I was becoming somewhat proficient. Flight in a helicopter is akin to flight in a fixed wing airplane; it's in the transition from ground hover to flight and vice versa where all the training is focused. By my fifth hour, I was doing full on auto rotations to the ground, a maneuver to simulate a mechanical failure. Sid loved the horrified expressions on my face whenever he gave me a demonstration.

Later, when I had six hours of helicopter flight instruction under my belt and close to soloing, Sid took off for the weekend. As soon as I saw him depart, I had the Hughes rolled out to the ramp. It was a lovely March afternoon, perfect for doing my first solo hovering. I did that so well I decided to do a flight solo as well. I requested a departure north from the airport to a spot just beside the Rio Grande where Sid and I had practiced landings. I did several solo landings and takeoffs and then returned to the airport, a competent but unlicensed helicopter pilot.

The next day I flew the chopper up to Taos and landed in the pasture next to my house. The subsequent takeoff from 7,000 feet was severely inhibited by the extra 2,000 feet of altitude. I had to skid-bump forward through the grass until the machine bumped high enough into the air to gain speed and lift with the rotor blades. I was so busy trying to fight myself off the ground that I failed to notice the power lines overhead and blew right through them. I had to keep the chopper hidden in the back pasture behind the house after I reported the mysterious power outage that morning. I had the helicopter back in Albuquerque on Sunday and was ready for my official solo on Monday.

While the Hughes was being assembled at Cutter's hangar, I had sold it before I even started flying it. I had told the buyer that I would deliver it to Denver when vital parts arrived. After my legal solo, at seven hours, I had to add at least thirty more of actual flight time so I could take my commercial check ride the following week. The next weekend I took the chopper to Taos and then flew back to Albuquerque with Hueri. We stopped on top of several buttes and ship rocks overlooking the Rio Grande, once for a picnic and a couple of times for the hell of it.

A week after my first official solo I had amassed the requisite hours, and on an early Saturday morning an FAA examiner signed me off. An hour later I headed for my friend Norman's two-story apartment complex in downtown Albuquerque. I was now a licensed commercial helicopter pilot, and I wanted to land in his courtyard and have coffee with him. It seemed like a cool thing to do. I settled down into the courtyard, then suddenly visibility went to zero. A landscaper had just finished spreading manure on the lawn and I was repositioning it. A shit storm enveloped everything. The noise and rotor wash of the helicopter rattled the windows and doors of all the units that fronted on my landing spot. Tenants opened their doors only to be blasted back. I pulled full collective and twisted the throttle and rose out of the murk and departed without anyone getting a look at me or the machine. Norman was never able to get me to admit to the deed. Consumed by guilt, I flew directly back to Taos to pick up Hueri and fly on to Denver. I had promised delivery no later than Sunday, the following day.

We took off in the early afternoon from the Taos Airport; it was too warm to leave from my pasture. By the time we got to La Veta Pass the temperature was too high to fly over the mountains with both of us aboard. I had to go back to Fort Garland on the west side of the pass and land on the highway so Hueri could hitch a ride over to the east side. I was barely able to keep abreast of her transport as I was still woefully underpowered. I spent most of the forty-mile flight trying to climb high enough to make the crossing at 10,000 feet. On the east side, before Walsenburg, I picked Hueri up at a gas station and we continued along the east slope of the mountains chasing coyotes. A poor coyote would make a couple of desperate running turns and give up. No wolf or coyote has a chance from those hunter/killer thugs in helicopters.

Just north of Pueblo we saw a freight train running north at about thirty mph beside the interstate. I pulled alongside and landed on one of the boxcars about midway between the engine and the caboose, not all that hard to do in a chopper. There was a guy on top of the engine watching us and another guy standing on top of the caboose jumping around and waving at us. We rode the train for a few moments, exhilarated by the insanity of it.

By now it was late afternoon and we had only an hour left to get to Denver and the end of my helicopter flying career. I finished the flight into Stapleton Airport very conservatively. The next day the buyer, while heading back to Billings in his new Hughes 269A, had to do a real autorotation due to a broken fuel line. He survived but the machine did not as he was forced to land in uneven terrain.

* * *

Twenty years passed, and except for time spent as a passenger in helicopters on ski trips, I hadn't flown one. However, I was active in buying and selling aircraft with my partner Don in Arizona, who one day mentioned that there was a little Enstrom for sale in Butte, Montana. It was springtime, 1988, and adventure called. A few days later in Salt Lake I rented an Enstrom for an hour's check ride with an instructor. Although I was rusty, I thought I still had the touch.

The next day I arrived in Butte on a commercial flight. The helicopter was in the air racketing around. I walked over to the machine when it landed and introduced myself to Ken, the pilot. Ken had received his flight training for Viet Nam. We flew a short circuit around Butte and when we landed, I delivered my cashier's check and he passed over a bill of sale. The machine was mine. It had a lovely candy-apple-red paint job and, like my earlier Hughes, had three blades and a turbo 200 hp Lycoming engine. The turbo would solve the altitude problems that I had encountered two decades earlier. I expected to spend a few minutes reading the Enstrom's manual, then head to Salt Lake City that afternoon. I was used to picking up airplanes, briefly inspecting whatever I was buying and, if I had never flown that type of aircraft before, quickly scan the manual, especially the part about the fuel delivery system. If the engine would start, I'd fly the plane back to our base in Phoenix.

After a quick look at the manual, I started the familiar Lycoming engine, engaged the rotors, lifted the machine off the ground, and all hell broke loose. The machine and I caromed around the large empty concrete pad for a half minute while I tried to stick it back down which, thankfully, I managed to do.

I shut down, got out, and walked back to the nearby office where I could see a crowd watching me; Ken and his cronies were probably doubled over in laughter. I suggested that if he was for hire, I might need a couple of hours of flight instruction in my new machine. He was available and we began immediately. I was more than rusty. It was like starting over from the beginning. I had had the idea that piloting a helicopter was like learning how to ride a bike — that it would all come back. It didn't. For the first couple of hours I was again a complete novice. The next day my landings started to show some coordination and then, suddenly, it all came together, but not before I had received five full hours of instruction. Ken's most common refrain to me over the intercom was, "Now, don't get shaky on me."

On the second day after my arrival I was getting ready for my solo that would also be my flight to Salt Lake. A cold front was beginning to affect the local weather so I told Ken I had to leave. By then I had accumulated around six hours, close to the amount of instruction I had taken before I soloed twenty years earlier. Ken looked at me dubiously and suggested that he could go with me as far as Salt Lake. I insisted I was ready to solo on out of there. He said, "Well, your license says you're a

commercial helicopter pilot and you own the machine, but ..."
He signed off my biannual flight review and I took off for Utah.

I flew off, leaving the foul weather behind me. With a full
fuel tank, I could stay in the air for two hours so my first stop
was Idaho Falls, where I made a shaky landing beside the gas
pumps. From there I continued south through strong westerly
winds that allowed me to surf the western side of the north/
south mountain ranges, giving me extra ground speed. I barely
resisted the urge to make some mountain peak landings. I hit
the Great Salt Lake and to avoid active airspace around the
Salt Lake Airport, I flew down the east side of Antelope Island
where, at the south end, I spotted a dock sticking about 40 feet
into the water. I was tired and thought it would be a good place
to rest. As I settled down into a twenty-knot head wind, the
right end corner of the dock let go and tilted sharply toward
the water. I was still maintaining power so I was instantly airborne and away to Provo, only sixty miles further south. That
would have been an ignominious end to the trip—the Enstrom
in the lake with me stranded on an island awaiting rescue. I
arrived in Provo miraculously still alive.

I departed early the next morning through the Wasatch
Mountains to Price and Moab. With five solo hours under my
belt, I was feeling somewhat confident flying my new helicopter. The winds were calm and the temperature was cool so I
had no problem passing over Soldier Summit east of Provo. I
refueled in Moab without incident and then took off for Farmington, but by then the winds were howling. I headed directly for the windward side of the 12,000-foot La Sal Mountains,
just southeast of Moab, where I found ridgeline lift along their
western flank. I topped out at 12,000 feet as I passed the highest peak and then I turned south. With no visible means of

support, I was becoming anxious in my little plastic bubble. I was looking down 6,000 vertical feet to the ground, held up by a two-inch spinning shaft attached to frail, articulating blades trying to fling themselves off the shaft.

Despite my fears, everything was working well and I would be able to make Farmington without an intermediate fuel stop. During some earlier turbulence, my chart for the last segment of the flight had slipped onto the floor. I released my shoulder harness and when I reached over for it, I had to let go of the collective. I had set the friction lock but I let the cyclic between my knees slip back so the nose pitched up, causing a rotor stall. The machine rolled over and went into a diving 180-degree turn, a minor acrobatic maneuver in a fixed wing, but for me in a chopper, extremely disorienting. For a minute, the machine was upside down but it quickly stabilized right side up. I regained my position in the seat and control of the cyclic. Whatever phobic feelings I had been experiencing moments before were replaced by the euphoria of surviving.

An hour later I was descending through the canyons of Mesa Verde. I was tracking for a landing just forty miles ahead, but meanwhile I was flying by Anasazi cliff dwellings where I spotted ruins not yet open to the public. Even with a little ground level turbulence I could hover beside and view some ancient granaries.

A short time later I was landing into a forty-to-fifty-mph gale in Farmington. I should have shut down and spent the night there but I was on my last short leg home with a tail wind and only ninety miles from my ranch. I decided to push on.

Forty minutes later I was settling down on my own landing strip. The trip was all but over and the machine was finally planted firmly on the ground. I was starting to shut down when I thought, *Boy, you're in a chopper. Park the machine in the meadow right below the house.* Because of the still-gusting wind I had to ground taxi sideways over a wire fence and then a flood control channel. I crossed the fence and was passing over the channel, setting up for ground contact when the machine bucked back from another rotor stall caused by some sudden gusts. I felt a slight shock run through the controls. Once on the ground, I opened the door and looked at my tail rotor and could see that its very delicate blades were deformed. They had hit a chamisa bush and, although they were only slightly bent, they would have to be replaced.

After two days of coping with one horror after another, I had damaged the machine during my final landing. The romance of owning a helicopter evaporated even before the rotor blades quit turning. If only I had left the machine on the runway. If only I had spent the night in Farmington and started out fresh the next morning. But then I had flown all the way from Montana without killing myself. That was the idiot reward; at least I hadn't hurt or killed myself or anyone else.

A couple of weeks later the helicopter was repaired but I had happily already sold it "As is, where is," minus the exorbitant cost of repairs. The new owner had agreed to pick it up at the ranch after it was fixed, but the day it was ready he begged off and asked me to fly it down to Albuquerque and I agreed. I wanted to vindicate myself by having one last flight. I flew over to the ranch in my plane and met the mechanic. He discovered he lacked a few items for repairs so I flew him to Albuquerque to pick up some screws. We flew back and he installed the screws and said the machine was ready for test hovering. I hopped in and fired it up. By now it was late afternoon and the spring winds were back.

I lifted the machine to hover and did some left/right turns. After each maneuver, the mechanic gave me a thumbs-up so I took the chopper for a short circuit of the valley. Upon returning I decided to do a conservative aircraft approach to the runway. I had just gone into ground effect hover and was about to set down onto the runway when suddenly the machine started to rotate to the right. My first thought was that it was another wind gust so I depressed the full left rudder. The rudder pedal collapsed on the floor. I had no tail rotor.

I had lost control and had to go into an autorotation hover. Despite my limited experience, I responded appropriately and dropped the collective. The machine touched down ninety degrees from its initial heading, and I had it on the ground in only a quarter turn. However, I failed to roll the power off, so the torque carried the chopper around almost three quarters of a turn after initial impact. The right skid strut collapsed, and as the machine started to roll onto its side, I pulled up on the collective and swung the cyclic away from the direction of the rotation to try and stay upright.

I was partially successful, but as we came around for a full revolution, the chopper bucked up on its nose then flopped back on its tail and finally rolled to its side like a beast in its death throes. When the dying helicopter hit the ground, the jolt caused the belts that couple the motor to the transmission to disengage. It was as if I had turned the power off. The tail rotors had impacted the ground, but without power they hadn't deformed. The machine finally ended up pointed down the runway with the blades still spinning free. Then it ended its death act by bucking up on its nose and the right chin bubble shattered, and the cockpit was inundated with dust and debris.

Throughout all this, I was still sitting in the seat, strapped in and uninjured. The engine was running, the main rotor blades still spinning and I was in a state of shock. If a fire had erupted from a ruptured fuel tank, I think I would have just stayed there, staring at the instrument panel following the normal shut-down procedure. Luckily, there was no fire and the mechanic came running, opened the door and reached across me to turn off the engine. With that I came to my senses, punched my harness quick release, and hopped out.

The problem was left over from the former incident. The tail rotor drive shaft hadn't been checked; it had a closed fracture which didn't separate until I was in a ground-effect hover after my short circuit of the valley. I flew the circuit in a couple of minutes, and never climbed more than a hundred feet. If the shaft had broken open during that time, I wouldn't have had speed or height to autorotate safely to the ground so I would have most likely lost control and crashed. And died.

I ended up flying the mechanic back to Albuquerque for the second time that day, and then I returned to Taos to, once again, celebrate my survival. I was elated to be alive, uninjured, and no longer the owner of the sadly damaged machine I had left lying on its side.

It turned out that the new, less-than-happy owner had not insured me for the flight to Albuquerque, so he paid for the repairs. The FAA arrived the next day along with two mechanics to haul the carcass back to Albuquerque. Although the FAA wouldn't exonerate me, they didn't file a violation. The shop that had made the initial repairs dodged their responsibility for not inspecting the drive shaft by saying the damage was caused by pilot error.

The Enstrom flew again with yet another buyer to Dallas, where it crashed on delivery, killing both the pilot and a passenger. I have wisely given up flying helicopters. I take heart in the fact that I safely completed an 800-mile trip through the mountains with less skill than any pilot in the history of rotor wing flight.

EASY MONEY

Chuck, the owner of New Mexico's Angel Fire Resort, called me at 6 p.m. on New Year's Eve, 1969; he needed to be in Vail, Colorado, only six hours away, before 1970. Something about money, foreclosure, and rescue. I was facing similar problems for similar reasons, but on a lesser scale.

I had recently acquired a new twin-engine plane for my faltering charter business out of Taos. I had also acquired an agreement with TWA to fly their ski-bound passengers to and from Albuquerque and Taos Ski Valley. The expected business had, however, not yet materialized, and I wasn't able to meet the monthly payments for my new Cessna T-337. Chuck and I were each facing the loss of our respective major assets.

Central Colorado was under a heavy snowstorm that night. I suggested we fly to Denver, but that wouldn't get him to Vail in time even if the passes were open. Chuck suggested we try for Eagle Airport, forty miles west of Vail, whereupon I negotiated a bonus of three golf course lots should we get there. He had nothing to lose, so why not? If we didn't get to Eagle he wouldn't have any lots in the morning anyway.

I had become intimately familiar with flights into high terrain and the weather of central Colorado. With my new twin-engine plane, loaded with all the bells and whistles that aviation could offer, I knew I could skirt the weather by staying on top of it, probably at around 18,000 feet where we could pass safely over the 14,000-foot peaks.

It would take Chuck an hour to drive to Taos from Angel Fire. If Eagle was open, we would be on the ground by 9:30. I might even be back in Taos to bring in the New Year at a gala party.

Chuck and I were in the air, heading north, shortly after 7:30 and climbing into a clear and very cold dark night. One hundred miles north of Taos, over the San Luis Basin, we started picking up cloud cover and lost sight of all ground lights. I started a climb. At 18,000 feet we leveled off, still in calm, clear air. We had to breathe supplemental oxygen with the plane controlled by autopilot. The outside air temperature was reading minus 55 degrees, but the cockpit heater provided us with adequate warmth. I had even taken off my down jacket and thrown it behind the seats.

I was navigating to a commercial radio station broadcasting from Leadville on my ADF that I frequently used when I did daylight weather approaches into Aspen. At Leadville, 8,000 feet below us, in clouds and snow, I switched to the Eagle Airport beacon and turned west toward its signal. The beacon was right on the airport and my automatic direction finder (ADF) picked up a strong transmission. We were only fifteen minutes away but beneath us were still those 14,000-foot peaks.

Then, even before my ADF indicated we were there, I spotted the green and white flashing airport lights adjacent to the Eagle runway. I keyed the microphone to the airport's common frequency and magically the runway lights came on. There was an opening in the clouds right on top of the airport so I pulled the power back on the engines, dropped the landing gear, lowered the flaps and down we went in a tight spiraling descent.

Chuck's ride was waiting beside the terminal building, so without me shutting down the engines, he got out and drove to Vail. He would make his appointment with his financial savior and find his own way home. My job was done and I was determined to get back to Taos to celebrate my newly acquired wealth and the New Year with friends.

I lifted off a few minutes after 10 p.m. and started a circling climb to 18,000 feet. I leveled off and headed south. I could soon be able pick up a navigational signal from Alamosa at the southern end of the San Luis Basin. Until I locked onto that signal I was just heading south by compass with the autopilot flying the plane.

Suddenly I smelled acrid smoke. I was somewhere around Taylor Pass, fifteen or so miles southwest of Aspen. Below me again were 14,000-foot peaks. I turned on the interior white light in the ceiling and could see a yellowish fog seeping out of the instrument panel, which indicated an electrical fire. I quickly turned off the electrical supply to the radios and opened the small pilot window beside me to exhaust the smoke. This only served to suck out the heat and did nothing to stop the smoke. I then had no option but to switch off the electrical master switch.

The smoke stopped, but so did the heater and the oxygen flow. All the lights for the instruments were off, but I had a small flashlight that helped me maintain an erratic southerly heading. My eyes adjusted to the darkness and there was just enough starlight to provide a vague outline of the clouds below.

Within minutes, however, I was affected by lack of oxygen and the cold. Without the heater, the interior was matching the ambient air temperature outside the plane. Without an autopilot, I couldn't risk leaving the controls to reach for my down jacket. I fortunately found several small survival blankets in the seatback pockets, which I quickly opened and draped over my lap and shoulders. Despite shivering violently, I was starting to feel drowsy, which allowed me to dispassionately imagine that I was in the early stages of physically shutting down.

I became aware of a string of colored lights, below and to my right, which my oxygen-deprived mind slowly deduced was from Gunnison, Colorado. I was on course. Ahead was the Continental Divide and the San Luis Basin where I would be able to descend to relatively warmer, denser air.

When I estimated that I had passed over the divide, I started a descent down to 12,000 feet and was soon passing through light cloud cover, and finally into clear air with the lights of Alamosa fifty miles ahead. I reasoned that if the temperature at 18,000 feet had been minus 55, it was still around minus thirty at 12,000 feet. Alamosa was almost always the coldest town in southern Colorado due to frigid air pooling in the basin. It had been minus ten degrees on the ground in Taos when I had left three hours earlier.

I continued my descent to 9,000 feet and passed over Alamosa, where I could have landed but I knew there were no services there. Since it was only another twenty minutes to Taos, I decided I would go all the way. I was shivering and my teeth chattered while I kept pounding my feet on the floor and pummeling my chest and shoulders with my right fist to stimulate circulation. By this time my left hand was numb and had frozen to the control yoke.

At 9,000 feet I was too low to fly directly to Taos. So, to avoid the old volcanoes at the southern end of the basin, I continued on top of the highway and then turned east at Tres Piedras for the last twenty miles to Taos Airport. Ten miles out I flipped the master switch back on just long enough to power the radio so I could tap the mic a couple of times to turn on the airport runway lights and lower the landing gear. In a hurry to rid myself of my flying refrigerator, I used all the runway and taxied quickly back to the ramp and coasted into the still-open hangar.

I was down and safe. My left hand was like a claw still clutching the yoke. I couldn't release my fingers except by pulling them off one by one. Even then I had no feeling. I drove home to the arrival of 1970 with no thought of the party. I only wanted a hot bath and a shot of Jim Beam. My core temperature had to be down a couple degrees and I mistakenly assumed a good shot of whisky would warm me up. Once home, I drew a bath and sipped. I quickly got warm and happily curled up, sweating, in my bed. But soon the shivering returned. I repeated the bath and whisky cycle and went back to bed still shivering, but I mercifully fell asleep.

Chuck kept his word about giving me the golf course lots, but it took a couple of years for their titles to clear from liens that encumbered the whole resort. In the meantime, I sold them to doctor friends who were willing to wait.

One snowy spring afternoon in 1973, finally having been paid for the lots, I was driving into Velarde, a small town on the Rio Grande thirty miles south of Taos. At the entrance to the village there were a couple of police cars parked by a low rider. Sitting on the fender talking to the cops was Richard, a friend from Taos. Richard told me he had been thrown out of his girlfriend's car in Española for some misdeed. They had just arrived back from Peru where they had acquired some cocaine that had been transformed to cash after landing in Albuquerque. Richard was carrying a large sum of money in his pockets, stuffed into his boots, and in several money belts around his waist. Seeing him hitchhiking, a lowrider stopped to pick him up.

Richard wasn't choosy and it wasn't a wise choice of rides. In the ten-mile drive from Española to Velarde, the two other passengers attempted to rob him. The passenger in the front seat turned around and tried to bang him on the head with a hammer, while the guy in the back seat grappled with him. Richard, only momentarily stunned, swung into action. A skilled street fighter, he grabbed the hammer, beat both passengers, and then suggested that the driver pull over. The driver wisely stopped at the Velarde gas station, where both he and his two bleeding friends vacated the car. I arrived in my VW bug shortly after the police and walked back to see Richard.

Witnesses from the gas station corroborated Richard's story and he, still loaded with drug money, was delighted to see me. The cops already knew his assailants and released Richard to my care. He joined me for the forty-mile drive to Taos and told me all about his trip to Peru and Bolivia and then suggested that I partner with him to buy some property. I had only recently been paid for the Angel Fire lots and had paid off my debts and had some cash. Believing strongly in synchronicity, I pledged my remaining funds and within the year I was done with commercial flying.

SMUGGLER

In the spring of 1970 I imported 600 pounds of marijuana, Mexico's most marketable agricultural product, into the United States. Long before that flight I had been accused of smuggling by many authorities: the U.S. Treasury, the Drug Enforcement Administration (DEA), the INS, the state police, the IRS, and the FAA. From 1965 to 1973 I operated a small commercial flying service and airport in Taos, New Mexico, which automatically made me suspect in the eyes of federal and state agencies. But I only did the one trip and there were extenuating circumstances.

Having a twin-engine plane on my hands at the end of a ski season was like having an albatross strapped to my back. There wasn't enough business to support its mortgage so when an acquaintance, Forest Smith from Aspen, asked if I would lease it to him for the summer, I jumped at the opportunity to rid myself of monthly payments.

Forest was introduced to me by my old grade school chum, Jock Craig, who operated the Ski Mart in Aspen. Forest was a real estate speculator who had west coast clients and needed my plane to bring them in and out of Aspen. His clients, later revealed to me by U.S. Treasury Agent Bud King, were kilo blocks of Culiacan Gold. My twin-engine Cessna T-337 was involved in several illegal cross-border entries from Mexico.

When King called, I was shocked to hear that I'd been set up by Jock. I was further shocked to hear that I could lose my airplane. During the call I told King that I would take the plane back immediately. "Wait a minute," he said, "don't do that. Keep it on the lease but let us know when and where it's going." I said that I couldn't keep track of the plane but I didn't want to risk having it seized. King then said, "If you cooperate with me, tell me what you know, you won't have to worry about losing your plane." Eager to keep it on the lucrative lease and believing in the authority and integrity of The Man, I took him at his word.

To further cover my ass, I flew up to Aspen the next morning and confronted Forest with the news I had received from King. I told him that I would report his activities to King, and that if I knew of any further flights into Mexico in my plane, I would personally see to his demise.

Several times during the summer I called King's office in the Federal Building in Denver to let him know the plane was in California. A couple of months later he called to inform me that my plane, piloted by Forest, had been seized at the Rifle Airport, down-valley from Aspen, with a load of dope aboard. He then told me that he was seizing my plane because I hadn't cooperated with him. I mentioned the phone calls and he blatantly lied that he hadn't received any. I resurrected phone bills but in his eyes I was already guilty of smuggling.

Surely, when the facts were presented, I would be exonerated and my plane returned and King punished. Forest, to his credit, had followed my demand about not smuggling across the border. However, he had been called by a friend to fly down to St. Johns, Arizona, and pick him up. His friend had said that his airplane had broken down there and needed a ride back to Aspen. When Forest arrived at St. Johns he found his friend with a broken plane filled with Mexican dope.

The friend pleaded with Forest to fly him on to Rifle with the load as payment. Forest capitulated. After all, he wasn't smuggling; the dope was already in the country. So off they went and when they landed at Rifle they were caught unloading the cargo into waiting vehicles. Somehow Agent King decided that justice would be served by getting me at the same time. He just knew I had to be involved. If he couldn't get me directly he would get me financially. With the seizure of my plane, the bank pulled the loan and the IRS called me in for a criminal fraud audit.

By the following spring I had reached a level of frustration that could be handled only through fantasies of vengeance against King. The government had stonewalled my appeal, standing behind King's lies. My three lawyers in Taos, Aspen, and Washington told me that King was most likely jealous of my apparently opulent lifestyle, which included flying in and out of Aspen on ski trips, something he could hardly afford. I couldn't either; my trips were paid for by my customers.

With my mini-empire going down the financial drain, I faced the spring with no small amount of fatalism. Fortunately, I received a call from Carl, an Aspen drug dealer and bar owner. His offer was for me to run a load of marijuana up from Mexico that would make me rich beyond my wildest dreams, or at least pay for the attorneys' fees I had recently incurred.

My motley fleet of planes included an elderly Cessna 180 tail dragger which I chose for the flight because it was worth the least. I took off for Mexico one Sunday afternoon in late April. The irony was not lost on me that if I was lucky, I might pay off all my legal fees by breaking the law.

The flight down to Culiacan was uneventful. I had taken everything out but the pilot seat so the plane was literally a large empty tube all the way back to the tail cone, something that signaled "smuggler" to anyone who might notice. I was supposed to meet Harry, Carl's associate, at a hotel in Culiacan that night and he was to have already organized a place and time to load the dope. I was to be back in the States the next day. But as things work in the dope trade, nothing goes as planned or, as in this case, unplanned.

I spent the next thee days on the coast waiting for Harry to get everything together. Harry, who looked sixteen but must have been twenty-five, knew the growers in the Culiacan area but hadn't been informed of my arrival. After arrangements had finally been made, Harry and I were to depart Culiacan before dawn and head to an irrigation dam forty miles northeast of the city to load the dope. Harry was then to return to the U.S. with me and the load. Harry was carrying a briefcase that contained the cash to buy dope and I would be in charge of dispensing it while the kilos were loaded into my plane.

I easily found the dam and airstrip in the early light and Harry spotted two pickup trucks inside the tree line. I landed and stopped where six guys were lounging around the trucks. They were all wearing cowboy boots, straw hats, and pistols tucked under their belts. The trucks were filled with white flour sacks of kilo bricks of marijuana, wrapped in Mexican newspapers.

For our defense I had a tiny .22 caliber automatic in my lap as well as the briefcase filled with hundred-dollar bills. The dope would be weighed on an ancient fish scale. The Mexicans would call out the weight and I would pay to the nearest 100-dollar bill as the sacks were loaded through the plane's passenger door. The first couple of sacks were shoved all the way down to the end of the tube on top of the elevator and rudder control cables. More sacks followed with the fuselage space and stack of bills diminishing accordingly. Meanwhile, I kept the engine running for a hasty departure. There had been a Huey Army helicopter back at Culiacan and we were all worried about the potential for its sudden arrival over a nearby ridge. I was also worried about the obvious exposure to the Mexican growers. Why not just shoot the gringos, keep the dope, keep the money and the airplane? My .22 wouldn't do much but I could sure make a quick departure if things started to get ugly.

I was parked pointing back down the runway and the transaction was taking place right beside me. As the sacks were pushed into the cabin I would pay out my side window. The cabin quickly filled up until I was squashed against my door. Beside me, but soon buried under the dope, were four five-gallon plastic containers of fuel for refilling the tanks close to the border. That would give me an extra hour and a half of flight time once I was back in the United States.

When all was loaded, it became apparent that Harry had underestimated the space required to carry six hundred pounds of Sinaloa's favorite export. There was absolutely no room left for Harry. I had limited visibility directly ahead and to my left; to my right and to the rear, my view was blocked by white flour sacks. Each sack weighed about forty pounds and I had fifteen sacks aboard. I was also carrying seventy gallons of fuel so including myself, I was at maximum take-off weight.

The last sack was squeezed in and the passenger door was pressed shut from the outside. I couldn't reach through the pile of sacks to the door handle to lock it but I hoped it would stay shut until I was airborne. After that, air pressure would keep the door closed and the load inside. I paid the guy for the final sack and sold him my pistol for one of the last hundred-dollar bills I had just given him. Harry came over to my window and took the briefcase. We said good bye and I rammed the throttle forward and was quickly in the air.

I turned east and headed toward barranca country and into the rising sun. The light streaming through the windshield illuminated my green haze-filled environment. I was in a cloud of marijuana dust and getting an unintended contact high. I opened the pilot side window to ventilate the cabin and kept it open; being stoned was not part of my plan for this trip.

For the next hour I flew over deepening barrancas, slowly gaining altitude until I reached the high plateau southwest of Parral at around 10,000 feet. From there I flew northeast into ranching country, all the while looking for a lonely strip or a road on which to land and refuel. After being in the air for a couple of hours, I was somewhere east of Chihuahua, less than an hour from the border. I found a long gravel road with clear views for miles in every direction and landed.

As before, I left the engine running and set the parking brake, then got out and pulled the fuel containers out from underneath the sacks. I slung the containers on top of the wings and crawled up and filled the two wing tanks. I was in a hurry and didn't want to be there when someone drove down the road. I threw the empty containers off to the side, climbed down off the wings and back into my sack-filled cave, and took off for the border.

The week before I had flown the general area where I would be crossing into the U.S. so I had a vague plan but nothing specific in mind. I would be flying very low on both sides of the border to stay below El Paso radar. As I approached the Rio Grande I was only sixty miles southeast of El Paso but well screened by a small mountain range. Once I entered the Rio Grande Valley I would easily be spotted if I was much above ground level.

As I approached an escarpment to the valley, I descended to sagebrush level. I even fit the fuselage down into a shallow gully which ran into the Rio Grande a couple of miles ahead. At one point, with the body of the plane in the gully and the wings just cresting the ridgetop, I nearly ran down two Mexican cowboys on horseback. If they had been any closer, my left wing tip would have hit them. I crossed the Rio Grande and several miles ahead I could see the green iridescent highway signs of the interstate glowing in the morning sun. I crossed the highway to clear some power lines and then dropped back down to the desert floor.

Sixty miles ahead was Guadalupe Peak and just to the west were some dry salt pans that would be an excellent place to stash my cargo. I spotted one that would be particularly easy to identify later; it seemed to be almost round with a small vegetated pimple right in its center. It was a quarter mile across and blinding white in the sunlight; the white flour sacks would blend in perfectly. I made a low circling approach to check that there were no vehicle tracks into the salt pan. It was clear so I landed from the north. I coasted to a stop and climbed out of the plane. I was still too paranoid to shut down the engine in case I had to make a hasty departure. As it was, it didn't take much time to haul the sacks out of the plane and dump them on the embankment.

I checked the now-empty interior of my plane for any signs of cargo and then turned the tail on the pile of sacks and blasted them with a propeller-made dust storm to cover them. Next, I slowly taxied forward, blasting my tracks behind me into what I hoped would be oblivion. Half way to the other side of the dry lake, I lifted the tail with full power and started a takeoff roll. I continued my takeoff right in my earlier landing track. If anyone came down to the lake bed they would see tracks that indicated someone had landed and immediately taken off. I circled back over the sacks and, even knowing where they were, I could just barely make them out. They would be safe, I hoped. My job was done. Someone else would take them from there. I would give Carl my treasure map and be through as a smuggler. Or so I thought.

Two hours later, flying with the side window still open to cleanse the interior of the marijuana smell and dust, I was gleefully back in Taos. I thoroughly vacuumed the interior and then sprayed some toilet deodorant to ameliorate the distinct smell that still lingered. Under the edge of the carpet against the side of the fuselage I found a marijuana bud that had escaped one of the sacks during the hasty unloading. I replaced the seats and the baggage bulkhead and left the plane, its interior smelling like a recently cleaned urinal.

Drug dealer Carl was now in Miami aboard his large trimaran. When I told him the load of dope was safely in the country he asked that I finish my job and deliver it to him, whereupon I would be paid. There would also be a handsome bonus. I wasn't happy about the additional journey but it became clear that we were at a standoff. Without delivery to Miami there would be no payday. Of course I knew where the dope was, but he had the money, so a week later I returned to the dry lake to transport it on to Miami. I was filled with misgivings but I'd survived the first leg. Would I be so lucky on the second?

This time I was flying a bigger single engine plane; it was a six-seater with a large nose compartment with plenty of room in the fuselage for the load. I was carrying a batch of flattened cardboard boxes in which to repack the kilo bricks. The bricks themselves, however, were still wrapped in Mexican newspapers, which telegraphed their suspicious nature. I naively thought that if they were neatly packed in boxes I might disguise them, thereby obviating some risk.

I planned on arriving at the lake just after sunset and spending an hour, aided by a lamp, repacking the bricks into boxes. After a couple of hours the big plane was crammed but there were still twenty-eight Mexican-newspaper-wrapped kilos left that I had to put in the forward luggage compartment. By now it was 10 p.m. and pitch dark. I gathered up all the remaining white flour sacks, mixed with a lot of Mexican newspapers that had fallen off the bricks, and lit a big bonfire. I taxied to the far side of the dry lake, turned the plane around and took off toward the flames that helped me orient in the moonless night. Although the plane was full it was well under its maximum takeoff weight and I was a hundred feet in the air when I passed over the remains of the fire.

My plan was to stay low until I was over the road that ran northeast of the dry lake and skirt the south end of the Guadalupe Mountains. Then I would start climbing while continuing east until I was over central Texas, where I would land for the night. I still had at least three hours of fuel left but my misgivings about the whole venture were increasing. A nagging voice insisted that I was running out of luck. *Go home"* it said, so I turned north. Two hours later the lights of Taos appeared as I crossed the tops of the Sangres and landed after midnight. I was exhausted but I tucked the plane back in the hangar and spent another hour unloading the boxes into the bed of the airport's pickup truck which, ironically, was labeled "U.S. Dept. of Agriculture" on both side doors.

I drove home and collapsed in my empty house. My soon-to-be-ex wife was away and I planned on storing some of the boxes under our king size bed. In the morning I started hauling the boxes upstairs and soon the storage area under the bed was full. I took the remaining boxes down to a shed that was attached to my guest house two hundred feet away. My friend Bill and his wife were living there, but they were at work so I filled up what unused space there was and then called my brother-in-law, Mark. I asked him to relieve me of the fifty pounds of Culiacan Gold still in the nose compartment of the plane and make a sales trip to Phoenix and San Francisco. Mark showed up in his black Mercedes and off we went for a gala dinner with the last of the kilos in his trunk. After dinner I went home for my own quiet and introspective celebration of survival, and slept like the dead on top of three hundred-odd pounds of Mexico's finest.

Next day Hueri came back and I left for my sad motel room in town. I soon received complaints from both her and the tenant about a smell permeating the interior of both homes. I agreed to take care of the odor, which I did with bathroom deodorant.

Then I started to get calls from Carl. "Where's the dope, good buddy? You trying to do something on your own with my product?" This was a not-so-veiled threat to produce or else. I was stuck with a 500-pound albatross around my neck that I had to get rid of. I loaded the boxes from both locations into the pickup, drove to the plaza and parked in front of the Rexall Drug Store. I left the dope-laden truck out front smelling like a skunk while I fatalistically enjoyed a chocolate malt. Then I drove out to the plane and loaded it with fuel and the boxes. I took off in the afternoon and flew east into the night, heading for Miami.

After six hours in the air I dropped down out of the darkness to bless Sulfur Springs, Texas, with my presence. The airport was close to town so I walked to its only hotel, slept until dawn, and walked back to the airport to wait for someone to show up and fuel the plane. From a hundred yards away I could smell the rotting marijuana and when I got to the plane I could see that the boxes were splitting open. The marijuana was absorbing the Texas humidity and the bricks were bursting. I started the engine and taxied the plane to the fuel pump and positioned it so the morning breeze would blow the stench away. I watched as more of the boxes split open, exposing the newspaper-wrapped bricks. I was doomed. I would have to refuel once more before Miami if I could even escape Sulfur Springs unscathed. The airport manager arrived and without any questions fueled the plane and I departed for Miami, six hours away.

Somewhere over southeastern Georgia I decided to stop for fuel and make a call to Carl, asking him to meet me at the Ft. Lauderdale Airport with a van. I landed at a small airport and again situated the plane so it was facing into a wind. After paying, I called Carl but was only able to leave a message. I walked back to the plane, hoping no one was calling the police after smelling my cargo. It was over a hundred degrees and either because of a vapor lock in the fuel line or a flooded engine, the plane wouldn't start. I cranked it over trying to get it going but the battery was on its last legs. I sat there pleading with fate, promising I would never do this or *anything* bad ever again, *please*. I fully expected police cars to show up at any moment. With increasing despair and desperation I twisted the starter key again and the prop grudgingly turned, then stopped. The starter groaned, but with its last erg of energy it caught, the prop spun, the engine fired and I was on my way.

Two hours later I landed at Ft. Lauderdale and taxied into a maze of parked airplanes. The wind was blowing so the odor, I hoped, would be defused throughout the parking area. I walked to the office to await Carl, all the while keeping an eye on the plane. The meeting time arrived and passed and still no Carl. I was calling him every five minutes on the office pay phone but got no answer. By six o'clock I was desperate, so I rented a large Ford station wagon and drove it out to the plane and loaded up the ruptured boxes. I had boxes stacked to the roof and kilo bricks that had fallen out jammed under the seats and on any floor space, trying to keep them below window levels. By then it was dark and still no sign of Carl. I moved the wagon around the public parking areas of the airport so that the smell and location would be hard to trace.

I finally gave up waiting at the airport and drove to the beach. I found parking areas with beach access, stayed awhile, and then moved on to another location. Later in the night I found a beachfront hotel with an open multi-level parking structure with the wind blowing through it. I was able to sleep until dawn. I called Carl and he finally answered. He was delighted to hear from me and said he must have gotten the date wrong. In any case, his crew had already rented a van and he would meet me at a shopping mall within an hour. We met in an empty parking area, where I immediately vacated the wagon for a nearby restaurant to eat breakfast. Carl joined me a short time later. The van left with all the goods and my smuggling sojourn was over.

Carl and I walked back to the wagon. Carl lit a large joint, which he smoked as we drove down a side street. Out of nowhere, a police car pulled up alongside us and the cop inside gave us a once over. Carl swallowed the joint and I went from feeling relaxed to paranoid hysteria. I was going to prison. But then the cop pulled ahead and drove off. We drove on as I hyperventilated, expecting to be surrounded and arrested any minute. We drove on to a marina in North Miami where Carl kept his yacht and I spent the day sleeping, trying to recover.

I didn't want any more of Carl's activities. I wanted out. I drove back to the airport that evening with a bundle of cash— not nearly what I'd been promised—but I'd be able to pay my attorneys. And I was free. I had been so lucky! Carl said he'd send more money soon. Later that night I landed at Shreveport, Louisiana, and caught a cab to a famous barbecue joint beside the river. I ate and drank like a king and slept through most of the next day.

Carl never paid me and I never heard from him again. No one in Aspen has ever heard from him, either. The story is that he was lost at sea making another delivery. Jock also disappeared and, although his family has asked me if I had any knowledge of his whereabouts, I've only heard the vaguest of rumors.

Harry, Carl's contact in Culiacan, appeared one day when I sailed into a tiny island anchorage in the Cayos Cochinos off the coast of Honduras, where he was running a small eco dive camp. I had gone ashore for dinner and we recognized each other from the time, thirty years earlier, when we were arranging the Culiacan Gold shipment. We had drinks, toasted our mutual survival, and he confirmed that I might have been the last person to have seen Carl.

As for the release of my airplane, my efforts continued through the summer until, in August, I contacted Dr. Al, a friend in Taos who knew U.S. Senator Joe Montoya. Dr. Al put in a call to him on my behalf, almost a year to the day of the seizure, and by early afternoon he called me, suggesting I get my ass up to a small east Denver airport where my plane was parked in a dilapidated tin hangar. One of my pilots and I immediately flew to the small airport and found the plane. With the aid of a bolt cutter we freed it from its year-long impoundment. It was covered in pigeon shit, the tires and front strut were flat, and the battery was dead. We got the plane flyable and I was soon in the air on my way home.

The plane was soon sold to a nearby resort to cover the balance of its mortgage, and then leased back to me to operate. There were no repercussions from the government except for the IRS audit which was reduced to civil fraud, and after four years of harassment, reduced even further. It was finally resolved at a fraction of what was initially filed. Over the years I have often wondered what the senator said to whomever he called, and if Agent King and his career survived as well as I did. At the time, I was too happy to care.

POJOAQUE

When I moved out from our home in 1970, Hueri became filled with wifely vengeance after discovering another woman's clothing hanging in my rented apartment's closet. She confronted me in the town's most popular watering hole with the Other Woman in tow. Hueri had convinced her that I was a sick and deceptive bastard, which was true enough, but considering her role in co-opting and seducing my lawyer over our property settlement, she was, if nothing, a hypocrite.

I was sitting with a friend when I noticed him backing his chair away from the table and trying to stand up. His face was a picture of horror as he looked over my shoulder. I turned and saw the two women advancing through the bar, weaving between tables of late-Friday-afternoon drinkers. Talk died in the room as all eyes followed the course of the Valkeries. It was too late for me to bolt, so I was left to face them alone. For the next several minutes Hueri rained down pure hypocrisy upon me while my new love interest stood by the table glaring. I had apparently deceived them both by allowing *yet another* woman's clothes to also hang in my closet.

Hueri had arrived from Los Angles and had come over to to thank me for signing the deed over to her. I had hoped that we would sell it and share the proceeds, but she and my erstwhile attorney, now her lover, had decided that with the IRS and the DEA waiting to pounce on me, it would be far better for her to take them all than let the government get a dime.

There I was, sitting at my table, a rictus grin on my face, trying to be cool while my mind suffered the social mortification of it all. I indured her diatribe while the whole bar looked on. Lines of cocaine, carefully drawn across the bar, were left unattended as everyone nodded in agreement as Hueri laid out her grievances.

She finally finished and hurled a final insult about my shallow character and lack of integrity, then spun on her heels and walked out followed by my hoped-to-be new girlfriend. They were two good looking woman so being the focus of their contempt was enough to buoy me with pride. The bar noise returned to normal. I fumbled some money onto the table, got up and started walking out with friendly comments and slaps on the back from the patrons sitting at the bar. The bartender, Steve, a good friend, rolled his eyes at me. His almost-ex-wife was the other woman. Taos was such a small town that almost all relationships were recycled.

The two women stood talking outside by my car. In the several minutes since they had vacated the bar they had decided that I was less someone to be despised and more like a wretch needing help. The fact that Hueri needed to get to Albuquerque that evening for her flight to L.A. mitigated my depravity in her eyes, and I had been elected to drive her to the airport.

By the time we reached Pojoaque we were alternating between operatic drama and being at each others' throats. Hueri was driving when suddenly, in a quick fluid grab, she unzipped my pants and adroitly plucked out my flaccid member and proceeded to stimulate me with her luscious mouth. She still had her foot on the accelerator but her hands off the wheel and her head in my lap. Our car passed through heavy traffic at the Los Alamos interchange at seventy mph while we moved diagonally across three lanes of slower traffic. I was horrified but perversely delighted, and I somehow managed to steer from the passenger seat. I willed myself a quick finish. Within a half mile and in a record thirty seconds we had achieved success. But I was spent and still in a bit of shock at our preposterously crazed run through speeding, merging traffic. It was fortunate we weren't cited for disorderly conduct and reckless driving, not to mention we narrowly escaped dismemberment and death.

BEER-CAN CAPER

In 1970, I was on my way to making it big. *Really Big.* My friend Mike Reynolds, an architect and bold genius, had invented a waste-product building block composed of six derelict steel beer cans set together with four upright corner cans and two center cans laid horizontally. The six-pack was then wired together.

Those of us who came of beer-drinking age in the '50s and '60s will remember how steel cans were opened by what was known as a church key, a small blade that punched a triangular hole in the can's top. This was in the days before the pop top. Undented steel beer cans have exceptional compression strength, a quality Mike recognized and exploited. He believed a wall built from stacking these blocks with a layer of mortar in between could be made quickly and easily from litter found along the roadsides of America. Rural labor could benefit from gathering the free materials and building beer-can houses could become a prosperous new industry. Mike related this vision to me as we sat, stoned on pot, inside a miniature Cheops Pyramid set up in his living room in Taos. I seized upon his inventive idea; dollar signs bedazzled me and that summer we became partners.

We set in motion the first step: to collect beer cans and have them assembled into blocks. We acquired enough money to buy a small lot on a windswept, sagebrush-covered mesa. Soon construction began on a prototype, funded by a grant from the Can People, a group of companies that manufactured and distributed food and beverages, including beer, in steel cans.

The house was completed and sold to our mutual friend and attorney, Nate, who by then had become another partner. We three were bonded by the enterprise, its potential, and the delightfully bent lifestyle of Taos—dope, women, rafting, and skiing, and the need for financial survival. With the house successfully completed, we set out for Manhattan to negotiate the sale of the construction-block concept with the Can People, a song of imminent wealth in our hearts.

We arrived in New York on a flight that allowed Mike and Nate to rehearse their can-block presentation for the entertainment of our fellow passengers, some of whom would have happily invested in the venture. I carried a slide projector that illustrated how the house was built.

The Can People offices were located on Fifth Avenue in an imposing glass-walled structure. We had every expectation of being warmly welcomed by the highest level of Can People hierarchy. After all, they had financed the house where Mike had successfully proved his concept. We were directed to a small office on the fourth floor and moments later the occupant arrived. Without any pleasantries, he curtly told us to leave and never darken the Can People's headquarters again. I vaguely remember he had a security detail escort us to the imposing front door. Apparently, the corporate factotum who had disbursed the construction funds for the prototype had been told by those on the higher floors to get rid of us. Something was afoot and we weren't privileged to know what it was.

Nate left us there on the street corner, but Mike and I went on to D.C. to give HUD a presentation. Mike's delivery of his concept was like that of a charismatic religious leader. We left with dignity and a certain future with HUD.

The next day, in Milwaukee, Mike and I were treated to beer and bratwurst sandwiches by another factotum of Corporate America. We were gently informed that the entire beverage industry would soon convert from steel to aluminum cans that have the structural strength of toilet paper. The beer-can house in Taos still stands, a monument to bad timing.

SHARING A RIDE

By June of 1970, Hueri had packed her things, leased our house, and moved to Los Angeles. Living with me in a Hacienda de Valdez condo were my two boys, Michael and Cobie—her son from a prior marriage whom I had legally adopted. We three males were on our own for most of that summer.

Toward the end of August both boys were going back to their respective mothers, Cobie to Hueri and Michael to Judy. In her departure from Taos, Hueri had taken two large oil paintings of mine as I then had no place to store them. I now had somewhere to hang them. I decided to drive the boys to Los Angeles in my VW van and return with the paintings to give my new home some decor.

Although both boys were still preteens, the trip would be an opportunity for them to learn how to drive. Each had a turn at freeway driving while I sat in the right seat or lounged on the rear bed. We arrived without mishap and both boys became competent drivers.

Several days later, with the paintings stashed behind the front seats, I was ready to return to New Mexico. On the way to Los Angeles on I-40 we had seen hitchhikers at most freeway entrances. My plan was to pick up a couple for driving duty while I slept or read. I departed Los Angeles in the early evening and was back on I-40 east of San Bernardino.

On the access ramp at the San Bernardino interchange there was a line of at least twenty hitchhikers waiting for rides.

I got off the road, circled back and stopped at the head of the line where two grungy guys stood among the sweet-faced, clean-cut college students. What to do? Could I choose? I told the two to hop in the back and we pulled onto the freeway. I turned off at the next exit and parked at a gas station. I explained to the guys that their job was to deliver me safely to Albuquerque. They were delighted. I then sent them into the store with cash to buy snacks and drinks for their night of driving while I gassed up the VW.

When they returned, probably after plotting how they would do me in during the night, I was lounging on the bed in the back of the van. The two large paintings were blocking the tiny aisle between me and the two front seats and I felt quite secure. It was almost dark by then and as they pulled back onto the freeway we chatted amicably. They were headed back to Detroit. They had come out west in the early part of the summer looking for jobs but things hadn't worked out. They were destitute and had been living in the San Bernardino City Park most of the summer. They had survived on odd jobs but after a couple of months their dreams and expectations of sunny California had evaporated. One of them had been bitten by a brown recluse spider and he showed me a festering wound on his forearm. Their luggage was only a couple of blankets wrapped in tattered plastic.

While there was still enough light to see inside the cabin of the VW, I told them what I expected and what their duties were. Then, from under my pillow, I casually eased out a large stainless steel revolver. I kindly suggested that there was nothing personal in my gesture but should the camper pull off the freeway and into any unlit area, for whatever reason, things would become unpleasant. To avoid any development of nighttime paranoia they should inform me, well in advance, of future fuel stops. "Do you understand?" I asked. By their expressions and widening eyes, both seemed to indicate that indeed they did, so we drove on through the night.

I was informed twice of the need for fuel and provisions; once in Flagstaff, Arizona, and again in Grants, New Mexico, where the sun was coming over the Sandia Mountains to the east. I had slept well and they had done their job. On the east side of Albuquerque, at the last exit before Tijeras Canyon, I had them pull off at a truck stop, gave them each a $20-bill and bid them good luck and farewell. I suspect the stories of the road they later told were more harrowing than mine.

MIDAIRS

Of my many flying mishaps, two near misses stand out for their immediacy; from beginning to end, only one or two seconds elapsed in each case. There was no time for reaction. In one instance my mind calculated the time to impact and I responded by doing nothing but squeezing my eyes shut and waiting for the inevitable. In the other I watched my entire view become instantly occluded by aluminum and again did nothing.

In the first event I was flying a twin-engine Cessna T-337 down the Rio Grande Valley from Taos to Albuquerque on a calm summer afternoon in 1971. Chuck, a frequent passenger, was in the right front seat. The two of us had taken off a half an hour earlier and were just starting a gradual descent from 10,000 feet for landing. Albuquerque was beginning to appear around the corner of the 11,000-foot Sandia Mountains.

Suddenly, Chuck punched my right shoulder with his fist and tried to say something while pointing out the upper right corner of the windshield. I couldn't see anything, so I raised the right wing and bent my head forward so I could look in the direction he was pointing. In that tenth of a second I saw two rectangular jet engine air intakes separated by the very narrow cross section of a fighter fuselage, coming at me from a few hundred feet above.

There was no time to do anything. My reaction was simple: I lowered the wing, closed my eyes, hunched my shoulders and waited for impact. No impact. I opened my eyes and saw a mass of aluminum hurtle past, so close I couldn't make out any form, only rivet patterns and fluid streaks on a fuselage. It was there, and then in an instant it was gone, out of sight. I rolled the plane to the left and watched a jet falling flat like a barn door, all its control surfaces helplessly flapping, hundreds of feet below me. The pilot had stalled a fighter—probably an aptly named Phantom—when he saw me, which was probably at the same time I saw him. He had instinctively jerked the nose up to avoid me. Without sufficient speed and power, the sleek machine had stalled.

I later surmised that the pilot, probably an Iranian being trained by our air force out of Clovis, had tried to do a loop in heavily traveled Albuquerque civil air space. He was out of control. A thousand feet below me, twin stalks of blue flame shot out of his engines as his afterburners kicked in and he accelerated out of sight behind me.

Chuck and I droned on, saying nothing. After a few minutes, I started talking to approach control, asking for a radar explanation for what had just happened. They had none. The incident had occurred between 8,000 and 10,000 feet in a radar blind spot caused by the bulk of the Sandia Mountains. I reported the mid-air but never heard another word on the matter. Back then the Iranians were our allies and best friends in the Islamic World.

Several years later, on a perfect summer late afternoon, I was flying north from Albuquerque to Taos in a single-engine Beech Bonanza with two elderly ladies and a small dog. The dog was beside me in a dog box and the two ladies sat in the back seat. I was relaxed and flying with the autopilot at 9,500 feet. I was approximately ten miles northwest of Santa Fe Airport. The ladies were chatting and laughing. Suddenly the windshield of the Bonanza was filled with an aluminum mass. It was so close I couldn't see any design to the structure, just aluminum with a green stripe. Again, I did nothing. I didn't call out or jerk or even lift my hands to the controls.

In that fraction of a second I recognized the green stripe as belonging to Frontier Airlines, probably a twin propjet Convair that had taken off from Santa Fe about the same time I had passed over the airport. I had been on a northerly heading to Taos and as the jet climbed, I had always been to the pilot's left. The Frontier had climbed northwest and closed in on me. He came at me from below at my right rear quarter and passed me both vertically and horizontally. I sat there, watching the jet climb off to the northwest, leaving two faint streaks of exhaust in its wake. Neither of my two backseat passengers had seen a thing. Their conversation sparkled on. Like the earlier event with the fighter, there was no turbulence. I have no idea why we didn't collide with the Convair's left wingtip vortices as it came up from beneath us. We were so close that we were in the triangle formed by its left wing and fuselage. For an instant, we were almost one.

Over the years, radar coverage has vastly increased, especially in proximity to airports. Today, the Santa Fe control tower would probably have notified the Frontier pilot of my location. Or not, since I was well outside the controlled airspace of the airport. So even with our advanced technology, collision avoidance at low altitudes is still dependent on pilot skill. Or luck.

CREVASSE

In the early fall of 1971, after the collapse of my second marriage and my financial life, I responded by purchasing round-the-world airline tickets for myself and my girlfriend, Linda. Back then tickets were $900 including, as we happily found out, unlimited zigzags around the globe. Linda and I left for Hawaii on an early evening flight from San Francisco. We arrived late and woke late in a hotel tower on Waikiki Beach.

After viewing the crowds on the beach from the twelfth floor, we caught our first zig from our planned itinerary and ended up later that night on the island of American Samoa or Pago Pago. Pago was dominated by tuna canneries and gigantic indigeni. It was just a stopover while we waited for the next plane south to romantic Fiji.

While waiting, we took out the hotel's sunfish, a vessel slightly larger and sturdier than a windsurfer, and spent the afternoon trying desperately to get back to the hotel beach. Foolishly, we had left the protected area inside Pago Harbor and sailed past the headlands out into the open Pacific. There had been no discernable transition from calm, orderly breezes and gentle wavelets to enormous rollers with breaking crests and steady twenty-knot winds. The wave troughs were so steep and deep that the wind blanked out at the bottom. The sunfish sail would suddenly backfill from our rapid forward progress, but we would then be buffeted onto the crests of the rollers. We spent an interminable amount of time trying to keep from pitchpoling down the waves and being swamped by the breaking crests. All the while we were getting further away from the protected harbor. Obviously we got back, but my memory fails regarding how. Maybe we were picked up by an inbound tuna boat? The evening was spent being deeply introspective.

Bye bye, Pago Pago. On to romantic Fiji where we were told about one of the great old hotels on the southern coast where steamships traded passengers en route from Australia to the States. The isolated hotel was packed with gentle New Zealand teachers on their vacations. Our room was above the kitchen in an unairconditioned dormer. The nightly luau feast was canned tuna fish salad, canned fruit cocktail, and a punch that reminded me of Boy Scout camp. The tropical air was redolent with the smell of kerosene from tiki torches.

As we had done in Hawaii, we left Fiji within twenty-four hours, for. The next morning we were introduced to the quaint New Zealand culture during an intimate moment in our hotel bed. A tea dolly propelled by the Kiwi equivalent of the 300-pound Fijian maiden came through the doorway with a crash. "Tea, duckies?" she chirped.

A week later we were at the Hermitage Hotel on the South Island below glacier-draped, 12,360-foot Mt. Cook, where I hoped to ski. Access would be via a ski-equipped Cessna 185. I joined a group of two couples with a guide. We would be flown up to the end of the Tasman Glacier and then climb to a hut perched on a crag shadowed by the Hochstetter Dome which overlooked the glacier, 1,000 vertical feet below the hut. That night a not-infrequent gale blew through the mountains. The already wind-polished snow was burnished to a gleaming steel-like surface by the seventy-to-ninety-mph gusts that buffeted our precarious perch.

The next morning we started out on a 3,000 foot climb to the top of the Hochstetter Dome, which was to be our routine for the next three days. Each morning we would climb different routes up for lunch and then descend leisurely in the afternoon. The last morning was crystal clear and absolutely calm. Halfway up we met a group of glacier experts descending to the hut. They had been with us the night before but had left for their climb hours earlier. They suggested that we return to the hut because the glacier tongue was shifting and it was becoming too dangerous to continue.

Our guide was a mountain-climbing guide, not a ski guide. The day before, we had impressed upon him the fact that we, his clients, were incredibly experienced skiers. Our experience was legendary, from the ice fields of the Canadian Rockies to the snowy crags of Europe. He was mistakenly impressed. We elected to continue our climb but roped up for safety. We would be crossing snow-covered crevasses that were impossible to discern because of the wind-polished snow. The slight concavities on the glacier that might indicate snow bridges were hidden by a covering of snow from the previous night's gale. We plowed steadily up the ice tongue and finally crested at the top of the dome. To the south, and towering above us, was Mt. Cook. To the west we could look down to the Tasman Sea. To the east we could see endlessly to the Pacific side of the island. We sat on our packs on the snow-covered dome and ate lunch.

Apparently my exaggerations about my skiing experience were more grandiose than those from the rest of our group because our guide deferred to me about the route down. I said that I would lead, but not roped together. Our speed would carry us over any of the snow bridges that had been weakened by the glacier's movement; anyway, we had just climbed up and across them without incident.

The most dangerous spot was just below the crest of the dome where the ice angle changed. Black rock cliffs edged both sides of the steeply descending ice tongue for a full 3,000-foot descent to the hut. The group we had passed was talking about the possibility, even likelihood, of it pulling downward from the top of the dome. The crevasses would widen and what was solid ice could split apart, forming new ones.

Determined to make check turns as I descended over the critical band of ice, I set my edge and fell. I was sliding on my back, not overly concerned except for my dented ego. I planned to roll quickly back onto my skis when suddenly I was falling. Just as suddenly I stopped. I had fallen with a saucer-shaped piece of wind-slabbed snow that lodged between the two sides of a crevasse. The snow bridge that had covered the abyss collapsed, probably from my impact. I was eight feet down inside the crevasse. On either side of me was a vertical blue world of ice with no bottom.

My first thought was to not move. I was still on my back and any movement might crumble my fragile, wedged platform. The wall above me was snow. I still had my skis and pack on, and I still held my poles. My head was almost against the wall of snow.

My resolve not do anything quickly dissolved as I realized what little was holding me up and what might be yawning below. Only a few seconds had passed. My visual environment was suffused in shining blue ice crystals blown up from the bottom of the crevasse when the snow bridge had collapsed. I was able to reach the wall behind me and, with all my strength, I plunged a ski pole almost to its basket into the stiff snow just above my head. I now had an anchor besides the fragile snow saucer.

The next thing I remember was crawling away from the crevasse with my skis still on. I was back on the surface. I had apparently gotten up on the protruding end of the pole and plunged the other pole just below the top and popped out like a jack-in-the-box. I don't remember the struggle to pull myself out, but I was out. I had shed my pack and left it on the snow saucer inside the crevasse. I dragged myself to the nearest exposed rocks, which provided some security. I was on the down side of the crevasse and I could hear voices, but an ice crystal curtain hung thirty feet above and obscured everything uphill. I was able to talk to my companions through the curtain that was slowly defusing in the still air.

I happily relinquished all leadership and the guide retrieved my pack and poles. Roped together now, we continued our descent to the hut where the guide called on the radio phone for a pick up five miles farther down the Tasman Glacier. We spent the late afternoon skiing unroped down the gentle glacial slope, gliding effortlessly to the landing spot.

Although I secretly pondered what lesson there was to be learned, that evening I celebrated my thrilling crevasse adventure with champagne and dinner with Linda and my new friends in the elegant dining room of the Hermitage.

SNAKES IN A TAXI

Linda and I had been on the road for two months and we were flying from Colombo, Sri Lanka, to Calcutta with an overnight stop in Madras. The flight from Colombo was on Indian Airlines, not Air India. There is a big difference. We were in a French-made Caravel, circa the sixties. Ever wonder where old airplanes go? They go to India after having worked their way from America or Europe to South America and Africa. By the time they reach India they are a cobbled-together collection of parts. Many junked cars on blocks, as frequently seen in Taos County, are an essential supply of parts for these hulks still flying in India.

The pilots for Indian Airlines are as seemingly expendable as the patchwork equipment. So are the passengers, judging by our approach into Madras. We were cruising along the East Indian coastline at 30,000 feet when a large city came into view, which I assumed was our destination. An airport appeared below and when we got over it, still at cruising altitude, the pilot popped the spoilers—the large rails on the upper surface of the wings that thrust up to spoil the lift. This turns the wings into brakes, which makes the plane's fuselage fly like an object without wings, not unlike a rock hitting a brick wall. Anyone standing or sitting without restraint is hurtled forward.

After having eaten Indian Airline's onboard cuisine of rice and part of a chicken foot, I realized that, like the food, the airline equipment was highly questionable. Linda and I had attached ourselves firmly to our seats for the duration of the flight but observed, with some dismay, our fellow passengers piling up at the front of the cabin after the spoiler had been deployed with a loud thud. We were welcomed to India by plunging downward, spiraling like a lawn dart into the Madras Airport. This tactic was apparently the approach used if the airport was suddenly under attack from Pakistan; it was 1971 and indeed, war was to break out only a month later.

We stayed at a hotel in the city center. Although the airline had warned us to stay indoors and not tour Madras after dark, we went out on the street looking for adventure. The first thing we found was a burlap bundle in a sewage-laden gutter. The bundle moaned. There was a beggar's bowl by the figure and the figure must have been a leper or the remains of one. The moaning was chanting or singing, I suppose. That was our first night of adventure in India. We spent the next day touring Madras, from the lovely beach south of the city to the straggly Bodhi Tree where Buddha became enlightened.

Despite our earlier traumatic flight, we flew on to Calcutta the next evening. The ride into Calcutta from Dum Dum Airport was in an open-sided bus. The people of Calcutta, it seemed, lived on the sidewalks; families gathered outside around cooking fires. We were dropped off at The Oberoi Grand, a faded colonial-era hotel. From our experience in Madras the night before, we decided to stay in and wait to venture out the next day. Morning would put a better light on things.

Or at least it did at first; the morning air was fresh and water trucks were sprinkling down the streets. The real Calcutta began to reveal itself soon enough as the body wagon came by, picking up the dead who had expired during the night. The Maidan, the central park of Calcutta, was actually a parking lot filled with heavy trucks that were supposedly used to ship international food aid to starving people in the countryside. Instead, the food was being kept, stockpiled for the impending war with Pakistan. As tourists, we had no idea what was really going on.

Not far from the hotel stood the walled British Hospital, which was completely encircled by sick people hoping to become patients; many would die on the sidewalks before being admitted. They say it could take you up to a year to circle the four blocks to the main entrance before you finally received care.

Our intention that morning was to get a permit to go to Darjeeling. We took a cab to an imposing block of Victorian government buildings. The cab driver drove around the square looking for the appropriate number and paused, coincidentally, by a naked gentleman who was holding on to a steel lamp-post while shitting his life away into the gutter. While we waited, stunned, a suave man in business attire approached and asked if we would share the cab with him. He was a dapper Lebanese silk merchant determined to sell us his wares and to show us some of the better aspects of his adopted city. We bought some silk from him, which, to our surprise and delight, arrived in Taos months later. His idea of showing us the city included a trip to the burning ghats on the Hoolie River, and to a mongoose and snake fight.

The snake/mongoose thing was illegal but could be arranged by finding a snake guy with a mongoose on his shoulder, his not-too-concealed advertisement. He would also have a burlap bag filled with several cobras. We quickly located a snake guy and he piled in with us.

The taxi was a tiny prewar Morris Minor. Linda and I sat in the back. In front of us, from left to right, sat the silk guy and the snake guy who shared the tiny front passenger seat, and on the far right was the driver mixed up with the snake-filled burlap bag and the mongoose. We sped through the now steaming streets of Calcutta looking for a quiet hideaway where the snake guy could put on his show.

The streets were packed with humanity: great wooden-wheeled bullock carts rumbled along in the throng, soot from open-hearth forges drifted through the streets while bodies were being burned just a block away along the river, their ashes mixing with every other imaginable combustion aftermath and settling on all of us as we looked for a quiet spot. Our driver, clearly a maniac, forced his way through the crowd with his horn.

Suddenly, I noticed that my comrades in the front had assumed extremely rigid and contorted body positions. All three suddenly levitated so that their feet were on the dashboard, their torsos were free of the seats and they were screaming in Hindi at each other. The mongoose was chittering and running back and forth, upside down, across the ceiling of the taxi. The driver, who must have had a hand throttle, amazingly kept up his speed and partial control of the vehicle.

The snakes had gotten out and were slithering around the bottom of the tiny car. Linda and I instinctively assumed the same pose with our feet on the top of the back of the front seats and our heads resting on the top of the back of our seats which allowed us to elevate our bottoms. We needed no prompting, as just below us were squirming cobras and just above us ran the enraged mongoose. Somehow the snake guy grabbed the cobras and stuffed them back into the burlap bag. We found a secluded park with only a few hundred locals and proceeded to watch the mongoose anticlimactically kill a cobra. The next morning, eschewing another attempt for a Darjeeling permit, we fled Calcutta for Kathmandu.

NEPAL

Linda and I arrived in Kathmandu in early October. Our itinerary across the Pacific had already included Hawaii, Samoa, Fiji, New Zealand, Australia, Bali, Singapore, Thailand, Malaysia, Sri Lanka, India, and now Nepal. The brother of a friend from graduate school was married to a member of the Nepalese royal family and he had just started a small trekking business. I was going to be turning thirty-four shortly and I hoped to have my birthday in some memorable spot high in the Himalayas. Doug, the brother of my friend, would organize our trek. As it turned out, he was easily located and quickly set us up with a guide, a pleasant young sherpa named Ahn Kami. Within a couple of days of arriving in Kathmandu, we were ready for a two-week trek to Helambu on the Tibetan border.

Doug had ended up in Kathmandu doing research for his Ph.D. in anthropology. While in northern India, he had been commissioned by the village where he was staying to kill a tiger. It was an early evening hunt and a goat was staked out not far from the threatened village. After dinner Doug was led to where the goat was; it was still light enough to see it tethered in a small clearing, a hundred feet away. The idea was to stake out the cleared area so when the tiger came he would simply pull the trigger. Doug's only claim as a hunter was that he was from Denver. He was also extremely short sighted and wore thick glasses but, nevertheless, he had once shot a deer in Colorado.

Doug lay in wait for the tiger, along with one of his friends from the village. They were lying side by side, staring into the increasing gloom of the evening. Doug stared through the open sights of the rifle, which was leveled on the goat. After a short time and, as if on cue, the goat started bleating and nervously moving back and forth on its short tether. At that point, Doug was doing some serious soul searching about the predicament he had volunteered for; it had sounded like an interesting adventure until, with visibility dropping and the goat's sudden unrest, he became more and more aware of the vulnerability of his situation.

After several minutes of nervously looking down the barrel of the rifle, there was still no sign of the tiger except for the now frantic bleating of the goat. Doug and his friend were nervously scanning the small clearing, wondering if they might also be prey for the tiger that was obviously close by, undoubtedly watching them. Doug returned to staring through the sights of the old rifle and realized with horror that he was staring directly into the eyes of a huge tiger, staring directly back at him. His first reaction was an involuntary loss of bladder control but then he pulled the trigger. He never had to move the gun. The bullet struck the tiger through the neck, which severed its spine. It dropped in its tracks, dead. Linda and I had seen the tiger skin in the family home in Denver just before we left for the trip. It was quite impressive; its huge teeth and jaws in a huge head and an appropriately sized tiger skin were draped across the family's living room floor.

Word spread of Doug's expertise and he was called upon several more times. On one occasion, he was invited to take out a tiger in Nepal. After successfully dispatching it, he was invited to meet the Nepalese royal family where he met a cousin of the king, a young well-educated princess. They fell in love, married, and settled in Kathmandu. When I first met Doug, he was just setting up his trekking business, and Linda and I became his first clients.

The month of October is the end of the monsoon season so we were soon outfitted with a patch of plastic for a tent and a couple of ratty sleeping bags. We had our own boots and flip flops we had bought in the local market. Although the sale of hashish in Kathmandu wasn't legal, it was everywhere on the streets. Every western coffee shop advertised it, but I couldn't brave the idea of walking up to the counter to ask for some.

Late one evening Linda, Ahn Kami, and I were eating pie in a tea shop. We had just finished equipping ourselves with provisions for the trek. We were to leave early the next morning from the central market, with two porters carrying our shabby gear and food. I mentioned to Ahn Kami that I had heard that a caravan from Mustang had arrived in Pokara and wondered if any of their infamous hashish had been brought down to Kathmandu yet. Maybe an enterprising merchant had air-freighted some already? Ahn Kami said he would check. He left and returned with a teenage boy who would take us to some people who might know.

We left Ahn Kami on the street and followed our new guide into the old town composed of pagoda-like warehouses. This was the Chinese merchant part of the city; the architecture was all Chinese and some of the buildings were as high as five floors. There were no streetlights. It was very quiet, with no traffic of any kind. We were the only people on the street and I was starting to wonder why I was going to all the trouble to find some mythic hash when regular street hash was readily available in all tea houses. We could have easily ordered some along with a water pipe when we had ordered our apple pies. But no, we would trek with the best hash in the world.

Our guide stopped by a small door on a dark street and rapped on the entrance. There was no noise from inside but finally the door was opened and another young Nepalese, who recognized our guide, bid us enter. The two had a short conversation and our guide indicated that we should go with the new guy. The interior of the building was lit by a few dim electric lights; it was a huge building with many small rooms, some for storage and others for sleeping. We walked down a long corridor to a bamboo ladder that went up to a second floor, and then up to another. We were the only people moving about. From behind closed doors we could hear the murmur of voices and smell cooking. By now we were on a third level with still another, smaller bamboo ladder that led up to a trap door. Our guide climbed and rapped on its underside. There was a short conversation between him and another guy on the other side. The door was lifted and our guide scrambled into a brightly lit space under the eaves of the pagoda's roof. There was more conversation and then our guide beckoned us to come up.

Both Linda and I were more than ready to flee but, realizing we could never find our way out, we climbed up the spindly ladder. As we entered the room we found three men with evil Mongol faces and leering smiles. They were sitting on cardboard boxes surrounded with more boxes and, as I quickly found out, they were repackaging Swiss Sandoz Lab medical-grade cocaine with milk powder into tiny ziplock bags for retail sales in Thailand. The tension was quickly broken when the leader of the thugs asked me with a New Jersey accent, "Hi guys, where you from?" We were offered some of the product being packaged, but all I wanted was to depart.

We declined the coke and purchased a stick of Mustang hash-ish. Our guide took us back to the bright lights of downtown where we left him with a large gratuity, and fled to the safety of our hotel.

The next day we met Ahn Kami and our two porters at the market. One was a teenager and the other his grandfather. We filled the porters' wicker baskets with our limited gear and some food. Ahn Kami selected a bag of rice, some tea, salt, and sugar. We then departed out the back of the market to a concrete stairway and started climbing into the clouds. After the first 1,000 vertical feet, the stairway turned into a dirt trail of switchbacks up the first ridge on the northern side of the Kathmandu Valley. We were heading due north across several 12,000-foot ridges directly to the village of Helambu, which was right beneath the main range of the Himalayas. It was also the headwaters of the Kosi Sun River, one of the main rivers flowing from the mountains to the lowlands and into the Ganges. We would later return down the Kosi Sun to the soon-to-be-finished Chinese highway from Tibet.

The first day we started out bravely carrying our light day packs but, by lunch, and at the urging of Ahn Kami, we piled them on top of the wicker packs of our geriatric porter and his grandson. Pride goes before exhaustion, I soon found out. In the afternoon, after salt chai, a beverage that tastes like its components—salt, sugar, yak butter, rice brandy, and hot water, we continued up to the top of the first ridge where we fell into a coma-like sleep. The Mustang hash we'd picked up was so powerful that swallowing a bb-sized ball would allow me to fall asleep with granary rats, head down on temple steps, in a running rivulet, and amid stinging poison nettles, and to deliver political rants to yaks along the path.

We would usually find ourselves in the evening on a ridge-top in the clouds. Sometimes we slept under cover in mangers, granaries, and homes, and sometimes out in the open under our piece of plastic. I remember one rainy night we slept beside a stream in a rhododendron forest. The stream jumped its banks and we became part of the new stream bed. I complained to Linda that we should do something about it, although the water seemed warmer than the night air. Her response was, "Don't do anything, it will just get worse." I lay there in the water trying to figure out how it could get any worse. But it did.

Before conditions became totally intolerable, I called out to Ahn Kami, who was nestled under a rock with the two porters, happy and dry: "Ahn Kami, I'm wet and unhappy." They grudgingly roused themselves and in the pitch darkness we broke camp and stumbled back down the track to some terraces where we had passed a small rock granary. Linda was in front of me, walking along a terrace and, in the dark, she plunged off the edge, five feet down to a lower terrace where a poison nettle bush broke her fall. There were no great injuries but she developed an instant allergic reaction to the nettles which caused her so much discomfort she couldn't sleep in our dry, but rat-infested, shelter.

The trek to Helambu went on for a week as we crossed the ridges, working our way to the Tibetan border. The trail was an old pilgrimage route and every day we passed numerous shrines where the devout made stops to pray. On one of the first days, we rested among a group of pilgrims leaning against a steep bank on the trail. I felt an itching between my thumb and forefinger and I looked down and saw something hanging there, like another finger. It was my first encounter with a Himalayan leech. They were all over us in the rhododendron forests, dropping off leaves like tiny silver threads as we passed under the branches. The pilgrims were highly amused by my initial reaction to discovering the leech, engorged with my blood, attached to my hand. Leeches are particularly attracted to the sock line at the top of boots. There they would swell until they burst, leaving my socks red with blood. We quickly adapted to trekking in flip flops, which allowed us to pick or flick them off. How quickly we adapted. I awoke one morning nestled against Linda. Her face was slightly transformed by a fully engorged leech hanging off the corner of her upper lip. I gently removed it before she awoke and found it herself.

One morning we heard bells ringing across the valley from a village that would be our destination for the night. It was only a half mile away but across a gorge 4,000 feet deep. We were mildly disheartened to have to descend to the river, cross it on a swinging rope bridge, and hike up to the village, when we heard rhythmic chanting from below. I thought it might be from another Buddhist shrine, but looking down I saw a line of maybe fifty men trotting up the switchbacks, carrying one long piece of steel cable for a new suspension bridge somewhere ahead of us. They passed us long before we reached the village. Ahn Kami told me they had left Katmandu only the day before. They had been on the trail for a day and a half when they passed us, while we had been out almost four full days.

Because it was the end of the monsoon season, erosion was ever present. Terraces built on forty and sixty-degree slopes, laden with rain, were collapsing and plummeting thousands of feet to the bottom of the gorges, wiping out trails and terraces beneath. We often found ourselves shuffling sideways across one of the terrace slides. The new trail was barely a boot width wide and, although the slope wasn't vertical, it's not easy to walk across a sixty-degree slant; to the senses it registers as vertical. The porters held their wicker baskets against their chests and shuffled across effortlessly.

On the fifth day, Ahn Kami let the grandfather porter go. He would probably be back in Kathmandu the following day. The next day we arrived at the upper end of the Helambu Valley. We crossed the headwaters of the Kosi Sun, just a small creek at 10,000 feet. We walked the ridgetop that formed the border between Tibet and Nepal in dense fog; visibility was only twenty feet or so. Suddenly, out of the mist in front of us, came a line of six soldiers dressed in ragged uniforms but carrying small Chinese burp guns and wearing red stars on their hats. We passed each other with nervous salutations. Had we already passed into Tibet? Were they actual Chinese soldiers? Ahn Kami was just as startled as we were. I asked him what was going on but he didn't have an answer. The line of men disappeared quickly into the fog behind us. Then one of the soldiers came running back, calling Ahn Kami by name. He was a cousin on border patrol. Ahn Kami explained that they, too, had been startled by our sudden appearance through the fog. They had been out for a month, moving in and out of Nepal or Tibet as the physical terrain required, sometimes trading uniforms and weapons as souvenirs. We regrouped in the fog and talked and laughed.

Now a week into our two-week trek, I was beginning to fantasize about the upcoming delights of the famous Yak and Yeti Hotel in Kathmandu, where we planned to celebrate my birthday. Three days later, by walking down and occasionally up and around the gorge of the Kosi Sun River, we came to the highway from Tibet. A couple of hours after that we were taking showers in our elegant room.

Four days later we were enjoying the view from the observation deck of the Kathmandu Airport. We were leaving for Delhi and there was one last thing we needed to do before boarding the plane: get rid of the last of our hash. We had been advised that most western passengers coming into India from Kathmandu were suspected of carrying some form of Nepalese drugs. An unofficial custom had therefore evolved: a final departure ceremony held at The Pipe of Sorrows, a vertical rainwater drainpipe where, after much equivocation, intelligent travelers say goodbye to their unused stash. Return visitors also know where to find the innocuous rain gutter below the observation deck when they arrive back in Kathmandu, so all is not lost. You can leave happy, knowing that someone will enjoy what you have left behind.

ACID AVALANCHE

In 1973 heli-skiing was an elitist sport that required deep pockets. There was only one place to do it then—an isolated lodge beneath the Bugaboo Spire in the heart of the Purcell Mountains of British Columbia. Viet Nam was as much a factor in developing the sport as was the B.C. climate and terrain. Besides flying troops and supplies into combat, Bell's military transport helicopters were ideally suited for lifting nine or more skiers to the tops of peaks within a ten-mile radius of the lodge.

I had been visiting my family in Calgary that March when I heard that an all-new heli-ski operation had recently opened, and it was offering access to immense wilderness terrain in British Columbia. I called to check and was told that, indeed, there was such an operation and a vacancy was available for the coming week. I could ski for half price, $600. The package included lodging and a minimum of 80,000 vertical feet of powder snow.

I drove over to the Columbia River Valley from Calgary the next day. It was a typically dreary day of heavy, water-laden clouds that obscured the mountains. Beside the highway, in a farmer's muddy pasture, was a small parking area where a bus and a helicopter were parked. People from the previous week were leaving and the eager new group stood around asking the departing skiers the inevitable question: "How was your week?" The sport was so new, no one knew what to expect.

As I have subsequently learned, all heli-skiers lie. You can't admit to having spent your life's savings in conditions so miserable you would happily pay the week's cost again just to be shuttled away from the awfulness of having to sit in a lodge, fog-bound, waiting for good weather, reading magazines or playing board games with forty other suicidally depressed skiers. Conversely, how to describe one of the best weeks of your life? I have had both extremes and all the gray areas in between. But despite the escalating price, most heli-skiers find the sport addictive.

The first four days of that first heli-skiing trip were spectacular. On the fifth day it started to snow, part of the more than 500 inches that fall in the mountains each winter. The chopper was grounded because of fog, so the guests broke out the games and books. People develop their own weather-related neuroses while waiting for the weather to break. Mine was to stare at the barometer knowing it would only get worse. Generally I was correct. With this foresight, I had come to the lodge with a tab of acid.

After lunch I swallowed the acid and informed the lodge staff I was going cross-country skiing. I indicated the general direction where I was headed. The snow was falling in silver-dollar-sized flakes and not a breath of wind disturbed their descent; they hit the snowpack with audible plops. Loud, plopping snowflakes indicated to me that it was good acid. I followed a trail through a forest of standing fire-dead trees that writhed in vertical black and white patterns. It was really good acid.

The trail led to the base of Bugaboo Spire. I could barely see a hundred feet ahead of me. Farther along, the trail ascended the left side of the valley until I was above the tall trees on the valley floor. At this point, I started to notice a subtle vibration. I had no idea what its source was until I came upon the first of several avalanche chutes.

I crossed the first chute and then realized that the sound was the sensation of tremendous elastic tension given off by the snowpack above me that I sensed would soon be released in an avalanche. This revelation came in the midst of another chute, at the bottom of which was a conical mound where years of avalanche debris had built a pile thirty feet high. At the top was a little wind and snow blasted fir tree that had grown at an angle, beaten back by repeated avalanches.

In my altered state, I reasoned if that little tree had survived for years at the end of this avalanche path, so could I. I skied to the bottom of the chute and climbed to the top of the mound and settled against the weathered trunk of the stalwart little tree and waited, listening to the increasing tension.

When the release sounds of the snowpack came, I was exhilarated. The show had begun! From my location I could see up the avalanche path to a black cliff face above the trail I had just been on. Everything above was obscured by snow and mist. *Whoomph* echoed back and forth in the cirques high above me. Multiple avalanches! These were the first real sounds I had heard since leaving the lodge. That sound is nature's way of saying, "Bend over and kiss your ass goodbye." But in my acid-addled mind, I was filled with glee and expectation.

I concentrated on the black cliff band above the avalanche path. Suddenly, as snow poured down its face, it turned white. A loud hissing sound accompanied the tons of snow sweeping toward me. The rushing white torrent engulfed the old snow layer just opposite my position and then broke around the little hill I was relying on for safety. Then, immediately behind the slide, came a huge snowball, fifty to a hundred feet in diameter. I was doomed. But it, too, broke around the bottom of the hill, and for a few seconds I was engulfed in wind and ice crystals. The snowball was an ice crystal billow towed or rolling down the mountain by the vacuum created by the slide itself. It was breathtaking.

Suddenly, all was calm. The valley became silent again. From my secure perch I yelled, "Bravo!" and clapped my gloved hands together. I stood up, dusted myself off, skied back down the little hill, and returned to the lodge in time for tea and pastries. My weather-related depression was gone and the next morning we were back heli-skiing in fresh powder.

MISADVENTURES

The buyer of my flying operation, a young Frenchman named Bernard, and two passengers were killed in a violent crash just north of Albuquerque in mid-January 1974. Weather and pilot error were the cause of the crash. Bernard had picked up two passengers at the Angel Fire Airport for a flight to Albuquerque while, ironically, I was cross-country skiing as he passed over me, heading for the Rio Grande Valley. The weather was windy and mixed with clouds close to the mountain ridgelines. I congratulated myself that he was flying and I was skiing in the mountains. But further south there were intense snow showers.

Bernard flew into one just north of Albuquerque and we speculated that he became disoriented in the blizzard. The shower left a ground track of snow across the valley, five miles wide at most. It would have taken only a couple of minutes to penetrate and be out the other side into relatively clear weather, but it was enough for him to lose directional control of the single-engine plane and plunge to the ground.

Frank, another pilot who had flown for me, had been directed by Albuquerque Departure Control to fly to the site of an emergency locator beacon that was picked up by a Russian satellite. The transmission point was from one of the Indian pueblos between the interstate to Santa Fe and the Rio Grande. Frank was flying back to Santa Fe anyway so he passed over the wreckage for a look. When he got down he called me and said he thought it was one of my planes and that no one could have survived the crash. He was right. Bernard and two passengers had been killed on impact. The 5:30 news showed pictures of the crash site taken from a hovering helicopter. The National Transportation Safety Board (NTSB) figured that the plane hit sixty degrees nose down at full power. I flew over it the next morning to see for myself.

Bernard had come to town several months earlier to buy my charter company, Taos Air Taxi. He was a young businessman in love with flying. His enthusiasm reminded me of myself ten years earlier, at twenty-seven, when I started flying commercially. He arrived in Taos with his girlfriend and his six-year-old son from a recent divorce. I liked him immediately and, as I was burnt out on the business, I sold him the operation and one aircraft on a note with the hope that he would be able to pay me back within a couple of years. I was left with an old Bonanza with archaic radios, even for 1974.

Later that winter Linda and my friend Nate and I were flying up to Denver for an evening on the town. We hit a big bump on the east side of La Veta Pass, which reduced Linda to muffled sobs for the rest of the flight. Her fear was further renewed at Colorado Springs when we flew into deteriorating weather. I had just enough radio equipment to contact center and file for IFR approach into Stapleton Airport. When I tried the cockpit lighting system I found it wasn't functioning. Nate, fortunately, had a matchbook with a joint tucked behind the few matches left. Twenty minutes of flight time remained in a black, snowy void, only occasionally illuminated by Nate's judicious use of our diminishing match supply.

I was finally cleared to intercept the instrument landing system for runway 26. As soon as I turned down the localizer, the speaker inundated the cockpit with the sound of a mariachi band. I flew the localizer course with the ILS indicator swaying to the rhythm of Mexican ranchero music. Just as the last match was searing Nate's fingers, the approach lights showed up through the snow and we landed.

The flight back the next day was worse. Nate chose to stay over rather than return with us. We were trying to get out of Denver in the face of further bad weather. We headed back south, climbing steadily to clear the rising cloud deck beneath us. Icing over the Sangre del Cristo Mountains kept us from crossing La Veta Pass and into the upper Rio Grande Valley to Taos. I finally ended up at 16,000 feet but still within visual flight eighty miles east of Albuquerque. I spotted the ground through a small hole in the cloud cover. I circled down through the hole with the flaps and wheels extended. It was snowing heavily in all directions as I came out less than 500 feet above the ground. I was right over I-40 east of Albuquerque. There was a two-lane overpass across the freeway which I promptly landed on.

We thought of hitching a ride into Albuquerque but, after getting out of the plane and walking a couple hundred feet, I realized there was no traffic; the interstate was closed due to the weather. The sun was setting through a narrow slit in the western sky, and to the north I could see a thin clear horizon between the lowering clouds and the ground. There was at least five miles of horizontal visibility and the Las Vegas airport was only thirty miles in that direction. We could either stay in the plane and freeze to death or get back in the air for the short hop to Las Vegas. Linda demanded to be left there rather than fly again but I coerced her into staying aboard. We took off and flew into Las Vegas without a problem. A friend drove over from Taos and picked us up at a diner and drove us back that evening.

On another flight, Linda and I were returning from Denver just before dark. The weather began deteriorating at the Colorado border until finally, just north of Questa and only twenty miles from Taos, it became dark, with visibility reduced down to a quarter mile. I was flying just above the highway which I could barely see, but just high enough to avoid any power lines. Linda was indicating that if I didn't get her on the ground, she would jump. I could see the arc lights by the state weighing station coming up and knew that there was a dirt airstrip to the west of the station. I jogged to the right and got the flaps and wheels down. I could just make out the outline of the snowbanks along the runway ahead of me.

I reduced power and descended to the strip, but just before touching down my landing lights illuminated deep tracks in the snow. The strip hadn't been plowed. I hit the throttle to go around. Instead, even with full power, the plane came to a dead stop in less than a hundred feet. The snow was crusty from an earlier melt so when the main wheels hit and broke through, they acted as brakes. Fortunately, I had pulled the nose up so the relatively fragile gear didn't collapse. I shut the engine down and we got out to walk over to a nearby farmhouse to use a telephone to call for a ride back to Taos. The house's owners offered us dinner while we waited.

When our ride came and we were on our way back to Taos, we saw several fire and rescue vehicles stuck in the snow at the far end of the runway. They must have been alerted by someone at the weigh station who had seen the plane disappear into the snow. The high banks along the runway obscured it from the road so witnesses had assumed we had crashed.

The next year, and under almost identical circumstances, I was flying down from Colorado and again ran into heavy snow just north of Questa. The visibility was so bad that I put the airplane down on the highway just north of the same weigh station and then taxied into the facility to get my plane off the road. The official was quite surprised to see me. I used his phone to call my friend Nate, who drove up and picked me up. The Taos News got a picture of the plane sitting at the station the next day with the caption, "Strange Visitor to Questa."

CANYON TALES

In late May of 1975, with several years of rafting behind me, Linda and I joined a three-boat group of ten people for the ultimate American rafting experience—paddling through the world class rapids of the Grand Canyon. We had flown into Marble Canyon to join our companions and had somehow crammed all our gear, including three eleven-foot wooden oars, into my plane.

The other rafters were all from Aspen and, like us, had never before experienced a big whitewater river. We dined that night at the Marble Canyon Inn surrounded by spectacular blown-up photos of large commercial rafts flipping in the three biggest rapids in the Grand: Hance, Crystal, and Lava, notorious whitewater we would be rowing through in the coming two weeks. The photos were of thirty-foot boats powered by forty hp engines and operated by professional boatmen, tipping over and throwing their helpless passengers into the raging water. Did those passengers survive? And how would we fare in our tiny fourteen-foot rafts powered by each boat's single oarsman? Fortunately, the Marble Canyon Inn had a well-stocked bar. We told ourselves by the time we got to Hance, the first of the big rapids, we would be seasoned and ready.

Two days later and thirty miles in, we rowed up on a Class V (five) rapid called House Rock. It was hardly rated although, for us, it was the biggest one we'd encountered so far. Although a Class V is generally considered not worth scouting, we stopped on a sand bar above it to examine our possible route. When I saw that it was a real horror, I resolved to stay there and await a helicopter evacuation. Clearly there was no way through.

The river jammed up against the left canyon wall and just to its side were two huge, mostly submerged, rocks the size of, well, houses. At the downstream end of each rock was a huge hole and the entire river was directed right into them. There looked to be no safe way through. Why hadn't someone told us about this, and if these were truly only Class V rapids, how would we possibly handle the Class IXs and Xs awaiting us below? I would sue the Park Service for failure to caution us. Someone would pay.

While I was silently raging, one of the thirty-foot commercial boats soared by into the rapid. They made it through easily and, with their 40 hp engine, they kept far enough right to avoid the dangers on the outer curve of the river. They made House Rock seem doable so my friend Baxter walked back to his boat and put in. I watched with glee, and more horror, as he was swept out into the left side, yet miraculously went through without flipping. He ran between the two huge rocks and the wall. With Baxter through, I had no choice but to try my own luck.

I had three passengers who fortunately knew nothing of rafting or how lucky Baxter's run had been. A flip would cause us to either hydraulic and drown under one of the two rocks, or be dashed against the left wall. I had neither the skill nor the strength to pull far enough right to avoid the looming hazards, so I would have to trust in luck. And once through, what awaited us at Hance, another forty miles down the river?

My passengers—Linda, a friend and business partner, plus his famous supermodel girlfriend—tightened their life jackets and affixed themselves to the raft's lifelines with death grips. I pulled off the shore, trying to keep the boat close to the right bank, but my right oar kept hitting the shallow bottom, causing me to miss my strokes. The current grabbed us and I found myself heading hopelessly for the left wall and the huge rocks and gaping holes.

I gave up trying to row to the right because that would probably set us up for the upper hole. All I could do was stroke to keep the bow facing into the oncoming maelstrom. I passed the first large hole and then a capricious current swung me across to the right of the next rock. Then I was through and pulling for an eddy below the rapid. It had been a spectacular run made without any benefit of skill whatsoever. The next boat came through and now we were river-bonded. We had made it and we were cool.

Two days later we came up on Grapevine, another Class V rapid, but by then we had already passed through several Fives. A quarter mile above the rapid, another commercial boat motored past, and at the lip of Grapevine it plunged out of sight into mist and spray. What had happened to them?

I stood up on my rowing frame but couldn't see anything but turbulent whitewater in a very narrow canyon. There was no place to pull out; the canyon walls were vertically sheer to the water, and the current was raging. All my pre-House Rock fears came back. I imagined this was what it was like for Colonel Powell a hundred years earlier. Powell was the one-armed Civil War veteran who led the first expedition through the Grand Canyon in 1869. For them, in their heavy wooden, high-sided, flat-bottomed dories, every rapid was potential doom.

I dropped back into the rowing frame to keep the bow heading into the tempest.

Two years earlier I had been knocked out of the stern while a friend had been rowing a rapid on the Green River that Powell had described as a "boulder-strewn maelstrom." What was ahead epitomized maelstrom. Below the falls was a narrow channel with huge waves crossing from both walls and collapsing on top of the only possible route through. The river had been reduced to a hundred-foot-wide torrent.

I locked my feet between the rowing frame and the inflated cross thwart. With my feet locked down I could be dislodged from my seat but not thrown over the side. My stability in the rowing frame was also augmented by keeping the oars in the water. We slid down the face and through the trough with little water coming in. We were through! What skill!

But enough of whitewater; the real horror of boating on the Grand is an upstream gale and an accompanying sand storm. On the afternoon of the fourth day, one caught us on a long straight section of the river. It was so strong that the gusts blew walls of spray upstream. It felt as if we were about to capsize but all three boats made it to shore safely. I crammed mine into a tamarisk thicket where we spent the night huddled, coated by sand, and listening to the wind howling off the rim five thousand feet above. When dawn arrived we could see fresh snow halfway down to the river. The temperature on the water was barely above freezing and the air was calm. By midmorning we came to Hance, our first Class X rapid, anti-climactic by now, and we ran it easily.

Some of our passengers departed at Phantom Ranch, including my friend and his girlfriend/model. She had adapted to river life and its attendant hardships, but the mogul couldn't adjust to the fact that there were no telephones and no way for him to follow the stock market on the river. At great expense, he ordered a helicopter to pick him up at Phantom Ranch and get him to the nearest pay phone.

Over the next ten days we passed through the rest of the major rapids with growing confidence as we began to read and understand the river. We spent many hours walking or standing on overlooks carefully analyzing the vagaries of the currents. Once through a rapid, you pose for the camera with the hole exploding beside you. I have a poster of a fourteen-footer taken with a telephoto lens showing a boat heading into a hole but, in reality, the boatman, having made it through, is relaxed and thanking the river gods for his safe passage.

* * *

The next year I signed up to raft the Grand with a group of doctor/kayakers from the East Coast. I had written to all the permit holders, introducing myself as an experienced Grand Canyon rafter. I would provide support, physically and emotionally, for a private party. I had several takers but chose a group for their early fall put-in date. They were all expert kayakers and only needed me and my boat to ferry their gear.

On a long side canyon hike to Thunder Hole, a spectacular spot where a stream flows out of a red wall cliff below the north rim, I was guiding three of the group up to and across a ridge and back down to Deer Creek. As we descended, we found we could clearly hear the delightful sounds of the stream, 1,000 feet below. There was a trail that led to the creek but we were soon out of water and the air felt like a furnace. On the way down the switchbacks, I realized that I had never really been thirsty before. I measured my descent by the increasing sound of the stream and my mounting urge to plunge underwater and swallow Deer Creek. On the valley floor, I stumbled through a screen of cottonwood trees and threw myself into the water, mouth opened wide.

My three companions soon joined me but, one, an athletic kayaker with little body fat, wasn't in good shape; he was severely dehydrated and suffering heat stroke. He desperately needed salt tablets and electrolytes, which were in the boats waiting for us at the river. We proceeded along the stream and from a ledge above, we saw our two boats tied below; the rest of the group had left us.

By now, the heat stroke victim was delirious. Never have so many doctors been so potentially available but were nowhere in sight.

Back at the river we rowed until dark forced us to quit with no dinner. During the night, we had to frequently immerse the kayaker in the fifty-degree river to try to control his body temperature. He was now in a coma and not responding so, at first light, my companions took off with the invalid to reach help. They found the main group by midmorning at Havasu Creek where they stabilized him. He survived, but was incapacitated for the rest of the trip. I vowed to never again forget salt tablets or to overestimate the physical conditioning of my companions.

* * *

My next trip through the Grand Canyon was semi-catered by an outfitter. He supplied us with his fourteen user days and we brought our own boats. It was the perfect arrangement. The proposed trip was in September, the best time for rafting the Grand.

I was invited to join a group of vacationing river guides. It was a mistake. They were hell-bent on staying drunk for the entire three weeks. There was an abundance of beer, and food was a recently road-killed elk. I lasted with them for ten interminable days before I gracefully exited.

After six days, I took off for a solo hike up to Thunder Hole and spent the night sleeping on a ledge overlooking the canyon under a full moon. In the early morning, I continued over to Deer Creek Falls where I joined the rest of the group for breakfast. I learned that one of our companions had fallen during the night and received a shoulder injury.

We decided that my boat would take off for Havasu, where one guy would run up to the Supai village to telephone for help. We would raft on to Lava Falls where the injured guy, his wife, and I would hike out a rough trail. The so-called injury turned out to be a ruse to escape the drunkards and I was happy to go along with it.

We got to Lava Falls in the late afternoon and started to prepare for a hot climb up the 2,000 vertical feet of black rock cliffs and lava ash. We prepped by soaking in the river to cool down. We each drank a cup of Kahlua, soaked towels in the river and wore them like turbans to keep our heads cool. We each carried a gallon of water for pouring over our turbans and for drinking.

Halfway up we stopped in the shade of a large boulder. The air was very still and we were too tired to talk. I was looking across the canyon when some movement on the far side caught my eye. A 300-foot vertical column of rock slowly detached from the canyon wall and, like a large tree, swung out from its base, intact. When it reached an angle of thirty degrees the column broke into segments and then plunged out of sight. There wasn't a sound until impact, which drifted up to us like thunder. The lower canyon filled with red dust. I found out later that both sides of the river were covered with rock fragments from that fall. What if we, or anyone, had been passing underneath that section?

When we had started the climb we had no idea whether or not the telephone call from Havasupai Village would result in a pick-up at the top. In the early evening we were still short of the rim and not sure where the trailhead was. We were also out of water. We heard someone call out above us. A friend of the evacuees had driven in sixty miles from Kanab bearing beer and lemonade.

The next morning, I flew down Kanab Canyon to the confluence, turned hard right, and at twenty feet over the water at 180 mph, I retraced my route through the Grand Canyon from the day before. I passed the rest of the group floating above Lava Falls and then I hurtled through the spray and mist of Lava.

Three hours later I was eating shrimp cocktail at the Santa Monica Pier.

* * *

In July 1983 I rafted the Grand at record-high water. Unpredicted winter snowmelt and a failure of the Bureau of Engineers to recognize the extent of the runoff, led to near disaster at the dam. Lake Powell filled to the point that they had to add height to the top of the dam with heavy wooden planks to control the lake, lest it spill down the face and wash away the power station at the bottom. They were discharging to the max through the emergency tunnels. For a half mile downstream the canyon was filled with spray and mist. While the dam was discharging, the rock was dissolving around the huge concrete pylons that anchored the dam to the canyon wall. The entire edifice was beginning to vibrate and they were worried the whole thing might let go.

At that time, we were in the narrowest part of the canyon at Phantom Ranch. A ranger at the suspension bridge suggested we evacuate; no one knew what was going to happen. I was with my son Josh and we declined. We had stopped to pick up Nate and his girlfriend who were joining us, and we didn't want to stick around for an evacuation order. We pulled out and headed for Horn Creek. The current was faster than I had ever encountered and the whirlpools and eddies were horrendous.

We swept down to Horn Creek which is not a rapid you normally have to check out but, because of the increased volume of water, I pulled over to a ledge to see what the river was doing. Horn was named for a horn-like projection of water that erupts right in the center of a spillover at normal flows of ten to twenty thousand cubic feet/second. The flow that day was 96,000 cfs. It was now more than a rapid; it was an enormous column of water being forced through a spout. The river was a hellish torrent, drowning out the rapid with its sheer volume and speed.

I was pulling in on the left side just above the spillover but, just as Josh was ready to jump to a ledge with the bow line, a capricious current grabbed the burlap beer bag hanging off the stern and proceeded to drag the boat backward toward the torrent. I tried desperately to row forward but the current was stronger, so inch by inch, we were drawn closer to the roaring hole. It took no longer than half a minute for the stern to pitch over into an abyss of thundering water and spray. We fell backward into a spray pool, ten feet below the top. Suddenly, there we were, beside and below the thundering river passing immediately beside us. From there we could easily climb to the viewpoint with the rest of our group, who had also successfully made it to the ledge. Later, when everyone had passed safely through the center of the torrent, we climbed back down to the raft and lowered it into an eddy and back into the current to rejoin the group at Granite, the next rapid below Horn.

In the morning, although we had camped well above river level, we found the kitchen area under four feet of water. There was no current there so everything was sitting, as we had left it, or floating in a slight eddy. Fortunately, the sleeping alcoves in the bushes were situated higher than the kitchen.

Granite and Hermit Rapids were completely drowned by the enormous volume of water pouring from the dam. The huge hole at Crystal, however, had just grown in proportion to the increased flow. The entire river flow was swallowed by the hole. I elected to take Crystal by choosing a route through the tamarisk bushes on the right side, going from one bush to the other, hand over hand. I'd had my thrill the day before at Horn.

Josh and I were leaving the group later that day at Bass/Shinumu. We were planning a two-day hike up Shinumu and White Creek to Swamp Point on the North Bass wilderness trail. When we swirled into Shinumu, the takeout and lower campsite were completely under water. There was no eddy at all, just strong current. We were barely able to hold onto the top of the tamarisk while we collected our gear and threw it ashore. We jumped after the gear. Meanwhile, the boat with our friends was swept away. The other three boats hadn't even tried to pull in.

Josh and I were alone at the bottom of the Grand Canyon with a two-day, 6,000-foot ascent ahead of us. Rather than camp on the river we decided to start hiking over the first ridge and stay at Bass Camp, a mile up Shinumu Creek. We climbed up to the ridgetop but, from our perch, the creek didn't sound right. It was roaring back at us. The snowmelt from Kaibab Plateau had turned it into a river. We descended, only to find the trail upstream completely under water. We tried wading in chest-deep snowmelt but there was no way; one slip while wading against the current and we would be on our way down to the Colorado River.

We climbed back over the ridge to find a campfire burning beside the river. A commercial boat had pulled in for the night and we joined its passengers for dinner. The next morning the boatman offered us a ride so we could rejoin our group. He was a stoner and he would deposit his passengers ashore for short exploration hikes to sacred Indian sites, manufactured solely by his imagination, so he could have time to load and relight his pipe. In one season, he would do fifteen five-day motorized runs on the river from May to September. In the winter, he drove a snow cat through the night, stoned, at a Colorado ski area.

By early afternoon we had rejoined our group.

Two days later, at Havasu Creek, we again left our friends to hike to the Supai Village upstream and get word out that we were safe. As I later learned, just after we left the boats at the confluence, a helicopter settled down on a rock ledge above my boat and a lady ranger stepped out on the skid with a question: "Has anybody seen or heard of someone named Fred Fair?" The search that had started earlier in the afternoon was called off. Meanwhile, I had incurred a bill for $800 in helicopter time.

Josh and I walked up Havasu and camped above Beaver Falls in a spooky valley of dead and dying cottonwood trees draped by morning glory vines. For dinner we pulled out a can of Dinty Moore stew. After starting our little campfire, we found we had no way of opening the can. I found a nail clipper in the bottom of my pack and chipped a hole in the can. Dinner was saved. We were traveling light because I had hoped to make the village and its ice cream parlor before dark that evening.

The next morning, we hiked up to Mooney Falls. I had never been that far up before so when we got to the falls we were stymied as to how to get out of the vertical canyon to the village above. I finally found a chain hanging down the travertine-layered cliffs beside the fall, and we climbed up a series of tunnels through the rock. We pulled ourselves through and over the top ledge like gophers and there, spread out before us, was a festive, multicolored tent village set up by a gay hiking club from Los Angeles. We passed through the still-sleeping encampment in a state of culture shock and went on up to the Indian village.

There, I saw someone standing in a small grass field talking on a hand-held radio. A tourist chopper was arriving from the South Rim. We'd had enough, so I booked the empty helicopter back to the South Rim on my credit card. An hour later we were eating MacDonald's French fries after a spectacular ride out of the canyon, listening to "Flight of the Valkyries" on the chopper's stereo headphones while we hallucinated being in "Apocalypse Now." I pointed out to Josh that it sometimes pays to have a credit card.

Later that afternoon we chartered a plane back across the canyon to Kanab, right over the North Bass Trail and Swamp Point. There was still plenty of snow dotting the forested part of the Kaibab. That evening, in my plane from Kanab to Taos, we flew upstream and over the dam to examine the tremendous volume of water still exiting from the emergency tubes. A full moon illuminated the canyon, and below the dam it was filled to the brim with moon-white mist and spray.

* * *

Five years later I completed the North Bass Trail hike that I hadn't been able to finish with Josh. I joined a group for an event-filled week to Shinumu where the trail begins. I had also invited my friend Will along for the hike out.

The first event was Hance Rapid, which I had always considered to be highly overrated. It's a half mile long and interspersed with holes, ledges, and a current set which puts you into an extremely large hole at the bottom right. On this run I entered the top of the rapid too far right and knew I had blown it. A vicious series of holes culminating in one huge horror at the bottom was my reward for my over-confident position at the top. Instead of futilely attempting to row left, I studied my course and announced to my three passengers that we were doomed.

Moments before they had looked to me with trusting eyes, as my record in the canyon had heretofore been unblemished. I reconfirmed that we were truly fucked and that they should all hover on the bottom of the raft with the gear.

I rowed furiously to keep the bow pointed into the oncoming holes. The raft, now full of water, wallowed from one hole to the next, with the big one up ahead crashing right on the nose. Down we went in a rush and then up the steep breaking side. The huge wave was just starting to collapse back into the hole as we struggled up its building face at such a steep angle that I thought we were going over backward. But it was so steep that all the water in the boat poured out over the stern and, with sudden buoyancy, we bounced free of the hole rather than sliding back and flipping. Suddenly we were through Hance with hardly a need to bail. Another lucky ride!

When we arrival at Shinumu, we had had several river incidents. My friend Feelgood had been rowing and flipping a new cataraft through the upper canyon. The boat was extremely unstable, and the day before he had flipped in Hance, Grapevine, and Horn Creek, not to mention lesser rapids in the earlier part of the trip. That morning he asked me if I would row his cataraft through Granite just below the campsite, followed by Hermit and Crystal. I agreed and, with Will aboard, promptly flipped in Granite.

It was my first flip in my rafting career and after getting the cataraft upright I flipped it again on top of a high wave in Hermit. As I felt it going, I bailed out from the top of the wave and had a lovely long fall before I hit water. An eddy carried me to where the pick-up boat couldn't retrieve me, so I floated in a whirlpool until someone threw me a line from shore. By then the fifty-degree water had sapped my strength, and all I could do was hold on until I was dragged to shore.

Meanwhile, one of the dories had hit the wall at Granite, emitting a sound like a kettledrum. The bow section was fractured, so we had to spend a few hours repairing it.

Crystal was the next rapid, and I bowed out of further catarafting. Crystal was particularly vicious and I had heard that the hole had recently enlarged from side canyon flooding. The hole had swallowed the entire river, but there was still a small strip of current against the right bank where we hoped to skirt it. We desperately rowed and all made it except for the dory. The rower was pulling so hard to avoid the hole that he snapped one of his fiberglass oars. The current grabbed the dory but, before he could respond, he and his passenger and the dory were swallowed whole and didn't reappear until a hundred feet below—minus the passenger.

The passenger reappeared, floating against the far wall, and he was then washed helplessly over the ledges at the bottom of Crystal. I rowed out from shore to catch him but, in the full current, he was moving faster than I was. He floated another mile before anyone caught up with him and, by then, he was unconscious from hypothermia. We spent another hour reviving him on some warm rocks.

It was then almost dark. With another ten miles to go to Shinumu we rowed until finally, far downstream, I saw Carl —my friend who had driven to Swamp Point and then hiked down to the river. He was taking my place on the river, and I would use his car to drive back to my plane at Marble Canyon.

Will, my friend and raft passenger for the past week, had survived the horror of Hance, the cataraft flips, and now was faced with an impending 6,000-foot ascent up the North Bass Trail to Swamp Point. We left the group for an early morning start, exchanging farewells with friends who, only a week earlier, had been strangers. We climbed over the ridge and back down to Shinumu Creek, the site of my earlier flooded turnaround with Josh. We bathed at Upper Bass Camp in an idyllic stream and then continued along Shinumu until White Creek intersected from the left. Earlier flash floods had filled this tight gorge with debris and boulders, but now it was dry.

About midday we popped out of the dark gorge onto a magnificent esplanade with 3,000-foot red wall cliffs on our right, while the Powell Plateau formed the walls to our left. The direct sun and heat were intense, a shock from the gorge's shade we had been in since leaving Shinumu Creek.

We walked for an hour, dwarfed by the cliffs, into an ever-narrowing canyon. By late afternoon we were into a deep gorge about fifty feet wide. Somewhere in there we were to find a rock cairn indicating a trail up the left wall. We wanted to get out of the gorge before dark in case of an evening thunderstorm and flash flood. We found the cairn and a vague track climbing up a steep dirt and shale slope. Using our hands and feet, we climbed up the sixty-degree incline. As we got higher, we emerged into early evening light. Finally, a thousand feet above the gorge floor, we came upon a narrow bench where a relatively clear trail was defined. By then it was too dark to proceed so we had to sleep on the trail. Dinner, like our earlier lunch, was an energy bar.

The next morning, we started out at first light, trying to beat the sun. Above us, at 2,000 feet, was the saddle between the Powell Plateau and Swamp Point on the edge of the Kaibab Plateau. We were racing to make the steep climb before the sun caught us.

The trail soon disappeared into a morass of gullies and heavy brush. We coursed back and forth, searching for another rock cairn that would indicate the start of the climb to the saddle. After long, slow struggling for over an hour, we found both it and the trail. As we climbed, the vegetation thinned. Swamp Point was finally visible, 1,500 feet above us. We were still in the cool shadows but the sun line was chasing us from below.

We were long out of water, but there was a seep at the bottom of the red wall where we could replenish our canteens. We made it to the seep just seconds ahead of the sun. For the last thousand feet, energized by water and the breakfast bar, Will tried to catch me so he could kill me for taking him on this adventure. But all was forgiven at the top where Carl's car waited.

From Swamp Point we could look down over the whole length of our day and the climb from Shinumu, 6,000 feet beneath us. It was autumn at this altitude and the aspen leaves were starting to turn as we drove across the Kaibab Plateau. An hour later I was drinking a chocolate malt at Jacob's Lake Lodge. Three hours after that I was back home in Taos enjoying a hot shower.

ARSON

On a brittle cold January morning in 1977, I drove twenty miles north of Taos to the small village of Questa. I was looking to buy a parcel of forested land on the lower slopes of Cabresto Peak. A local bank had acquired it to develop a subdivision to meet the expanding needs of the village; an old mine had just reopened. The mine, however, did not create a need for house lots. The land remained undeveloped except for an unfinished road leading up to a large aluminum trailer, placed like a shimmering blight on the once-pristine mountainside.

Joe Wilson, the listing realtor, prided himself on never leaving his office to show property, especially on snowy winter days. The most a potential buyer could expect from him was a hand-drawn map, which, along with some verbal directions, got me to the rough road that climbed to the trailer.

The acreage I had come to see ran north from the trailer in a rectangle. It was already platted into one and two-acre lots but lacked access roads. I bounced along the snow-covered dirt track and stopped fifty feet from the trailer. Smoke was coming out of the chimney and there was a car parked outside. This didn't surprise me. Joe had said something about a strange woman living there and he warned me to keep out of her way.

There were two feet of snow on the ground, and I was ready with my cross-country skis. I toured the land for a couple of hours then came back to my truck. As I was taking off my skis, I heard the trailer door open, and I imagined some grandmotherly figure calling out to invite me in for tea and cookies. Instead, looking up, I saw two orange, shaggy-haired primates bounding toward me, their knuckles dragging in the snow. They were only about twenty feet away and coming fast. I took it all in immediately and, without much thought, opened the door of the truck and jumped in. The larger ape stopped two feet from the door, drew himself fully upright, bared his yellow fangs, thrust out his chest, and then thumped it a couple of times with his fists while roaring at me in a decidedly aggressive fashion. I thought, *Boy, Joe is going to pay for this!*

The woman who lived in the trailer was, as I discovered later, an animal trainer. Behind and inside the trailer were wolves and lions and other beasts. Some guy, a lawyer from New York, owned the triple-wide trailer and rented it to her. I never laid eyes on her as she guarded her privacy, but the next day I brought the elderly realtor out under the guise that I wanted him to show me the property and introduce me to the lady in the trailer before I signed. I was going to pay him back by giving him an opportunity to meet the monkeys.

We arrived at the same time the next day and parked in the same place, hoping the lady would turn out the apes just as before. I wasn't disappointed. Joe had already gotten out of his car and was starting to walk toward her door when they catapulted out of the trailer and headed toward him. He was sixty but he responded like a much younger man, doing a quick about-face and racing to the car. As I hadn't abandoned the safety of the vehicle, I saved him the effort of opening the door by shoving it open for him. He threw himself inside and slammed it hard. I was delighted.

I bought the property with a short-term bank loan, which required that I sell a considerable number of lots that summer.

The lady with her menagerie moved out in the spring when road construction started. By mid-May, I'd provided some form of access to enough of the lots so when they sold, I could pay off the loan. I had to sell $200,000 worth of land before summer's end.

Meanwhile, I sold my friend Ozzie on a plan of setting up a telephone sales operation in Taos. With all my remaining money, we would blitz the Albuquerque market for one Memorial Day weekend sales effort. Ozzie would man the phone bank of two lines and induce potential buyers to drive 140 miles north to take advantage of this once-in-a-lifetime opportunity to own property in scenic northern New Mexico.

After putting everything in motion, paying for the advertising, and selling the skeptical Ozzie on the idea of making a fortune on commissions, I left for a long weekend in Aspen. I couldn't stand the tension of waiting for the phones to ring off the hook with eager buyers.

I left Ozzie with the phones in a rented office right off Taos Plaza with instructions not to call me even if he could find me. I wanted to return and sign sales agreements. When I saw him after the weekend his incredulous comment was, "At first I thought the phones were out of order." The only call that weekend was a wrong number. I was faced with imminent financial disaster. All my money had gone into the down payment and the sales blitz.

I anguished until later in the week, when I received a call from a Doug MacArthur, who wanted to buy my entire inventory. Doug was recently from North Carolina, where he and his team had recently fled from an indictment regarding land sales fraud. Land sales guys are gypsies; they must keep moving since the Consumer Protection Agency of whatever state they last worked catches up with them. I wept with gratitude.

Then he mentioned that, of course, he would buy it over time and that I should come to Albuquerque and talk terms. Two hours later, I was at his sales center, the entire top floor of a two-story building with enough space to house fifty salesmen with fifty copies of the Albuquerque phone book. Doug had a real phone bank. Every evening, all fifty guys would get a section of the directory and go through it, name by name, cold calling. If they weren't hung up on right away, they would hold their target's attention by offering all kinds of free inducements to drive to whatever property they were hustling.

I listened to Doug's pitch. What could I lose? This was his offer: he would take half the proceeds for selling the land, including the down payments, and I would keep most of the contracts they generated. He came up to Questa the following weekend to look at the property. He liked it, but said the ugly triple-wide had to go. It sat at the entrance to the property and was clearly in violation of Taos County subdivision regulations.

I called the lawyer guy in New York to explain. I was polite. He wasn't. He told me, "Go fuck yourself and sue me, shit-for-brains!"

The next Sunday, I was back on the property packing the weekend edition of the New York Times up a canyon on the backside. It was a hot, windless afternoon in early July. Fortunately, for my purposes, there had been thunderstorms up and down the Rio Grande Valley for much of the week, so the forested slopes were moisture-soaked and, in places, still muddy.

I scouted the trailer and boldly walked up and knocked on the door. The lock had been removed since the lady had moved out, so I went inside but came out quickly. The rank smell inside was like a lion's den at the zoo. I returned for a short foray to find a long corridor that ran the full length of the trailer. There were several wooden cabinets at opposite ends. My plan was simple. I would use newspaper to start two fires. A prior employee of mine had been an arsonist back East and he had advised: Always start fires with newspapers and plenty of draft; also makes sure to get a premium for the number of victims.

I dove back into the reeking lion's den, ran down the corridor and started crumpling newspaper and stuffing wads into the corner cabinets. I had to hold my breath each trip because of the urine stench. It took several trips to opposite ends of the trailer to fill the cabinets with crumpled papers. On my last trip, I struck a match and lit the pile of papers in one of the floor-to-ceiling cabinets. I ran back down the hall, stopping at the midpoint to open the door for a shot of fresh air. I ran back to the far corner cabinet, lit it, then turned to rush back to the door, thirty feet away. As I started down the narrow hallway, tongues of spiraling orange flames raced toward me. That end of the trailer was a raging conflagration. I jumped through the doorway with the fire right behind me.

Once outside, I could see flames already spiraling through the roof and out the door I had just exited. I grabbed my pack and ran into the trees where I stopped to admire my handiwork. The entire trailer was burning. There was a vertical, twisting pillar of flames rising fifty feet above. A hundred feet from the trailer, I could feel the intense heat.

I could hear the fire sirens in Questa. It was time to keep moving back up the hillside and over the ridge to the truck. If he had any fire insurance, the belligerent New York lawyer owed me.

A couple of weeks later, Doug started selling the property. Within six weeks his inventory was sold, and I was holding enough cash and contracts to pay off the bank. A month later, Doug was on the run again: New Mexico's land fraud investigator was coming after him and his band of gypsy salesmen. Just before he left town he called to ask if I would buy back his share of the paper for twenty cents on the dollar. I offered ten cents and we had a deal. Within two months I had gone from pitiful debtor to successful arsonist with cash flow.

BUYING BEAR PAW

Before Doug left New Mexico for good, he took me to see another subdivision for sale in the northern neck of Sandoval County. Although it was tied up in litigation, he thought I might be interested in it. Years before, Hueri and I had driven up that way but I had forgotten how pretty it was.

From the Rio Grande Valley, the road gradually rises from the badlands to the Colorado Plateau. Cabezon Peak to the west looks to be straight out of the Paleolithic, and the east side of the highway is dominated by convolutions of geological trauma. Then come the pristine forested slopes of the San Pedro Mountains, the western flanks of the Jemez Volcano. Just north of Cuba, the San Pedros become a designated wilderness area, a forty thousand-acre forested park at ten thousand feet. This plateau captures most of the moisture drifting east from the Pacific and acts as a great sponge or muskeg. One of its drainages is San Jose Creek, the most northern system that flows off the San Pedros. The San Jose is the upper headwater of the Rio Puerco stream system that flows into the Rio Grande just south of Albuquerque, although I doubt any of the San Pedro waters ever reach that far.

We arrived in Regina about noon. The village was nothing more than a gas station and a bar called the Coon Holler. There was a little shack for a post office and another dozen derelict houses or stores scattered on either side of the road.

Just north of the village we turned east toward the mountains and drove a mile up a dirt road, which crested over a low ridge, and there before us was an open valley filled with ponds and pasture. The valley was the stream floor of San Jose Creek; the ponds had been created by dams. The bottom pond could generously be described as a lake. The upper end of the valley was dominated by the San Pedros, which rise three thousand feet above the ranch. I was told there was a resident elk herd. Across the valley were rows of apple trees neatly lined up on irrigated terraces. Behind the orchard was more forest, all the way back to the mountains.

I fell in love. I couldn't believe such a lovely piece of property could have fallen into financial distress. Over the next two years I would find out why.

There was a subdivision attached to the forested side of the property which was what we had come to see. My only thought was to buy the entire package. I was *seriously* in love. That was the summer of 1978. Twenty-eight months later, after many tortured negotiations, a few shenanigans, some horse-trading, much wheeling and dealing, and a lot of sustained effort, I would become the owner of what would become Bear Paw Ranch, still my treasured getaway and retreat.

BAJA

As a child, I began sailing with my father on the coast of British Columbia. The first boat I owned was a share in *Gypsy*, a shiny, new fifty-foot Gulfstar sloop. *Gypsy* spent the summers in the northeast out of Sag Harbor, and winters exploring the Caribbean. I sailed her in both locations, with or without a crew. (A crew usually consisted of a live-aboard handyman/cook. Sometimes the live-aboard would upgrade to "captain" if he was able to attract a girlfriend who could *really* cook.)

In 1978, we (*Gypsy*'s four partners) upgraded to a Stevans 60. Within a couple years, as in a poker game, I folded my cards and left the table; expenses were growing exponentially. But instead of leaving the game forever, I moved it to the West Coast.

After a boatless year, I formed a new partnership consisting of lawyers, doctors, and other professionals who, at a certain age, sense a need for a boat or, as we like to call it, a yacht. The new partnership and our new boat were named *Mullet*.

We were the mid-life crisis set, drawn to planes and yachts, and suffering from a syndrome called "boat self-abuse." Every would-be boat owner could benefit from a support group. The first sign one needs help is when you catch yourself picking up yachting or sailing magazines and turning directly to the classified ads. This is a red flag. Everyone else who owns a boat is trying to sell it.

We Mullets were soon reading listings and making offers. Miraculously, we found the boat of our dreams, owned by a typically desperate seller. After a pre-purchase inspection, we traveled to Long Beach, California, for sea trials—a short sail to Catalina Island for dinner. This was the longest open-water crossing the boat had made since it had been delivered to the previous owner, five years earlier, on the deck of a freighter from Taiwan.

Our new boat, renamed *Mullet,* was a stout Peterson 44 sloop. Like most West Coast boats, it had been safely docked in a marina since its arrival in California. Our plan was to sail it in stages to New Zealand. In preparation for our trans-Pacific trip, we planned to first take it down to Cabo San Lucas and enjoy the Sea of Cortez. I hired a young guy to be the live-aboard. His duties would be to shop, handle maintenance, and deal with the Mexican port authorities for paperwork and bribes. Provisioning was carried out in the hour prior to our departure by giving the five-man crew shopping carts at Safeway and telling them to meet back at the checkout counter in twenty minutes. As a backup, I had stuffed the bilge with canned goods.

The crew for the 800-mile sail down the west coast of Baja consisted of my nineteen-year-old son Michael; Ted, a fellow boat partner; Tim, a friend from Taos with prior sailing experience; and Gordon, the young live-aboard. We left San Diego in early January 1980 at midnight and motored down to Ensenada, Mexico, to clear customs and have lunch. Later in the afternoon we sailed out to anchor for the night at Todos Santos Island, a few miles offshore from Ensenada.

We backed the boat into a rocky cove and pinned it to rocks on the shore with the bow anchor and two lines off the stern. Amazingly, we awoke the next morning still in the same location. Nothing had dragged or come loose in the night. We were on the lee side of the island, which was fortuitous as the weather had deteriorated during the night and the wind blew in fiercely from the west. Before we left the protected anchorage, we spent a couple of hours walking through a sea bird rookery on the grassy spine of the island.

Around noon we sailed out of the cove. By late afternoon the wind was blowing a steady twenty knots. I was on the verge of telling Gordon to reduce sails for the night when Ted delivered pork chops for dinner. This caused Captain Gordon to lunge to the rail from the cockpit, vomiting. We were sailing parallel to the coast, five miles offshore, with a major navigational hazard ahead—the Sacramento Reef, named for the passenger boat that sank there en route from Panama to California during the Gold Rush.

I was now in command. Gordon, seasick, had dragged himself below, not to reappear for three days. My main concern was to stay off the reef, so I corrected our course seaward. I continued to do so until we were running at a right angle to the coast to compensate for compass error. Around nine o'clock, the wind picked up to twenty-five knots and was gusting over thirty. We were passing the lights on the coast off San Quintin and, seaward a of couple miles, was a brightly lit cruise ship out of Long Beach, heading for Cabo with thousands of passengers. I pictured happy people on both sides of us, sitting in restaurants with white linen tablecloths, candles, and wine, while we battled the elements and fought our way down the Baja coast.

There was no joy at the helm that night. I was cold and slightly seasick. My teeth chattered all night, whether I was below in a damp sleeping bag or huddled on deck dressed in everything I had with me. I should have reduced the main sail and changed the large foresail for a working jib, but it was more expedient to stay in the cockpit rather than work on the deck in the dark. The boat roared along, twenty tons skidding down the faces of overtaking waves, making eight-plus knots through the dark night. The only illumination came from the infrequent use of the spreader lights above.

Each functioning member of the crew took two-hour watches at the wheel. This was enough time to induce serious doubt about making any future sailing commitments. When I wasn't in the cockpit or at the chart table, I was on my bunk, waiting. I waited for the boat to pitchpole at the bottom of a wave we had just skidded down or, failing that, surf a large wave onto the Sacramento Reef due to compass error, or for the mast to come crashing down from a violent wind gust. It was a long night.

A dirty gray dawn brightened the horizon just enough to give us an indication of the sea that had built up after dark. By noon, however, the wind dropped off. Things dried out. We began to think about eating and sleeping. I estimated our position to be about forty miles offshore, so I set a new course that would angle us back to the coast. I wanted to stop in Turtle Bay, one of the few anchorages on the west coast of Baja, and I figured we could be there late the next day.

The wind continued dropping until finally, at dark, we started motoring. What a difference from the night before. We had a leisurely dinner in the cockpit and everyone but Gordon took four-hour watches. Except for my nighttime fear of being plucked from the wheel by the tentacles of The Great Squid, the night went well. A fiberglass hull is a great sound box for sea creature serenades; many aquatic squeals, whistles, and moans could be heard through it during our lonely night watches. We were sailing among a migration of gray whales working their way down to the calving grounds on the Pacific coast of Baja. Occasionally, we could feel the boat shudder as one of these magnificent creatures came up for a back scratch on our keel.

By dawn, we were cruising between the coast and the eastern shore of Isla Cedros. This desolate and spiny island has an incongruous fringe of pine trees growing along its crest. They have stayed alive because of an evolutionary adaptive miracle wherein their pine needles cause moisture from the air to precipitate, which is crucial to their survival as it seldom rains there.

By late afternoon we were anchored in Turtle Bay. The anchorage was the only thing to commend the village. Under only the most desperate of circumstances would the village of Turtle Bay be an end in itself. To celebrate our arrival, we elected to go ashore in the dinghy, dressed in our finest. A wretched lightweight Sea Gull engine (mostly bought by people with doubtful claims to British maritime ancestry) powered the dinghy, an eight-foot inflatable. Fortunately, that Sea Gull vibrated off the transom of the dinghy and into deep water not long after we got to Cabo. It was not replaced with like-kind.

Some things transcend skill. Taking a dinghy ashore through a shore break is one of those sacred moments of command. About a hundred feet from the beach, I noted a diminutive shore break of churning waves about eight inches in height. Inside the break, the wave action kept both the sewage from the village and the turtle guts from the turtle-rendering plant concentrated in an indescribable porridge, washing against the shore. Undaunted, I sized up the break and turned in with a small overtaking wave as I accelerated the dinghy from behind. The wave overtook us, the dinghy broached, skidded sideways, and flipped us all out into the knee-deep goo. Never in maritime history has such a small wave created such misery.

Dripping sewage, sand, and turtle offal, we pulled ourselves from the water and wandered the sandy street. Nothing was open so we returned to the boat. It was Super Bowl Sunday, but for us it was a miserable wet evening.

The next morning, barely on speaking terms, we headed out for a two-day sail to Cabo San Lazaro, a western headland where navigational errors, compounded with strong onshore current, had littered the beach with the corpses of several large freighters. I planned a dawn arrival, but estimated that we would pick up the lighthouse off the cape in the early morning hours.

Miraculously, this two-day sail revived our enthusiasm for the trip. Light winds kept us moving at five knots, and we were frequently accompanied by pods of whales and porpoises. Night watches were so benign that even my fear of the Great Squid was dispelled. Gordon finally showed up on deck. All was well. We picked up the flash from Cabo San Lazaro's light right on the bow just after midnight on the second night. I was greatly admired as a navigator.

By 3 a.m., we could make out the headlands against the starlit sky. I turned parallel to the coast, and we motored until we could identify the anchorage. It was a large open bay but gave good protection from the large northwesterly swells and weather. In the anchorage, a quarter mile inshore, we could see the anchor lights of several Mexican shrimp boats. I continued off the point that marked the entrance to the bay. When I judged that we were far enough beyond the point, we lowered sail and cautiously motored in at reduced speed.

We were all on deck. The spreader lights were on in anticipation of anchoring. To the left, I could hear waves crashing against the point. Ahead, past the two shrimp boats, I could hear the metallic sound of rocks and gravel being dragged back into retreating waves on the rocky beach. Tim was at the bow playing a spotlight on the water ahead of us. It was calm and peaceful.

Then Tim screamed, "Get out of here!" and started running for the cockpit. At the same moment, a red mist from the port navigation light enveloped us. A huge wave broke with a roar on our left. The spreader lights illuminated a white arc of water falling into a black void below us. We rode the edge of a giant wave down in free fall and struck the bottom with our keel. Everyone was knocked over by the impact. Another towering wave came up and collapsed on top of us. Luckily, everyone had tumbled into the relative safety of the center cockpit just as we rode the first wave down. Nobody was washed overboard. The hatches were wide open and a good part of the wave flooded the boat. I was still at the helm holding on for my life.

I rammed the throttle forward trying to get power while spinning the wheel hard to the right. The next wave was coming upon us as the bow slowly started responding. Our world was total confusion; noise and spray in the dark maelstrom of pounding waves. The boat's bow slowly turned into the oncoming wave and rose, taking the wave directly. It felt as if we went almost vertical before the wave broke over us, but this time we took on very little water.

Just as suddenly as it started, it was over. Once again we were cruising on a calm, silent sea as if the previous tumultuous minutes had never happened. Tim, who had been up in the bow, was now huddled on the cockpit floor holding his head in his arms and moaning, "Oh, my God! Oh, my God!" I thought he had suffered a head injury but it was only aftershock. Everyone was still on board, uninjured, and except for a lot of water and gear strewn below, there was no damage.

We headed directly out to sea and spent the next several hours cruising off the entrance to the anchorage, waiting for dawn. When it came, I saw my error. The entrance course had been premature and we had been carried over a storm bar that had built up off the point. The point that I had seen in the dark against the night sky was set back a quarter mile from low, black lava cliffs, where long swells had built up as they compressed against the sudden shallowing.

The first wave had carried us across the bar sideways and deposited us just inside it in time for the next wave to crash down upon us. The third wave, the one we took on the bow, had given us the lift to cross back over the bar and into calm water. Between the bar and the lava cliffs 200 feet inshore, was a washing machine of contradictory seas smashing against each other and against the cliff. We had been right in the middle of it.

We finally entered the bay safely, and anchored. Had there been land transportation available, the crew would have left me there. As it was, we dried everything out and in the afternoon we hiked up the beach, north of the point, to look at the freighters that had washed ashore. Like us, they were victims of navigational errors.

Without further incident, we arrived in Cabo a few days later. For the next several years we used *Mullet* to explore the Sea of Cortez and to go down the coast to Puerto Vallarta, Barra de Navidad, and Manzanillo.

I've had no further sailing traumas. But then again, I haven't cruised offshore since that first *Mullet* sail down Baja. At night, I want to see the warm friendly glow of my favorite restaurants reflected in the waters of a calm marina.

I ended my dubious history of boat ownership with a forty-five-foot powerboat also called *Mullet*. It had two diesel engines, carpeting, air-conditioning, and another diesel for electricity. It was a floating house. I loved it. Alas, Hurricane Floyd sank it in November 1999, in the Bahamas. It had been safely docked in the shallow water port of Marsh Harbor, when a tornado in the eye wall of the hurricane gave it special attention. It lifted the thirty-ton boat out of the water, dropped it, skewering the hull on three dock pilings. The deck house with the dinghy and davit was ripped from the main deck and carried 300 feet and deposited on an exposed reef. The insurance check soothed my grief.

No longer a boat owner, I am proud to call myself a boat bitch—content to step and fetch it on my friends' boats in exchange for a day cruise inside a protected bay.

VALLECITOS

A friend of mine owned a cabin on the upper part of the Vallecitos, a mountain stream that gallops south from the highway that crosses the high country from Tres Piedras to Tierra Amarilla, New Mexico. Forty miles south, from its 10,000-foot beginning, the stream joins the Chama River, which then joins the Rio Grande.

The road was paved within six miles of the cabin. In the winter, when it was open, we could drive to Hopewell Lake and ski to the cabin above the valley floor of the Vallecitos. There was always a good chance that we would be able to ski in on a snowmobile track instead of having to break trail. Even though the trip in was gently downhill, a snowmobile track could ease the journey to a couple of hours.

The cabin was a two-story log structure situated at 9,000 feet, where the nights could get as cold as thirty below in January. One New Year's Day, it was so cold that the steaming beef stroganoff, brought from the kitchen to the large fieldstone fireplace where we were huddled, arrived covered in hoarfrost. The temperature that night was forty below. Our dog, to her dismay, was stuffed into our sleeping bags with us.

One of the great things about the cabin was the propane generator that was installed underground to insulate its sound. When you arrived, you walked inside through the kitchen door, pulled a chain to an overhead light, waited a few seconds for the generator to come silently to life, then watched the light bulb illuminate. The kitchen had a large commercial cook stove and a pump that provided water to the sink. We, being purists of a sort, eschewed turning on the hot water heater. After all, the cabin was part of an authentic winter wilderness experience.

Linda and our friend Larry and I went there in the late winter of 1980 for a one-night stay. There had been record snowpack that winter, and conditions were perfect for cross-country skiing. The next day, we decided to return via the Vallecitos stream to where Placer Creek comes down from Hopewell Lake. From there it was only a couple of miles up an old wagon trail to the lake where we had parked the car.

It was a lovely winter day as we meandered beside and on top of the frozen river, skirting midstream boulders sticking through the ice. In the early afternoon, we came out of the canyon into an open, blinding white valley with forested ridges on either side. On a rocky outcrop beside the ice-covered stream, and in the heat of intense solar radiation, we stripped topless and ate lunch. In the summer the valley is fenced pasture, but on that day the barbed wire fence was buried under the snowpack. Nothing broke the blindingly white expanse of the valley floor.

Although I had never returned to Hopewell Lake via the Vallecitos in the winter before, I was familiar with Placer Creek from mountain biking in the summertime, so I knew I would be able to identify where the creek came out of the mountains. I hadn't, however, reckoned on the whole area being buried under five feet of snow. There was absolutely no sign of the creek or the wagon trail that would lead us up to the lake. We had spent much of the afternoon relaxing in the calm air and radiant warmth, but when the sun slipped behind the western ridge of the Vallecitos Valley the temperature plunged to below freezing. There were several possible routes in the folds of the heavily forested ridge that could be the stream course. But which one? Only one would lead to the car.

I picked a gap where the old wagon trail might have been. We were soon climbing up a steep gully in deep snow. It was difficult and slow, but I was hoping we were over Placer Creek. The gully flattened out into a meadow where the lake should have been. In the dark, there was no indication of a lake. There was also no sign of the paved road or the parking area. Had I picked the wrong drainage? If so, we faced the threat of being lost at 9,500 feet on a freezing winter night.

I was staring ahead into the darkness when, just as I was about to voice my growing concerns, I spotted a red light skimming across the snowpack ahead of us. There was no sound as it streaked from right to left for no more than a couple of seconds before disappearing. Both Linda and Larry saw it too. I realized it was the upper light on top of a large truck. We were only a couple of hundred feet from the highway and the car. We were exactly where we wanted, and needed, to be. We had, indeed, come up a heavily snow-packed Placer Creek, but it was only luck that had us looking toward the road as the truck went by. An hour later we were safely home and soaking in the hot tub.

ROAD RAGE

In 1980 I had an old four-door, two-ton Chrysler. It had massive chrome bumpers with large tit-like protuberances. I used the Chrysler as an airport car in Denver, which meant that it often sat unused for months. On one occasion, I was in town for the day with Jim, a business friend. We were returning to the airport from a meeting in Boulder, and I had just driven through the interchange of I-70 and I-25 when a car pulled up alongside us. The driver leaned across his seat toward me and started waving a short steel bar indicating he would like me to pull over so that he could beat the shit out of me. I had some-how ruined his day back at the interchange.

My first reaction was to ignore the threat. I stared ahead and proceeded to drive a steady fifty-five mph. Meanwhile, the guy pulled ahead in front of me and put on his brakes. I swerved left to avoid him but neatly clipped his bumper as I passed. It was four in the afternoon and traffic was starting to build. Ahead was the tunnel that passed under the runways at Stapleton Airport.

I pulled back into the right lane, a couple of cars ahead of him. In the rearview mirror, I saw him maneuvering in and out of traffic, trying to catch up with me, which he finally did as we entered the tunnel. He passed me and then pulled in front, again braking. This time I didn't have room to pull away, so I drove into the rear of his car. He was driving a lightweight two-door Chevy, so when I hit it, his car pivoted sideways, causing the grill and bumper to skid against the tunnel guardrail. The rear of his car was propped up on my front bumper, giving off a stream of sparks like a welding machine, while the Chrysler was hardly burdened by the load. I was starting to feel a little better, even invulnerable.

Halfway through the tunnel, I shrugged the Chevy off my bumper by braking suddenly. There was no traffic behind me and the tunnel was empty; drivers averse to road rage had stopped to let us have at each other. The Chevy driver drove on ahead. He had no place to go except to the end of the tunnel, either under his own power or riding on my bumper. When we were finally clear of the tunnel I accelerated to pass, but again he pulled out in front, trying to block me. I drove into his left side and noted with some satisfaction that a side panel fell off. He lurched off the road onto the right shoulder and I thought he had stopped chasing me.

I was hoping a cop was on our tail by now but I could see there was still no traffic behind us. I sped up to try and lose the Chevy or exit the interstate without being seen. I was doing eighty mph, and when I got to the next interchange I slowed and fitted back into a heavy stream of southbound traffic on I-225. Jim and I were just starting to relax and talk about the crazy driver when suddenly the passenger window exploded. Our assailant had driven up unnoticed and swung his steel bar as he passed. We were in the left lane and he swung ahead and braked.

Until then I had been driving somewhat defensively with only one goal, to not be stopped. This time when I saw him pulling in front, I stomped on the accelerator at about the same time he started braking. The Chrysler's rear squatted down and leapt into the side of the Chevy. The sudden deceleration caused Jim and me to be thrown forward against our seat belts.

The right front tit on the Chrysler bumper hit the Chevy on its driver's side, just behind the door, causing the Chevy to pivot 180 degrees. It landed facing me, engulfed in blue tire smoke, tipped over on its passenger side, and slid off the highway down into the grassy median while we flashed by. The driver's arm, with the steel bar still in his hand, was clinging to the outside driver's door to keep him from falling across the inside of his car. I could see the Chevy slide to a stop, still on its side. Again, there was no traffic behind us, still no witnesses.

I got off the freeway and drove to a friend's house to have a drink and negotiate with the police, who by now probably had a helicopter out looking for us. They were and they wanted me to turn myself in. As I was an owner of a condo development in the district and paid hefty taxes, I called the city manager and explained my situation: I wanted him as my representative when I talked to the police.

He agreed, so Jim and I drove to the station. The police already had the punk in custody. Jim looked like the businessman he was, which was good, as I was in my usual jeans and t-shirt. The City Manager was already there, which allowed me to tell my story. They put me in a cell with the driver, who turned out to be a nineteen-year-old thug. He was blubbering about his car and what his old man was going to do to him. I told him how lucky he was and that if I'd had a gun, I would have shot him on the interstate in self-defense.

Except for a slightly scuffed bumper and the broken window glass littering the interior, the Chrysler was unscathed. The punk's car, on the other hand, was a total wreck. The investigating cop came in and separated us. I told him I wanted to prosecute, but the cop told me to forget it. The kid's father was a cop with a bad reputation and would probably make things difficult for me. He gave the punk a reckless driving ticket and a careless driving ticket to me.

The Chrysler continued to be an airport car for several more years, in various locations. The road rage event coincided with my selling the condo project, and I happily extricated myself from any further business endeavors in Denver.

SEE YOU IN COURT

In late September 1981, I was at Bear Paw eating lunch with JB, my ranch manager, when a boy knocked on the door. He had ridden his bike up from the highway, a mile away. "The police want you down on the road." I told him to go back and tell the police to come up if they wanted to talk to me. The kid left and, twenty minutes later, he peddled back into the yard with another demand, "You'd better come down now or they're going to tow your airplane!"

JB and I had just finished eating, so we ambled out to my old Dodge Power Wagon and headed to the road. A highway patrol car with two cops was parked in front of my elderly single-engine Cessna 182, where I had driven it off the highway. A thunderstorm had passed through earlier, leaving my landing strip muddy, so I had put down on the road.

One of the cops appeared to be a boy, probably from the bottom of his class. That's all that's available for duty in the backwoods of northern Sandoval County. He was wearing what looked like an oversized Nazi uniform. I didn't get out of the truck. He and I just stared at each other.

"You're goin' to move that plane right now or I'm goin' to git it towed," he said.

"Can't. My strip is too muddy. I'm completely off the road here. Been landing here for years when it gets wet. What's the deal?" I replied.

"Move it now or I'll call the tow truck and cite you for a bunch of violations. Let me see your pilot's license!"

"I'm driving my truck." I offered him my driver's license. From that point, things went further downhill.

When I finally produced my pilot's license, he commanded: "Step out of the truck, Sir!"

The truck door was already ajar, so I opened it. I caught the kid with the extended side mirror, and he went down on his back. The other cop, an unarmed deputy who had been in the car, was backpedaling away from the altercation as fast as his toady little body could move. He tripped and sat down hard on his ass. Meanwhile, the boy cop was trying to get up and draw his holstered pistol at the same time. When he hit the ground, I was having second thoughts about my pissy attitude. Nothing cools the Walter Mitty in me faster than violence. I got out of the truck and said, solicitously, "Sorry about that, Officer. Damned side mirrors, they sure stick out, don't they?" I offered him my hand to help get him off his butt. Fortunately, he took it rather than going for his gun.

I agreed to move the plane. I knew the dirt strip at Lindrith, ten miles west, was dry enough to land on. I could fly over there, and JB could drive over to pick me up. The cop and deputy got back in their patrol car, winners for the moment. Their car was parked in front of me on the road's shoulder, with the deputy in the back seat keeping an eye on me. I was instructed to follow their vehicle until I was safely past some power lines.

I had the plane's engine running, so I started lurching across the shallow bar ditch toward their car. Not a total dummy, the boy cop stopped issuing instructions and started driving. I was right on him as I swung the airplane onto the center of the highway. I had a good view of the deputy sitting in the back seat, his moon eyes looking up at me through the spinning propeller disk. I stayed right on the cop car, then popped up over its roof.

A short while later, I was back in the truck with JB. He was chuckling and I was asking him if he wouldn't mind being my witness in court. I knew the takeoff scene was going to earn me some violations.

The morning after the cop/plane incident, Fran, JB's wife, woke me. "What's goin' on over in the orchard?" she asked. She was standing on the front steps of the ranch house, looking across the valley where 800 apple trees grew on terraces. From a quarter mile away, even without binoculars, I could see flashing lights atop a police car driving through the orchard. Fran said that just moments before, a cop had pulled into her driveway asking where I was and telling her to let me know that if I showed up, I should consider myself under arrest.

What to do? Run, run for home. Run for bail money. Run! And I did. I hopped in the truck and drove back to the plane and took off for Taos. An hour later, I was home, ridding the house of dope paraphernalia and picking up some cash. Then I headed into town to check with Nate, my counselor. His response was loud and unsympathetic laughter. He recommended that I stuff my jeans with hundred dollar bills for my imminent bail needs. I returned to the airport with a plan: fly back to the ranch to see what was happening.

By the time I got back, the ranch was its normal bucolic self. The police had left with B, the 18-year-old head of my construction crew, a young entrepreneur who had been funded to grow a large marijuana crop by an Albuquerque attorney. I had earlier spotted B running ahead of a police car. The cops plucked him off the eight-foot-high deer fence that surrounded the orchard. B, now in police custody, along with a truck carrying a large pile of recently harvested pot, was heading south with a group of law enforcement agents to the county court house, seventy miles away.

As I drove back to the ranch, I noted a lot of marijuana plants lying on the side of the road. They had fallen off the overloaded truck. I headed over to a cabin where the construction crew lived. It was in shambles. There was enough dope scattered on the floor to light up the neighboring Apache reservation.

There was an old ramshackle trailer connected to the cabin by a hundred-foot electrical cord. During the bust, the cops had gone over to inspect it. Unknown to them, two of the crew were ensconced inside, busy trimming the harvest. The trailer was literally stuffed with sinsemilla, hanging from the ceiling. There were fans aiding the drying and their noise had drowned out the sounds of activity. When the boys finally heard something, the cops were already at the door. They stayed silent and listened. Then they heard the cops say that they didn't want to waste any more time and miss lunch at El Bruno's, a restaurant in Cuba famous for its fishbowl margaritas. When they left, the boys fled like deer into the forest.

I showed up a couple of hours after the bust. I checked out the cabin and then walked over to the nearby trailer and opened the door. The aroma of rich, thick sinsemilla leaked out the doors and windows. Obviously, the cops hadn't been able to smell it because they had previously been in the cabin with the same intense odor and their olfactory senses had been dulled. Lucky boys. The bulk of the crop was safe.

I drove the Power Wagon over and hitched it up to the trailer, figuring I had nothing to lose. There might still be some cops around ready to jump me. Or there might not be. I charged off through the forest, making a trail of shattered lodge pole pines as the wider trailer busted its way into the national forest. I got it through my fence, well into the trees, and then jammed it backward into a tight grove of small, spindly pines. By then the trailer was a total wreck, windows broken out, whole sections of aluminum siding hanging off. All its corners were smashed. The crew found it later in the afternoon and emptied it of its contents. I flew back to Taos, exhausted.

B was let off with a slap on the wrist if he completed a year of probation. His attorney partner/backer was the same lawyer who successfully represented him at the hearing.

Early the next year, I was flying back to Taos from Albuquerque with clients who requested an under-the-bridge approach. The Rio Grande Gorge is 700 feet deep at that point, so it's not like you're going to hit something, unless it's one of New Mexico's Air National Guard A7 fighters coming the other way. I've been told that the Guard had even flown under the bridge in a Boeing four-engine refueling tanker.

This was not the first time I'd flown under the bridge, but on that day the regional director of the National Transportation Safety Board (NTSB) happened to be on top, eating his lunch. He was in town for a trial, so on his break he went out to the Gorge Bridge to enjoy the view. According to his testimony, he was standing on the bridge and heard a truck, which he couldn't see. Then, out of the corner of his eye, he saw the tail of my plane disappearing under him. He raced to the other side to see it climb out of the gorge and turn toward the airport. He ran to his car with his associates and raced off to apprehend me.

Meanwhile, I had landed, my clients had departed, and I was ready to do the same. Suddenly, his car sped onto the ramp and came to a stop in front of my plane. The car doors opened and the three government employees leapt out to confront me. The leader marched over to where I was standing and brandished his wallet with a big silver star.

"Are you the pilot of this airplane?" he demanded in a falsetto scream while thrusting the silver star in my face. I said, "Yes," and grabbed his wallet so I could read the tiny letters written in the center circle of his badge: "National Transportation Safety Board." Was I supposed to be impressed?

While I was trying to read the small print in the tiny circle with no beginning or end at the center of the tin star, my mind was coming alive with rage. I handed him back his wallet and proceeded to roar, "Get out of my face, get your car off the ramp! You can see me in court, but you'll have to wait your turn, asshole!" He was stunned. By this time, I had my face in his face and was spraying foaming spittle on him.

The next time I was in Albuquerque we were all in federal court, a bunch of us. It had taken eight months to hold a hearing, as I had demanded a circuit judge rather than a local one. My reputation preceded me. I was there to defend myself against the fifteen-odd violations from both the state police and the bridge incident. The local General Aviation District Office (GADO) took the afternoon off to attend. They were asking for a revocation of my license, as I was not unknown to their office. The boy cop was there from the state police. Without his uniform and jackboots, he was a frightened kid in a slightly too-large suit.

The morning session was dedicated to the state police. The afternoon would be for the bridge incident. I was armed with a lawyer and JB as a witness. The judge had a sense of humor and threw out the state police charges.

After lunch, the NTSB guy testified about what he had seen during his break. A structural engineer had been brought out from D.C. to testify what would have happened to the bridge if my plane's 300-pound engine block had hit its weakest part at 200 mph. Apparently, they hadn't put their stories together, because he said that nothing would have happened; the bridge had been built with a failsafe design. Any part of it could be destroyed, but it would remain structurally sound.

I finally had my moment. The judge asked me what I thought was dangerous about my antics. I told him the Air National Guard frequently flew under the bridge back then, and if I had flown under at the same time with them coming through the other way, it might have been a disaster. The judge and some others in the small courtroom laughed. There was no avoiding the regulation about flying within 500 feet of a structure, so my pilot's license was suspended for ninety days, an acceptable slap on the wrist. The FAA/GADO contingent was clearly upset. The NTSB guy left the court in ill humor.

As I had flown down for the trial in my plane, and the judge who had come out to New Mexico to officiate the proceedings planned to spend the weekend skiing in Taos, I offered him a ride up. He politely declined my offer.

BIKE TRIP

In early May of 1983, I started what I hoped would be a twenty-day odyssey on my new pearl-white touring bike to Kitty Hawk, North Carolina. It seemed as good as any destination and it was almost due east of Taos, some two thousand miles. I would pedal to the Atlantic coast, then step off my bike and fling it into the surf. I figured that once I got in shape I would be cranking out at least a hundred miles a day.

The first day out of Taos, I rode east across the mountains and down through Cimarron Canyon to Springer, on the western edge of the Great Plains. Linda and Daisy drove over later in the afternoon and met me. We drove back to Cimarron for dinner, then spent the night at the remodeled, but truly haunted, St. James Hotel.

The next day they dropped me back at Springer where, with great trepidation, I started the trip east. The spring wind was blowing at my back at thirty miles an hour. It was eighty-five miles across the rolling grasslands to Clayton, my destination for the night on the New Mexico/Texas border. With a little pedaling I stayed in a wonderful windless state the entire way. Although blowing steadily, the air was serene and silent. With little or no effort, I moved as fast as the wind. I could hear windmills creaking and cows bawling out of sight, all sounds carried to me clearly across the grasslands. Four hours later I rode into the bleak town of Clayton, the wind still at my back.

Although I was tired, I still had most of the day ahead of me, so I rode on to Boise City in the panhandle of Oklahoma. A couple of hours later I crashed in a modest motel on the east side of town, where I could have been on the Russian Steppe. These western towns have no frills; no trees, just pickup trucks and farm equipment dealers. Boise City, the epicenter for the Dust Bowl in the thirties, was now a serious farm and ranch town.

When I awoke in the morning, a dust dune had filtered under the motel room door. A northern had come in during the night, and the wind was now blowing west to north, ninety degrees across my path. I started out in the morning with a destination a hundred miles down the road, but after a few miles another road branched off to the southeast, and I was seduced by the idea of a quartering tail wind. Riding with the wind across the highway was difficult because passing trucks buffeted me away, but as they passed I was sucked back onto the road in their vacuum. This had already happened twice, so at the junction I headed southeast for Amarillo, one hundred and thirty miles away.

By early afternoon I was exhausted and feeling less and less adventurous about my journey east. At every gas station I would fill my water bottle with Gatorade, and at every Dairy Queen I would toss down a chocolate malt. By the early afternoon, the wind dropped off and the temperature started to climb. Ten miles from Amarillo I could see its tall office buildings from across the plains. I felt I could make it, but then I came to the Canadian River Canyon that dropped into what seemed like an endless abyss, with a corresponding climb back up. I coasted down the three or four-mile hill and then struggled up to the city. I was wind-blasted, dehydrated, and totally exhausted. I had been agonizing over whether to continue or not. At the edge of the city I called Texas International Airlines from a phone booth, thinking that if there was a flight back to Albuquerque, I would grab it. If not, I would stay overnight and push on the next day.

I found that a flight would be leaving for Albuquerque within the hour. I could make it, even though I was still five miles from the airport. Infused with strength, I pedaled madly for the airport tower, which I could see in the distance. I knew I didn't have time to pack the bike so when I cycled into the airport I went to a rental car agency and paid one of the line guys thirty dollars to pack my bike for air shipment the next day.

With twenty minutes left, I grabbed my saddle bags and raced for the gate, forgetting that one contained a small .22 pistol. Security caught it on the x-ray and I was pulled aside. Instead of being subjected to a full-blown investigation, I was returned to the airline counter where they calmly took the gun and passed it on to the cockpit crew, who delivered it back to me when I got to Albuquerque an hour later.

A day later I went to pick up the bike. No bike. I called the car agency in Amarillo and was told the guy I left it with had stated that my "agent" had come to pick it up. In other words, he stole it. For weeks, I had Walter Mitty dreams of flying to Amarillo to confront the thief.

The following October, my friend Jon flew me to scenic Dumas, Texas, to pick up where I had left off and continue my biking folly. I started zig-zagging east by south for two days through the oil patch of Texas to Sayre, Oklahoma. Each night ended with despair and exhaustion and the hopelessness of traveling across the flat, never-ending plains.

It was my forty-sixth birthday the next day, and ahead was a ninety-five-mile stretch due east, without even the slightest twitch in the road. From a slight rise that gave me an unbroken horizon, the road disappeared into infinity. At the limit of my vision a slight pimple appeared and, as I rode on, the pimple slowly broke above the horizon and grew into the county court house of Cordell, Oklahoma. The road ran straight to the court house steps, and then broke around both sides of the building and went eastward over the horizon again. I stopped for lunch at a diner just past the court house and, in despair over what awaited me that afternoon, I broke into tears. My destination for the night was the town of Binger. The road curved there so I built up high expectations for Binger; I would stay in the best place and eat at the finest restaurant.

The landscape was beginning to show signs of fertility. Pump jacks and drilling debris were giving way to increasing greenery as I penetrated eastward. Half way between Cordell and Binger, a hill appeared south of my route. A few farm buildings could be seen in the distance on either side of the road. My spirits, which had sunk at the diner in Cordell, started to revive as the scenery improved. A hill! What a treat.

Ten miles short of fabled Binger, a few evergreen trees dotted the edge of the road that was running along the top of a slight ridge. Suddenly, I realized there was a bend in the road ahead. I had arrived at the ninety-mile curve and Binger was just beyond. My spirits soared. A fine meal and a good room and I would be as good as new.

Like the night before in Sayre, thunderstorms were brewing around me, and it would be dark in half an hour. My timing was exquisite. Just ahead the road started downhill, slipping off the ridge and into greater downtown Binger. As I coasted along, the first of the buildings appeared. They were boarded up shacks; I was biking through a ghost town. I continued coasting to the bottom of the hill when it started to rain. I was beyond despair and it was dark. I got off the bike. It was too dark to continue, and I was too tired to think about pedaling further. I thought I would just lie down in the ditch beside the road and expire of despair. The nearest town was thirty miles away, and Oklahoma City was fifty more miles.

Headlights! A truck was coming down the hill. I was a pathetic figure standing with my bike in the rain, occasionally illuminated by a flash of lightning. The truck pulled over and the driver asked me if I wanted a ride to Oklahoma City. Two hours later I was snug in my room in the Airport Holiday Inn. I had a reservation out the next morning back to Albuquerque, and I was about to dine at the luxurious International House of Pancakes next door. I was in heaven. A gulf hurricane was heading into Texas and Oklahoma, and heavy rain was forecast for the next three days. The next day I cobbled together enough cardboard to pack up my bike and check it through to Albuquerque.

The Great Bike Trip to the Atlantic ended there. I still have the bike with the map indicating my proposed route from Binger onward, waiting. In case…

JUMP

Several events or coincidences found me standing on a small peg with one foot while holding onto the wing strut of an aging Cessna, with the air howling past at seventy miles an hour, and the ground six thousand feet below me. Against all reason, I was going to throw myself off my perch when the jump instructor, sitting safely in the plane, tapped me on the knee.

I suddenly empathized with soldiers in the trenches of the First World War. When the whistles shrilled, the soldiers filling the entire trench would stand up, struggle out of their muddy haven, and advance into a blizzard of lead, knowing they were all going to die. They knew because the rank that had left moments before were all dead or dying in the blasted landscape where they, too, were heading. Still they went. I knew that when the instructor tapped me on the leg I would let go of the strut and that I would fall with the consciousness of a rock and that I was doomed.

I had just completed a cursory forty-minute course, some of it directed toward *What to do when the chute doesn't open or doesn't open completely*. There was a mantra, "Reach right, reach left, pull right, pull left." Or was it, "Pull left, reach right?"

Why and how had I gotten myself into this dilemma? It was my son Josh's eighteenth birthday, April, 1987, and I had come from Taos to his boarding school near Portland, Oregon, to celebrate with him. What to do? What to do? Forget the usual birthday crap, the movies, the dinner. The poor kid was being forced to spend meaningful time with me, the distant parent, when he would surely rather be smoking dope with his friends.

Just down the road from his school on the valley floor was a small airport, and I noticed a sign as I passed, "Introductory Jump, $99!" Something clicked. Josh and I would jump the afternoon away. I would buy the entire skydiving package: four static line jumps, followed by a free fall, which required having to prove your ability to fall correctly during the first four jumps. The chute would be pulled out of the pack by a static line attached to the airplane, so that by the time you were clear of the plane, the chute would be opening. On the fifth jump you would pull your own rip cord after counting off five slow seconds. The jump guy would grade you on your performance during the static line jumps. If you didn't fall to your death in the first attempts, you could graduate to free fall, then fall to your death on the fifth. I was told that an entire college sorority had qualified the previous week.

So, there I was, at the mercy of my own self-inflicted pressure, ready to throw myself into oblivion so that Josh and I would have a heartfelt, bonding father-son birthday celebration. I had elected to go first because I couldn't stand the thought of watching him fall six thousand feet to the ground and die before me.

When the tap on my knee came, my last view was like looking at a religious painting on black velvet: the sun's rays slanted through broken clouds just above us, highlighting the rich green Oregon countryside below. I would be a mere pock mark in those fields within a minute, I thought, as I shoved off. My brain, horrified from the first moments, turned off as I let go. I had no more vision, sound or thought until I was jolted upright by the chute opening as promised. I was saved! I was ecstatic! I was safe under the paraglider winged chute.

I was in my element now. The first oscillations had stabilized and I was flying the glider winged chute in wide gyres around the airport. It was still a long way down and, after a couple of controlled turns, vague boredom set in. I partially collapsed one of the wings and started a tight spiral to try and get some falling sensation and scare the shit out of the jump guy if he was watching. Then it was time to start setting up for landing. With the glider chute I could enter the pattern like an airplane flying downwind, base, and then final to the bullseye landing site. I landed in the outer ring of the target with a couple of skipping steps, then pulled the collapsing chute down into my arms, trying to keep the fabric folds from touching the ground, a feat I had watched incoming jumpers do earlier; it was a demonstration of proficiency that broadcast that I was cool.

Josh was only a minute behind me and he shortly glided in for a perfect landing on the center of the target. We were now complete, bonded by shared experience. On the way down, I had made a vow that I would politely decline further jumps, explaining something about a sudden illness in the family, or some such. I had cheated almost certain death and I wasn't about to try my luck a second time. Josh, however, was elated and before I could explain about the sudden illness, the chute packer was in our face with a couple of freshly packed chutes. The jump plane had already landed with its engine still running and was waiting for us to go again.

I found myself back in the wretched airplane climbing back up to jump altitude. I complained inwardly about the unfairness of it all. How had I let myself become intimidated by the enthusiastic skydiving instructor? What if I had just been lucky the first jump? Too many of my aviation acquaintances had been killed, not by their flying careers, but for something stupid like parachuting. Five thousand hours of mountain flying and I die jumping out of an airplane for fun?

Josh jumped first this time. His chute opened and I watched him drift down below me as we circled back over the strip. I climbed back on the peg and when tapped, threw myself free of the plane. My brain didn't totally shut off this time. The horror of it all was much more acute. I could hear but couldn't see, and then came the jolt from the chute opening. With the jolt my vision came back and I looked up for the fully opened chute. It wasn't there. The right side of the paraglider wing was partially collapsed. Three of the riser lines hung over the top of the canopy, causing it to be only partially opened. I was in a tightly descending gyre, rotating around the partially opened wing panel. My options were wait and see if it would correct itself by jerking the risers over the top of the panel until the chute fully inflated or, failing that, I could do the mantra, "Reach right," etc., which would free me. I would automatically accelerate the process to free fall and have the pleasure of pulling a ripcord if my mantra sequence was correct.

But before I had to rescue myself, I was gratified to see the risers slowly slipping over and off the panel, one by one. The chute was soon fully inflated, and twenty minutes later we were driving away from the landing field. I was in ecstasy and the jump guy happily clutched a $20 tip for letting me bail out of further lessons. Josh and I headed for an afternoon movie and a traditional birthday dinner.

COPPERMINE

In midsummer 1987, I left Taos in my plane with some young friends to float the Coppermine River from Yellowknife in the Northwest Territories to the Arctic Ocean. There were five aboard—me, my son Josh, Rick, Tim and Bret, my house boy and friend of the past eleven years. Two friends from Utah, Willy and Rick, would meet us in Yellowknife, and Alex Cserhat, son of my good friend Joe, would also be meeting us there. We took a roundabout way north via San Diego, then up the coast to Portland for two days of windsurfing at Hood River. We then flew into Vancouver for another two days at the World's Fair.

We left Vancouver for a seven-hour flight to Yellowknife with one fuel stop midway. Willy and Rick had arrived a day earlier with the equipment and supplies for our ten-day river adventure above the Arctic Circle.

Willy was a classic Grand Canyon river rat from Kanab, Utah. During the summers he rowed tourists down the river, and the rest of the year he worked the oil fields. On prior trips down the Grand with Willy, he had become quite taken with our group, particularly the mostly-naked ladies. Except for his heavy drinking, Willy was a great boatman/philosopher. He had been the initial organizer for this trip, and I had agreed to gather together the group with his promise that he wouldn't imbibe. He agreed, but his interpretation of the agreement meant not drinking his own liquor. As the trip and tensions matured so did his need for booze.

We camped that first night in a campground near the Yellowknife Airport. Bret had brought a queen size air mattress, and I won the coin toss to spend the night on it. All the baffles had broken, so it had lost its rectangular dimension and filled the interior of the tent. Mosquitoes drove Josh and Bret into the tent, and the three of us slept precariously balanced on the large balloon.

The next day Alex showed up on a commercial flight, sporting a porkpie derby and wearing a flowery shirt, looking like a pimp.

Yellowknife was an incongruous combination of new glass-walled buildings and an old town section of log cabins. We would leave from there in a chartered Twin Otter later that evening. All our gear, three rafts, a canoe, and supplies for two weeks in the wilderness would be loaded into the plane along with the eight of us. By the time we had finished loading, the plane's floats were under water. We were to be flown 250 miles north into the Barren Lands and dropped off on Rocknest Lake, one of the sources of the Coppermine River. The lake was approximately sixty miles south of the Arctic Circle and, as migratory birds fly, 150 miles from our destination, the Eskimo village of Kugluktuk or Coppermine, on the Arctic Ocean.

It was eight in the evening before the Otter wallowed out onto an arm of Great Slave Lake. At full power, the pilot brought the tips of the floats out of the water and, after a three-mile takeoff, the overloaded float plane made it into the air. We were sitting in a row of jump seats on the left side, while the rest of the interior was jammed floor to ceiling with our gear. The canoe was lashed to one of the float struts outside. Two hours later, flying over featureless lakes and swamps, we touched down at our destination, a small island in the middle of the lake where we set up camp to avoid any wandering bears that might be about on the shore.

As we stepped out of the seaplane, we were greeted by the infamous black flies and gnats of the Arctic Tundra. These tiny insects erupt from the moss and make life miserable for both man and beast. We had been warned about them, but nothing can prepare you for their onslaught; they try to burrow into anything with moisture, such as your eyes, nose, and ears. We had brought seven mosquito hats for the eight of us. The loser got to spend the evening in a tent that we set up immediately. The plane was quickly unloaded and then flew off to civilization; we were suddenly on our own. The bugs took the steam out of a campfire sing-along that night, and we were soon all in our tents. I was worried about a repetition of the gnat attack in the morning. Could we stand spending the next two weeks with them, plus the mosquitoes?

I woke up early to the sound of wind and rain lashing the side of my tent, but it quickly ended. Fortunately, the rain and colder temperatures were enough to keep the bugs buried in the moss. Except for one other afternoon, we weren't bothered by them again.

We broke camp early and began inflating the rafts, and sorting and loading equipment. At some point, Willy proudly pointed out that we would be taking our journey without food. He had been responsible for provisions but had unilaterally decided we would learn to survive by doing, that is, by catching and shooting our provisions. It was an exciting announcement. We had several shotguns, originally for bear protection, a .22 rifle, and fishing gear. He did bring coffee and chocolate powder for me, and a thirty-pound sack of red russet potatoes, which turned out to be mostly rotten.

Our next challenge was to find the beginning of the river. We were in the middle of the lake with no map detailed enough to show where the river exited the lake. We decided to start rowing north against the western side of the lake until we detected some current. Every few minutes we would pause and try to determine if we were in one. After a couple of hours, our efforts were rewarded. We were funneled off the lake into a small river moving at a swift, smooth pace. The transition from still lake to river was completed within a half mile. At the mouth of the first side stream we all caught eddies and started fishing. Although I knew nothing about it, I immediately caught a five-pound lake trout. Within a few minutes, we had all caught trout.

Just below the fishing spot we came upon our first rapid. It wasn't much, but enough for the two canoeists put on their wet suits. The canoe quickly swamped in the first hundred yards, so we pulled in for lunch on a rock ledge and cooked the trout. After the fishing experience we knew there wouldn't be any problem eating. We wouldn't starve, but would we want to survive primarily on lake trout for two weeks?

Any time we came ashore we had to be alert for bears— Barren Land "grizz" was to be our unseen nemesis for the entire trip. We had acquired several long-barrel, twelve gauge goose guns for protection, but we never saw any bears, just plenty of bear signs. They were fishing along the banks and were territorial about their fishing rights. Each gun was loaded with a round of bird shot, a couple of buck shot, and then, as the coup de grace, two shotgun slugs. We figured we could escalate with each shot and save the slug for a bear at close range. It sounded great in theory, but I hoped we wouldn't need to test it.

Shotguns were required to get a travel permit for the Coppermine that summer, as there had already been a couple of bear attacks. One had occurred near where we were that first day on the river. A helicopter had dropped off three geologists and was going to pick them up at the same location later in the day. They were hiking inland and saw a bear on another ridge, a short distance away. The bear was standing, looking their way. He caught their scent, dropped, and started charging down the ridge toward them. He disappeared at the bottom in heavy brush, but then reappeared only a couple hundred feet away. The three geologists took off running toward the river, and the two with their packs on jumped in and drowned. The third guy stopped, turned, and realized the bear wasn't behind him, so he survived.

The RCMP guy who checked us out told us that the only way to stop a charging bear was a shoulder shot with a twelve gauge slug. With a broken shoulder or front leg, a bear would go down before it could get to you. Any other wound wouldn't stop a large bear before it was on you. Barren Land trees were only stunted pines about ten feet tall, so there weren't many options for escape.

Just below our luncheon spot was some good whitewater with fast current over gravel, the water crystal-clear to the bottom. The maps we had were general, and only showed major topographical features. We knew the river was a series of narrow lakes connected by short elevation changes. Toward the end of each lake, current would materialize and we would be swept along to the next level. We had put in at thousand feet above sea level at a good angle to the ocean, 150 miles away. The angles only occurred between the lakes, so we had current for less than fifty miles. The rest of the trip we rowed.

Shortly after running the second length of whitewater, the river turned flat and became a ten-mile lake, so we rowed our inflated barges for the rest of the afternoon. We camped that night on banks just above the river. It had been raining off and on all afternoon, but by the time we quit, there was a steady drizzle.

The river or lake banks were generally clay. If you stood in one place long enough, the ground would shimmy as if you were standing on jello. The campfire area was the worst because everyone liked to stand near the flames. We would try to arrange tarps over the fire and eating area to keep it dry, but my lasting memory was of tasteless food and cups and spoons filled with rainwater. This was not a catered gourmet Grand Canyon river trip. One early morning, I was walking below our campsite and came upon Alex squatting beside the river, eating a ptarmigan he had just shot with the .22. He had ripped open the bird's craw and was eating partially digested tundra cranberries with gleeful primitive pleasure. Such was our desire for sugar.

We had chosen to take the trip during the end of July because of an early mosquito-killing frost. Between the frost and the rain, we had few mosquito problems and the only bad bug incident was that first night with the black flies. I knew that without protection they would drive me crazy. One afternoon, Bret and I were coming back to the river from a hike and the temperature had climbed into the eighties, which brought the flies out. They chased us into the river, but that was the last time we were bothered.

Maybe it was the low angle of the summer sun above the Arctic Circle, but the green spectrum of colors was spectacular. On sunny days the hillsides shimmered with inner illumination. The growing season was so compressed that the forest was giving off its year's supply of color in a six-week blast of intensity.

On the morning of the third day we encountered a large male wolverine. I was rowing in a slight current just off the left bank when the big fellow slouched down to the river's edge. Although a full-grown wolverine can weigh around fifty pounds, up close at ten feet they appear to weigh hundreds of pounds. We were just upstream when he appeared out of the draw and gave us a contemptuous look. As we passed, he proceeded to swagger along the bank, keeping us abreast. This went on for a couple of hundred yards until he grew bored and swung up the bank and out of view. I had the oars in the water to keep the boat aligned, so we had a head-on view of him. No one had moved or spoken. His body language was eloquently "tough guy."

One lovely evening about midtrip, we took off for a midnight hike up a small mountain on the opposite side of the river from where we had set up camp. It didn't get dark at night, and there was always enough light to read by; but it did get spooky walking in the stunted forests. At the top of the five-hundred-foot hill, we startled a covey of ptarmigan, which reminded us we were still in bear country without our weapons. We had become pretty casual about bear protection by then. Our trip back to the river was hurried and I was looking over my shoulder for Mr. Grizz for the entire descent.

After six isolated days on the Coppermine River, I saw some unusual colored dots on the river bank. As we paddled up, they became dome tents peopled by ten teenage girls on an Outward Bound trip. They had been on the river for two weeks, and had a hundred more miles on them than we had. Their leader was only twenty years old. So much for feeling heroic.

The next day we came to Dismal Lake, which ran directly into the Coppermine. There were some fishing resorts on the lake, and a couple of float planes had landed with fishermen who were fishing for Arctic char, now our staple food supply. I insisted that Josh paddle over to the float planes to beg for food. He came away with two lunch sacks that had the most exquisite chicken breast and roast beef sandwiches, and even cookies and apples. We told the rest of our group about our feast, but only after we had safely consumed it.

One particularly pleasant sunny afternoon in good current, I spotted tree limbs floating below us. Looking a little closer, the limbs turned out to be antlers attached to swimming caribou. We were in the migratory route of the Athabasca caribou herd. We paddled through the swimmers, part of the great herd of fifty to a hundred thousand animals that would be crossing the river for the next few days. We had to use our oars to keep them away from the sides of the boats as we floated through. That night we camped just downstream from the crossing, and a couple times we had to protect the boats from the animals' spiky hooves as they tried to come ashore.

Every evening we would meet at a host's tent. The finest joint roller would present his artistry and, depending on how many days we'd been on the trip, we might share a treasured beer. The beer we brought, even judiciously consumed, lasted for only half the trip. Hard stuff lasted longer because there was no mix and no ice, and, anyway, we were more inclined to get high. Willy didn't participate with us in our evening socials, but instead simmered alone and sober in his resentment over being older than everyone but me, and much less educated than any of us.

One evening, as we were being hosted by Tim and Rick, smoking dope and enjoying the view down the river, Tim rummaged around and introduced the evening's surprise—a bag of bite-size candy bars. Now, years later and with Tim long dead from an avalanche in Taos, I still appreciate his generosity in sharing that bag of chocolates with us. At this stage of the trip a candy bar was of inestimable value. That evening, as always, Willy had been invited to join us but declined, declaring he had cooking responsibilities or, in other words, he was angry.

After the primitive, repetitive dinner of fish or tough, gamey ptarmigan, half-rotten potatoes, and Tim's candy, we all went off for short hikes. I went up on a ridge above our campsite to enjoy the evening's eerie Arctic light. While sitting on a sandy ridge, I heard scuffling sounds behind me. I turned to see three fox cubs playing outside their den, five feet away. They were either unaware of my presence or, like the wolverine, didn't care that I was sharing their space.

When I came down to the camp there was a meeting going on about Willy. He had gotten into my bottle of tequila and had become verbally abusive and threatening. The consensus was that Willy should be disarmed and tied up. He had already passed out in his tent and Rick, his tent mate, promised to take charge of him and the twelve gauge. I felt bad that Willy had fallen apart. He couldn't adjust to the younger guys, but I was willing to put up with him as we had known each other through prior trips on the Grand.

Willy had once invited me on a season's-end river guides' trip, and I was all puffed up about it at the time. But I quit that trip before it started as it became evident it would be a three-week drinking bout. There had been a party at the Marble Canyon Lodge the night before, and, as far as I could tell, everyone but Linda and I got blind, staggering drunk. In the early morning Linda called a friend in Taos and had her call the lodge to get a message to us regarding a "home emergency"— the babysitter had fallen ill, so we had to leave immediately.

By late morning we were winging our way back to Taos. We weren't cut out to be part of river rat culture.

The next morning, Willy was repentant, hung over, and, as he described himself, "a whipped-down toad." But the Willy problem resurfaced a couple of days later, the last float day. It started out with a loud shotgun blast outside my tent, and I thought someone had blown Willy away. The wind was blowing upstream at 30 mph as I crawled out into the rainy gloom. It was also foggy, with visibility down to less than a hundred feet, and there was fresh ice along the river's edge. It made all the rest of the trip look like a tropical cruise. The shotgun blast was Willy announcing that he was finished with us and off to Coppermine Village.

We quickly stowed gear and chose boat mates. Bret lost a toss and ended up with Willy. As soon as we were launched, we lost sight of each other in the fog. If you were rowing you could maintain some warmth while the passenger froze, so every thirty minutes we would switch places. As I found out later, Willy wouldn't let Bret row. The current was relentless on this part of the river and it was braiding between gravel channels. At one point Bret demanded to get off before he froze to death; spray from the rapids and high winds were drenching him, and the chill factor was way below freezing. Willy nosed into a gravel bar and Bret jumped to shore while Willy pulled away and disappeared into the fog, leaving Bret stranded in the middle of the Coppermine. Fortunately, just minutes later, the canoe passed by only a few feet from where Bret stood. He ran through the shallow water and jumped in, surprising the hell out of the canoe paddlers.

I pulled to shore to start an emergency fire to warm up. The other two boats, minus the canoe, joined me. We had brought along some piñon pitch all the way from Bear Paw for just such an emergency. It had been soaked in kerosene so it would light under any conditions. In minutes we had a roaring fire going.

When Willy showed up without Bret, he explained that Bret had asked to be put ashore, and Willy had happily obliged. We were dumbfounded. This would mean trying to work our way upstream against swift current while trying to find the gravel bar where Bret was stranded. Fortunately, the fog was starting to lift, and as visibility increased, we could see across to the west side. There on the bank was the canoe, upside down with three pairs of legs walking underneath. We put back in the river and quickly joined the canoeists who were now beside a lake with a solid rock wall a half mile ahead.

The wind was blowing head on and, although the canoe continued its walk, we in the rafts struggled to make any headway by poling with the oars. After an hour of this, we came to where the current became choppy whitewater running through a fifty-foot vertical gorge. This was known as Bloody Falls, where, a century earlier, a band of Athabascan Indians had killed a group of Eskimos.

We found a draw out of the wind to the side of the gorge to make a pot of hot soup from the remains of our rotten potatoes. We were long out of food, humor, and patience but, in the next half hour, the weather changed dramatically from a gale to a calm sunny day, and so did our attitude. We became companions again, and even Willy and Bret made amends.

A half mile through the gorge the river entered an open coastal plain and became a tidal estuary. After lunch, we walked the western wall of the gorge, following a trail through solid rock that had been worn down by a millennium of portages by Indians, Eskimos, explorers, and traders.

Before lunch, Alex had walked along the top of the gorge and returned saying there was nothing worth scouting. The first quarter of the river mile bore that out. Fortunately, we decided to again scout the rapids to the far end of the gorge. Just beyond the point, the river turned hard left and dropped over a ledge, which formed a severe hydraulic across the hundred-yard-wide river. Beside the western cliff was a twenty-foot-wide slot to skirt the hydraulic. The rest of the river was unrunnable due to the ledge, and thus the reason for the long portages by centuries of travelers.

I pushed off first with Alex as my passenger, and rowed uneventfully through choppy whitewater. I then set the boat for the narrow slot against the west wall. Suddenly, the boat rose up on a big current boil and was held for a few moments. Then it moved, diabolically, to the right, taking us over and just upstream of the ledge. There it stopped, then slowly started back, exactly where we had been captured, and let us go for a safe passage through the slot. Just below the slot, the river entered a short stretch of whitewater that I wasn't expecting, and we nearly flipped backward in a large hole. We were soon through and into the tidal estuary.

What an exciting ending the Coppermine gave us with that final hundred yards. We had arrived at the Arctic Ocean. Willy was rowing a raft behind me and had the same thing happen to him. The River Gods were having a last bit of fun with us. I have seen similar boils erupt and hold boats before. Once at Lava Falls in the Grand, a boil in mid-rapid held one of our boats for a minute and spun it around and around with the boatman trying to row off. Like our experience at Bloody Falls, the boil finally subsided, and the boat continued safely down the river.

We regrouped at the bottom with the canoeists who had wisely portaged the falls. Then we continued for a mile and came upon a cabin on the shore. We rowed over and were invited in for tea and sandwiches by a missionary couple from the village of Coppermine, just three miles away. This was their vacation cabin and they had come up in their power boat for the weekend. I was in tears over their hospitality and the peanut butter and jelly sandwiches. We left them with our canoe and the pitiful remains of our food. We had borrowed the canoe from the aircraft operator and he had said to leave it anywhere on the Coppermine that had a good landmark; he would pick it up on a later flight, if ever.

We were a couple of days ahead of schedule and I knew the last flight out of Coppermine was going to leave late that afternoon. Rather than stay over for two more days, Alex and I decided to hike across the tundra to the airport to try and hold the flight until the rest of the group could get there. I could see the airport radio antennas sticking up over the horizon so we struck off, making a beeline for the airport. After two hours of arduous bog hopping, we found we were still a mile short of the runway when we heard the incoming aircraft, a four-engine Electra. We saw it land and taxi to the little terminal, and then a half hour later saw it depart south to civilization. We had put our hopes on that flight, but, as consolation, I took a partial bath in a washbasin and used a role of paper towels to dry myself off after we reached the empty terminal. Clean after ten days of camping, we walked into the village and hired an outboard to take us up the coast to collect our group. We found the boats just a mile from the village and towed them back.

The village was a garbage heap at the ocean's edge. We unloaded our gear and set up our tents right there among the trash, and then we went into the village which was marginally cleaner. At the Eskimo Cafe we ordered chicken nuggets fried in seal blubber. By then it was after midnight and we had covered a lot of ground. Rather than continue our celebration we went back to our campsite to sleep.

There was a hotel—a collection of trailers stacked together—in the village that had a dining room, which served us a wonderful breakfast. The proprietor was also the airline agent. Recognizing my desperation to get out, she organized a pick-up flight to Yellowknife that evening. We had all day to wait so we packed gear and lazed around in the sunny weather. Some of the group went swimming in the ocean. The village itself wasn't much: a Hudson Bay store, a school, and a bunch of prefab shacks that came up the Mackenzie River on barges each summer. Alcoholism is very high among the Eskimos, so no liquor is sold in the village. Instead, they have it flown in by the case from Yellowknife. The village was littered with the carcasses of wrecked and dismantled snowmobiles and ATVs. The beach was littered with the carcasses of dead seals and whatever else the Eskimos could shoot.

Around ten in the evening the Electra landed after having been diverted from its regular run from Yellowknife to Victoria Island. It was a large plane and in the back end there was a first-class passenger capsule that could hold twenty. It came with a stewardess, drinks, and snacks. We sank back in the seats for a short hop to an Eskimo village to drop cases of liquor and pick up a few more passengers for the two-hour trip down to Yellowknife. Even after midnight we could clearly see the permanent offshore ice pack with supply barges still imbedded in the ice.

We arrived back in Yellowknife around 3 a.m., and camped out in the same campground where we had stayed two weeks earlier. Before going to sleep, atop a picnic table, I enjoyed a spectacular display of northern lights.

Early the next morning we all woke drenched in heavy dew. Willy drove us back to the airport for an early breakfast before we took off for our long flight south. We flew down the east side of the Rockies until I turned back into the high mountains of Jasper and Banff National Parks, where we surfed across the glaciers for the next two hundred miles to Kalispell and then, more asleep than awake, we flew on to Idaho Falls.

Pity the poor restaurant in Idaho Falls who played host to our first dinner. We ravaged their salad bar. The motel was treated in like fashion. We had been two weeks in the Arctic without really bathing. The next morning we flew home, clean and well fed.

ARAVAIPA

Later in the summer of 1987, I enjoyed returning to the dry heat of the southwest after the rains of the Arctic Circle. Aravaipa Canyon bisects a low range of desert mountains in southeastern Arizona at an altitude that allows cottonwoods and saguaro cactus to share the same landscape. Aravaipa is a modest stream that flows northwest, collecting water from mostly dry washes that flow down from snow melt or summer thunderstorms in the Santa Teresa and the Aravaipa Wilderness. At its eastern entrance, the canyon arcs west through low mountains, where the cottonwoods grow next to the stream, while saguaro grow above on the bare, south-facing sides of the desert canyon.

Over the years, I have hiked this lovely canyon several times. On this trip two friends and I came in from the east, walking in the shade of cottonwoods, and sometimes wading down the small stream. We weren't camping so we carried only water bottles. A couple of miles downstream, a dry canyon comes in from the north and then opens into a tree-filled valley. It's the first time you can see the cactus clinging to the steep south-facing slopes of the canyon. Many of the cottonwood trees have died, but just as many are reaching their full growth. The forest floor is a matchstick maze of fallen trees. A narrow trail winds through the labyrinth.

By early afternoon my friends had gone up the dry canyon to inspect some Indian ruins, while I chose to spend the afternoon by the stream, lazing along the trail. The midday heat had taken its toll, and, except for water bugs skittering across still water, nature and I were gloriously inactive. I climbed a large cottonwood and perched there on a branch, fifteen feet above the ground.

The branch extended out and over the stream. It was wide enough for me to lie on with my feet propped against the trunk. To my right, the narrow trail twisted through the cottonwood forest. I had been lying there for half an hour, occasionally adjusting my position. Only the hum of insects and the sound of the shallow stream running over rocks broke the afternoon silence.

Suddenly, a horse and rider appeared. I just happened to be gazing down the trail when he silently appeared thirty feet away. Behind him came nine other riders. They were on a trail ride coming from the western entrance to the canyon, seven miles downstream. I was just above their field of vision, seemingly just a bump on a log. As they came toward me, I wondered whether I should announce my presence or stay quiet. Although they were probably half awake from the heat like me, I didn't want to startle them; a stranger in the quiet wilderness lying like a snake on a limb. I chose to remain quiet and lie there, watching them approach.

The leader was wearing a working Stetson hat. He was leading a pack horse that had been carrying their lunches in saddlebags. He passed below me, unaware of my presence, as did the next eight riders. The ninth, a young woman, was just coming within range when she looked up at me and smiled. I was already grinning because of the strangeness of the non-encounter. Was she so open and friendly that, as our eyes met, she sent me a quiet greeting rather than a startled exclamation? The eye contact and smile were instantaneous, and, in that moment, we shared an intimate but unspoken exchange. She and the rest of the riders went silently up the trail and out of sight as I lay there, bemused. Would we ever meet again?

BLACK HILLS

In late August of 1988, my son Josh and I headed east from Taos to New York in my single-engine Bonanza for an end-of-summer sailing trip. We took off just before sunset and turned east to face the pink alpenglow on the 13,000-foot ridge of Wheeler Peak, the state's highest point. On the east side of the summit we started a gradual descent down to our 9,500-foot cruising altitude, while the outline of the Sangre del Cristo Mountains, now behind us, cast a shadow onto the plains of eastern New Mexico.

We flew on into the calm summer evening. After several hours, I checked our position. We were somewhere over central Iowa. A town ironically called Atlantic was seventy miles ahead. Atlantic had a lighted landing strip, and we began a steady descent out of the cool night sky into the clammy heat of Iowa. As we descended, the humidity increased and became a haze of moisture. The landing lights cast long shafts ahead of us, illuminating the increasing amount and size of flying creatures that soon became so large I started twisting away from imminent collisions. Were they bats?

I had taken the back seats out of the plane to leave room for our mountain bikes and camping gear. After landing, we pulled the bikes out and set up camp under the wing of the plane. We were parked in a pleasant grassy area, but after trying and failing to sleep in the heat, we decided to ride into town. It was midnight but we discovered that everyone else in Atlantic was awake and sitting in their screened porches, waiting for the weather to cool down. We returned to the airport and slept the rest of the night on couches inside a tiny dilapidated terminal that had a working air conditioner.

Early the next morning, we adjusted our itinerary and decided that the Black Hills of South Dakota might offer a break from the heat and humidity. I had checked the weather; the entire country, all the way to the Atlantic Ocean, was under the same humid blanket. We scrubbed sailing off our list.

A couple of hours later we settled down onto a grass strip in Custer State Park, near the famous State Game Lodge at the south end of the Black Hills of western South Dakota. It was hotter than Iowa but less humid. We pulled the bikes out and rode a short distance to the elegant old lodge where I bought a trail map. We chose a twelve-mile loop that left the lodge, headed north up a stream, and then looped back close to the backside of Mt. Rushmore, which we had just flown by. By then it was midafternoon. I knew we could do the loop in a few hours. We would be back for a wonderful meal in the lodge, and then set up camp in the grassy meadow where we had landed.

We followed the stream up a forested single track, where Josh's bike balked on a rock and he was launched over his handlebars into the stream. Nothing was broken and the stream was refreshing. Farther upstream we came to a reservoir where we both went swimming. Everything was going as planned. From the reservoir, we would start the loop back, but first we had to climb over a ridge and into another valley that would take us to the lodge.

We left the pleasant single track and started a gentle climb on an old overgrown logging road that led through a burned-out forest. After a mile, the track became steeper and ended with the ridge still hundreds of feet above. We now had to carry the bikes and bushwhack to the top. By the time we reached it, we were out of water and barely halfway through the loop. Ahead was a trackless wilderness filled with dragons.

The sun was low on the ridges to the west and it would be dark within the hour. We had to turn back. If we continued ahead, we would die, horribly gnat-bitten, dehydrated, and dinnerless. If we turned back, we would survive to sue the guy who sold me the map.

We turned around and, in despair, bushwhacked off the ridge and picked up our return track. By now it was dark. When we arrived at the reservoir, Josh was adamant about not continuing downstream. Instead, he wanted to follow a well-traveled vehicle track that led from the reservoir to somewhere that wasn't on the map. We were literally and figuratively in the dark. We could make out the road through the forest just enough to keep riding. We soon came to the pavement and a highway sign that pointed left saying "Game Park Lodge 12 miles." I assumed that the road would descend gently to the lodge and our much-anticipated dinner. It was still only eight o'clock. We were saved!

Shortly after coasting along a gentle descent, with a white line identifying the edge of the shoulder, the angle reversed and now we were climbing. As we continued, the angle kept getting steeper.

Why do I end most of my outdoor experiences like this? Is it a lack of careful planning or is it a sick desire to see if I can get out of bad situations? Thoughts of my wives and children, all of whom have had to put up with "Fred's Marvelous Adventures," bedeviled me.

When we left the reservoir, it was only two miles to the lodge on the single track along the stream. We were barely moving faster than a stroll up the endless mountainside, and our pleasant four-hour loop had turned into an eight-hour ordeal. I pleaded with Josh to lie down in the middle of the road with the bike feigning an accident, should any traffic show up behind us. But then we saw headlights cresting a distant rise. We had reached the top! All was forgiven. It was almost nine o'clock. We still had a chance for dinner or, at least, drinks and snacks in the bar and then a room and a shower. No camping for us after this.

We launched down the grade. It was steeper than our ascent and I was leading. We were flying and concentrating on keeping the front wheels of our bikes aligned with the dim white line marking the edge of the road. We were coasting at thirty to 40 mph. Exhilarating!

Finally, a car came down the hill behind us and its head-lights were just starting to illuminate the road in front, when I spotted a huge shaggy head with large horns and a large walleye staring directly at me. It was a bull buffalo, and he was standing on the shoulder with his head hanging over the white line, contemplating either his suicide or my imminent death. Headlines flashed through my mind. I swerved out of the way, missing the shaggy behemoth by inches. Josh did the same behind me. We were still laughing when we coasted to the lodge's entrance.

Soon we were seated in the elegant dining room with drinks in hand, followed by large buffalo steaks in memory of our near-miss. The next morning, rested and showered, we biked back to the plane and flew over the Rockies to Steamboat Springs and Aspen, and finally home to Taos.

LOOKING FOR CHUCK

One morning in late September 1993, Chuck Holden and I planned to take off from Taos to fly over to my ranch. Ripple, a cocktail waitress at Ogelvie's, would sit in the back seat. Chuck had met her the night before and had invited her to join us for the half-hour flight. He had assured her that she would be back in Taos in time for her shift, later that afternoon.

Chuck had recently received his pilot's license and had bought a small single-engine aircraft, a little hot rod the color of dirt. Even the white paint was brown, but it was mechanically sound. Just recently trained, he was a good pilot but he had an impetuous personality.

That morning the weather was clear, although thunderstorms were predicted for the early evening down the Rio Grande Valley. An early cold front was making its way through the Rockies, but Taos wouldn't experience its passage until the following morning. We met at the airport, and, like Ripple, I had to be back in Taos by midafternoon. I had to fly to Albuquerque later that day.

Due to a fouled spark plug that caused the engine to run rough, Chuck had to pull and clean several of the plugs. We weren't ready for flight until after 11 a.m. I had run out of time so I bowed out of the trip. They would fly to my ranch airstrip, where my son Michael would take them to lunch in Cuba, the nearest town. Even with their late departure, they could be back in Taos before 3 p.m.

An hour later, I was flying down the valley to Albuquerque. The Jemez Mountains were still clear, but I could tell by the moisture haze that there would be some storms coming into the valley. In the late afternoon, while returning from Albuquerque, I found myself flying parallel to a line of dirty thunderstorms that obscured most of the Jemez Mountains and the Chama River Valley. It was fortunate, I thought, that Ripple needed to be back as early as she did because by now, the route from the ranch would have been impossible to fly. When I landed in Taos, I had forgotten about them. An hour later, the thunderstorms were on top of Taos and it rained throughout the night.

I woke up the next morning filled with dread. It was just after six and I knew that Chuck was down. I called his house and my fear was confirmed by hearing the answering machine. I called Michael at the ranch to make sure that they had departed the day before. Michael confirmed that he had seen them off at the airstrip after lunch and that, yes, they had all had El Bruno's special margaritas beforehand. He also confirmed that when they left, the weather had been bad; there had been thunderstorms over the San Pedro Mountains. The mountains form a 10,000-foot barrier to the Jemez Volcano, which sits like a crenellated mountain Buddha, fold upon fold of tight canyons leading to the Jemez Caldera. The caldera is an ancient blown-out rim of a volcano of approximately 400 square miles, creating a grassy valley of more than ten square miles in the center. The eastern slopes of the Jemez drop 5,000 feet to the Rio Grande, and the northern side runs down to the Rio Chama. The San Pedros run fifty miles north/south on the western side of the volcano. Cuba is midway on the western side of the San Pedros. The gap I had looked toward from the confluence of the Chama and the Rio Grande the day before is the only significant terrain below 8,000 feet. If Chuck had made it through that gap it would have been clear all the way to Taos, seventy miles east.

The trouble with the gap was that it was just that, a narrowing half mile between rising terrain. If Chuck was trying to fly under the weather, there were spots where it would be too tight to turn around. But it would've been just like Chuck to try and get through. His options were, of course, to wait out the weather and talk Ripple into another margarita and spend the night at the ranch, or fly around the south end of the Jemez and up the Rio Grande Valley like I had done.

According to Michael they had departed for Taos around 2 p.m. with a line of thunderstorms already on top of the San Pedros. When I heard that, I definitely thought Chuck must have flown for the gap. The little village of Gallina sits in the gap's center at almost 8,000 feet. Somewhere in those eight miles, the weather must have closed in and Chuck would have tried to turn back. He either flew into rising terrain in a tight turn or inadvertently went into the clouds and lost control of the plane. In any case, he was surely down.

I drove to the Taos Airport in the drizzly morning. Chuck's plane wasn't parked at its customary spot. I went into the terminal, but it was too early for any activity. I called the state police and the FAA in Albuquerque to report that Chuck's airplane was down somewhere between Cuba and Taos. The FAA would begin checking local airports before initiating a search.

I planned to backtrack Chuck's most logical flight path to Taos. I would fly west across the mesa tops into the Rio Chama Valley to Abiquiú Lake and then, if the weather was open, through the gap from east to west. I didn't expect to find anything east of the gap as it was relatively open terrain. While flying, my dread turned to hope; perhaps they were down but still alive. They must be hurt because, if they weren't, they would've made it to the highway that runs close to their route.

From Abiquiú Lake I could see a 500-foot clearance between the clouds and the floor of the gap. I awaited the warble of the ELT (emergency locator transmitter) signal. I also realized there was a high probability that one wouldn't come for the simple reason that Chuck's ELT battery wasn't hooked up, or it hadn't been replaced, or was dead.

A signal can be inaccurate; a small twin-engine propjet had crashed after takeoff just off the Taos runway, and transmitted a signal that led rescuers ten miles away. The plane and its passengers weren't found until the next morning when someone spotted the tail of the downed craft sticking out of the sagebrush. The locator transmitter antenna had been damaged, and the search party had been combing mountainous terrain while the survivors spent the night entombed in the plane's fuselage.

On the other hand, Bernard, who had been working for me as a pilot, had gone down just north of Albuquerque with a couple of passengers. We surmised he had flown into a narrow band of intense snow that stretched across the Rio Grande Valley. The next day I could clearly see the track from the air, no wider than five miles. Another quarter mile and he would have flown into clear weather. In that five miles, Bernard had become disoriented and lost control of the plane. It crashed almost vertically with full power. The force of the crash killed the occupants instantly, but, ironically, the ELT transmitter worked perfectly. A Russian satellite picked up the signal and pinpointed its location.

Just after passing over the village of Gallina I suddenly got three distinct warbles on my radio receiver. I quickly turned back to pick it up again but heard nothing. I was right over a ridge of eroded white rock called Cerro Blanco. Although it was only a half mile long, dozens of deep, narrow gullies ran off its west side. I crossed and recrossed over, but couldn't pick up another sound. If Chuck was down in a gully in Cerro Blanco, a ground team or helicopter would be required to continue the search. I flew to land at Bear Paw where I talked to my son. He had heard from the post mistress in Regina that Chuck's plane had crossed right over the tiny village, heading south down the highway to Cuba, a couple of hundred feet above the ground. She had run out when she heard the plane flying above her, and she got a good description of its color as it disappeared south. According to her, the weather was horrible; the Gallina area had been enveloped in thunderstorms.

The sighting of Chuck flying southbound over Regina confirmed my earlier theory that he had tried to pass through the gap, but had been turned around by weather. It was right on top of him. He had nowhere to go but south.

By noon I had exhausted all my hunches. A full-blown search was being organized but the weather wasn't cooperating. I headed back to Taos without a peep from my radio receiver. Cerro Blanco was a discredited location now because of the reported sighting of the plane flying away from the gap.

Later that afternoon, back in Taos, I received a phone call from a local clairvoyant. She said she had some information for me. She knew Ripple and was "in contact" with her. She and Chuck were still alive. The plane had crashed. They were upside down, still strapped into their seats. They could see out the fuselage and were in a tight canyon facing west because they had seen the sunset the night before. This woman told me that we had to find them quickly because they wouldn't survive another twenty-four hours. I asked her if she had any idea where they were. "Is there a place called Eureka?" she asked. I had never heard of one but after we hung up, I called the forest service office in Cuba. They confirmed that their antennas were sitting on Eureka Mesa just east of Cuba. Eureka Mesa sits in a shallow gap of the San Pedros, just a mile east of the village, at 9,000 feet.

The hair on the back of my neck stood up. By then it was too late to search, but the next morning I would try again. I called Mike Reynolds, one of Ripple's good friends who was already organizing a ground search for the next day. I would fly the Mesa in the morning, spot the wreckage and direct the ground team to its location. I cleared my search location with the search and rescue people. A full air and ground search was going to start the next morning and cover hundreds of square miles.

Had Chuck flown south looking for an opening? When he came up on Eureka Mesa had he made a left turn into a canyon and then tried to make an about-face but spun in? Eureka Mesa was the perfect place to make that classic mistake.

Twenty years earlier I had been asked by a church group to look for a lost airplane. Four people were in a four-seater single-engine plane scouting for elk during hunting season on the high ridges of the Sangre de Cristos between Taos and Santa Fe. They never came back. Instead of the usual search and rescue operation by volunteer pilots, the Air Force got in the act. For days after the plane's disappearance, an Air Force C-130 aircraft flew down the range dragging instruments hanging from cables. No luck. The next spring, I was contacted. I could fly as much as I wanted until I was told otherwise. It was a heaven-sent opportunity to build my mountain flying time and create some income. Any time I was flying without passengers back from Albuquerque, or the reverse, I would range through the Sangres, looking down into tight forested canyons, hoping for a glint of sunlight on metal or glass.

The worst terrain stretched south of Truchas, a small village perched on a ridge overlooking the Rio Grande Valley, fifteen miles from Santa Fe. I didn't like flying in that area; if I got low enough to do an effective search, I was too low to glide out if I had engine trouble. There was no place to put a plane down with any expectation of walking away. I knew the lost plane had to be there.

Years later, the wreckage was, in fact, found there. A hunter sat on a log to rest and discovered he was on the fuselage of a plane. The bodies of the four hunters were still inside. The fuselage was covered with debris and vines in a heavy stand of timber. Before the plane was discovered, the rumor was that the men had been working at Sandia or Los Alamos Labs. Between the four, they had complete knowledge of one of our defense systems, so the government absolutely had to know that they were dead and not happily alive, swilling vodka in a seaside resort on the Black Sea.

The terrain east of the San Pedros/Eureka Mesa was just like the country I had searched years earlier. If Chuck had gotten past Eureka Mesa we would never find him.

Early the next morning we flew over Eureka Mesa. It was a clear and lovely day. Reynolds and his crew were already on the ground combing the edges of the mesa. We cleared the mesa top from the air and started concentrating on the canyons, especially those that could offer a scenic sunset for someone hanging upside down in a wrecked plane. We combed the canyons and gullies with no results. We returned to Taos defeated, the paranormal search over, for a while.

In the years that followed, there were several Chuck and Ripple sightings: on the west coast of Mexico, on a boat in the Caribbean. One day, my friend Dave, who runs an aviation repair shop in Albuquerque, called to tell me of a troubling dream. He had known Chuck and he also knew his plane. Dave is a pragmatic person, as far from the mystical as possible.

In his dream, Dave was driving with his son on a road not far from Eureka Mesa, where his family owned a mountain cabin. They were out looking for deer because the hunting season was to start the next day. In the dream, they drove down a road not far from their cabin. Some friends passed them going the other way and said that they had spotted deer in an oak thicket just below, in a gully. When they got to the spot, they got out of their truck and walked into the edge of a thicket. Before they got to the dense oak, Dave's son came running back, clutching a weathered ten-dollar bill he'd found in the grass. At that point, Dave's dream took on a nightmarish quality. He knew then that he was going to find Chuck's crash site. He and his son continued walking into the thicket when Dave spotted the nose gear door panel lying in the grass, upside down. They then came upon a fan of small bones that had been carried out of the fuselage by animals. Then he woke up.

Dave knew exactly where the gully was, and we arranged to meet there. I called Chuck's son and asked him and his wife Stacia to come with me to help in the post-dream search. We met on the road and Dave repeated what he had done in his dream. We walked down the gully and, in its center, was an eroded dry stream bed overhung with oak branches. It was a perfect place for a plane to go down and never be seen again. We walked for half a mile, spooked, but didn't find a thing. We could have gone further, but Chuck's son was getting freaked.

"Let them rest in peace," he said, and we were quite willing to accept his feelings.

Years have gone by. I continue to fly the route over Eureka Mesa, the dream gully, the Gallina gap, and the eroded white rock ridge. I find myself peeking down, looking for sunlight sparkle on metal or glass. Some fall, before the snow but after the leaves have fallen, maybe this rugged country will finally give up its secret. Maybe someday, someone will see something that doesn't conform to nature, maybe throw a stone into a west-facing gully and hear the ring of metal, or maybe choose a log to sit on to eat a sandwich and feel the metal surface of the log dimple.

BLACK ICE

Every year, around mid-December, there is a short window when the ponds freeze at Bear Paw Ranch, my mountain getaway just north of Cuba, New Mexico. It can freeze with a skim of ice in late November, but it's gone shortly after the sun comes over the edge of the San Pedro Mountains a mile to the east. Each day thereafter, the ice skim gets a little thicker until, finally, it holds throughout the day, but is still too thin for skating. But by mid-December the ice is ready. If it hasn't snowed during those critical two weeks, but remained cold, the pond becomes a velvet black coating of ice without a ripple on its surface, and it's a dream to skate on. Later, when it's safer for skating, after the snow has fallen and melted, the ice becomes lumpy from the freeze/thaw cycles. Instead of flowing gracefully across the ice you rumble over irregularities.

Each winter I anticipate that short skating window to take the first circuits around the pond. I hug the shore because I can clearly see fractures in the black ice, and hear it cracking under my weight. The early winter ice is no more than an inch thick, but, as I rationalize to myself, if I can keep moving, I can get across the weaker spots before I break through. Experience had always proved me right.

On a mid-December morning in 1994, I awoke at La Garita Creek Ranch, another property I owned for a while on the western side of the San Luis Valley in southern Colorado, often the coldest place in the United States. I knew that the pond at

Bear Paw was ready for my first skate, but, to get there, I'd have to start the plane with ether, an extremely volatile fluid. During the winter, I kept a can of spray in the plane to help the engine fire up with the propeller's first revolution. If it sputtered and quit, it meant that condensation in the engine would ice the plugs and I wouldn't be going anywhere until the midday sun had thawed it out.

I walked out of the lodge to my plane, a hundred feet away, and started turning the prop through several revolutions to break up the thick oil before trying to start the motor. I had the plane's controls set, the cylinders were primed with fuel, and then I sprayed ether into the air intake filter and raced to the cockpit. As I had hoped, the engine ignited. Although I was madly pumping the primer and throttle, the engine died after less than a half a minute.

I jumped back out to repeat the process, bent down to align the spray can with the air filter, and fired another shot. A jet of flame flared out and into my face. I dodged most of it but, that was the end of my mustache and eyebrows. What I didn't realize was that there was already a small fire burning in the air intake passage. When I resprayed the ether, the jet ignited right back to the can's orifice. I was lucky the can didn't explode in my face. I immediately dropped it and ran back to the controls to restart the engine. This time it fired up and ran steadily. I spent the next hour flying south, smelling the burnt hair of my mustache, and viewing some of the most beautiful parts of the snow-covered Rocky Mountain wilderness.

After landing, I walked down the runway to the pond, passed through the gate, and walked out onto the ice. The pond's surface was perfectly smooth. I walked across the shallow side, as the ice is always the weakest there because of ambient earth temperature. It was almost as cold at Bear Paw as it had been at La Garita an hour earlier. It was still only about 10 a.m. and, although a cloudless morning, there was no heat from the sun. The ice cracked, but held, so I walked up to the house to get my skates and put on a warm coat, and then walked back to the pond.

I put on my old hockey skates while sitting on a bench beside the pond, then launched tentatively onto the ice for the first time since the year before. The first circuit was perfect, the ice velvety smooth. The second was even better because I got my stride and rhythm down. The next couple of circuits were just as good. I was enjoying the view of the mountains, the thrill of having landed at my ranch and skating on my pond. Ah, the glory of it all (although I could still faintly smell the burnt hair under my nose).

Just as I worked myself into a euphoria of self-congratulation about the wonderful morning and my wonderful life, and just as I was putting my right skate down, coming out of a counterclockwise turn, the skate plunged through the ice. I went down hard on my chest, so hard that all the ice broke under me, and I was suddenly under water for a moment. I was no more than thirty feet from shore and on the shallow side of the pond, but it was still too deep to touch bottom. I lunged out of the water and could support myself on top of the ice that was in front of me. When I tried to lunge further it again broke under me. I repeated this maneuver several times with the same results.

I had no sensation of cold but I did realize that I was getting heavier by the second: My down jacket was absorbing water quickly, and I couldn't shed it because I couldn't find the zipper tab with my gloved fingers, and I couldn't take the time because whatever support I had from the ice required that I keep both my arms on top of it. Each lunge was getting me closer to the shore, so it was a race before the jacket dragged me off the fragile support or I eventually touched bottom. Twenty feet from shore, I finally felt the bottom with the tip of my skate blades. After several more walrus-like lunges, I could stand and walk on my skates through the broken ice until I was out of the water.

I doubt that I had spent more than two minutes flailing in the icy pond, but it wasn't until I had stumbled back over to the bench to change skates for boots that I started to feel cold. Adrenaline had kept the chill at bay for those few minutes in the water, but now, safe, I was starting to feel a penetrating, wet cold. My down jacket was stiff with ice and had gained twenty pounds from its watery immersion. When I reached the house, the cold had reached my core. I was shivering and hoping that the water heater had been left on since my last visit; that it hadn't been turned down to lukewarm to conserve energy. As usual, it hadn't, and seconds after entering the house and shedding my clothes I was in a steaming shower. The hot water warmed my surface, but it would take half an hour of continued soaking before my core warmed enough to stop shivering.

ADMIRE

My friend Jon Admire's memorial was held in Taos on Cibolla Mesa, four months after we pulled him from the blue waters of the Atlantic, in March 1998. Even at the memorial, it was hard to tell the story of how Jeb, Jon's 19-year-old son, and I found him 100 yards from where we had anchored the dinghy. Jon was floating face down, eyes open, staring at the reef under him. His view, if he had a last dispassionate moment, was of primary colors suffused into swirling shafts of midafternoon sunlight. Small reef fish swam undisturbed beneath him.

Jon was an easy friend from the first day we met in Taos. I had bought an airplane from his flying club in 1976, and knowing he wanted to continue flying, I offered him the opportunity to fly my regular clients back and forth to Albuquerque. Jon was laconic and sympathetic, and could play whatever role was required of him. He conversed amicably with his passengers, and would also carry their bags.

In 1984 Jon moved to Washington, D.C. to become a State Department "spook." One of his early overseas assignments was to spend several days in the new, but unfinished, American Embassy in Moscow. He was smuggled into the unheated building, along with a couple of specialists and a large x-ray device, to verify that the Russians had implanted listening devices in its concrete structure. They were outfitted like polar explorers to survive for several days in the sub-zero temperatures.

I'm looking at a photograph of Jon and me, taken by our friend Bitsy, aboard *Mullet*—a 45-foot motorboat we kept anchored at Marsh Harbor in the Abacos Islands in the Bahamas. In the picture, we're at Little Harbor at the southern end of the Abacos Cays, and it's Jon's first visit to *Mullet*. We're sitting on the aft deck, debating the choices for the day. We had been fishing from the dinghy, on the edge of the mangrove flats, earlier, but the heat from the morning sun had driven us back to the shade on *Mullet's* aft deck.

Later in the afternoon, we ran up the Cays to anchor at Pelican Reef. Two days earlier we had stopped there for snorkeling, but, because of the rough anchorage, we had moved on without getting in the water. Now there were no waves, just a gentle swell coming through the outer reef. We anchored in white sand between the outer and inner reef. I swam over to the inner reef's edge and waited for Jon and Bitsy to join me. They started off from *Mullet's* swim platform, but Jon quickly returned to the boat.

I asked about Jon when Bitsy joined me. She said he'd caught some water down his snorkel tube and had started choking. Bitsy and I snorkeled 100 yards up the reef, and then swam back to *Mullet*. When we joined Jon, he made no mention of having had any problem while he'd been in the water.

In late March 1998, Jon and Jeb joined me and my friend Philip in Marsh Harbor for a relaxing few days cruising in the northern Abacos. Phillip and I had already been aboard for a couple days, so when Jon and Jeb arrived on the afternoon flight from Fort Lauderdale, we immediately departed and headed to Great Guana Cay, an hour north. We anchored off Guana Village in sea-grass-covered sand, which makes for an uneasy night if the wind is blowing. One night, *Mullet* dragged anchor across a quarter mile anchorage and I awoke to the sound of waves breaking on a rocky cliff just feet off our stern.

In the late afternoon, Jon and Jeb took the dingy ashore to check out the small village. The tide had gone out while they were walking on the Atlantic side of the cay, and, when the two of them returned, we watched as they experienced the joy of dragging the heavy dinghy fifty feet to the water. That evening we barbecued steaks that Jon had brought from the mainland, and talked about our mutual interests. Jon, Philip, and I had known each other in Taos since the late '70s. Many amusing skeletons hung in our respective closets. The next morning, we all set out for a walk on the Atlantic beach. Jeb and Jon walked ahead of us. I was so taken with their father-son camaraderie that I took a picture of them walking side by side. Jon was slightly shorter than Jeb, and his shortness was accentuated by Jon walking on the waterside, his bald head bobbing along beside Jeb's shoulders.

Back on the aft deck, the dreaded *Mullet* ennui struck. We talked about what we should be doing and where. It was determined that we should run up to the north end of Guano for some snorkeling. Instead, though, we lazed around discussing the state of the world.

At noon, I took the dinghy ashore to pick up some beer for dinner. I walked through the sand dunes behind the village to find out how the water was over on the Atlantic side reef in case we decided to go snorkeling. The wind was blowing slightly from the north at ten knots, but the reef looked good.

Back on *Mullet*, I found Jeb and Jon buried in their books. Philip had gone below, taken by a nap attack. I fired up the diesel engines, which prompted a vague response from everyone about where we were going. I announced that the reef looked great and we were heading a couple miles north to the end of the cay. We would anchor just south of the point on the lee side at Baker's Bay. From there we would take the dinghy around the point and out into the Atlantic to the reef, 500 feet offshore. It was a large barrier reef that extended down the ocean side of the Abacos.

Half an hour later we were anchored in ten feet of calm, clear water. Just as Jeb and I were going to take the dinghy out, Jon muttered something about coming with us to make sure I wouldn't drown Jeb. I assumed he was going to sit in the dinghy while Jeb and I were in the water. Philip took a photo of the three of us, and then another as we sped off from *Mullet's* stern. We rounded the point, where I dropped anchor over white sand.

I went in the water. I was still assuming Jon was going to stay in the dinghy while Jeb and I snorkeled nearby. I swam fifty feet away to check the reef action for sharks. We would be snorkeling on top of the reef, so even if there were some in the deeper water, they wouldn't be a worry. I called to Jeb and told him to get in. The water was clear, and there were lots of colorful reef fish just a couple of feet beneath us as we drifted with the current.

When I turned to see how Jeb was doing, I saw that both Jeb and Jon were in the water and swimming toward me. As we swam down the reef fingers, several stingrays passed under us. I turned to Jeb to make sure he'd seen the rays. It was then that I realized that Jon wasn't with us. When I asked Jeb where he was he replied that he'd had gone back to the dinghy. I looked and saw what I thought was Jon's snorkel tube protruding from the water, only twenty or thirty feet from the dinghy.

Jeb and I continued floating down the reef and then started back. I couldn't see Jon in the dinghy, so I assumed he was still in the water, hanging on to the anchor line or the far side, still enjoying the reef.

But the closer I got the more apparent it became that Jon wasn't around. Maybe he was still hanging on to the dinghy from the far side. That thought was dashed when I rounded the dinghy. Fear took over. I scrambled over the side and removed my mask, snorkel, and fins, and stood up in the boat to scan the water. Jeb was also getting into the boat. I looked toward the beach hoping to spot Jon swimming to shore. Nothing.

As a parent and a worrier, my worst fears had never been realized; none of my family or friends had ever experienced the premonitions I have had about them. They always showed up, so I still held on to the hope that Jon would magically materialize.

Years earlier, we were running the Rio Grande Box in two rafts. Jon's wife Jean and Linda were with me, and behind us were Jon and Pierre, another friend, in my smaller raft. We had just run the worst part of the rapids. The water was up, and it had been very wet coming down that seventeen-mile section. I had just passed through a quarter mile of rough whitewater and turned the raft just in time to see them flip.

Both occupants were tossed into the torrent, but Pierre quickly reappeared and climbed on top of the overturned raft. Jon did not. We were floating fifty feet in front, still in heavy water. I was trying to keep them in sight, rowing against the current to close the gap while avoiding numerous holes we were still running through.

After a couple of minutes, we were getting concerned about Jon's whereabouts. I was hoping he was under the overturned boat clinging to the lifeline or the rowing frame. Still, I thought, he should be trying to get out and back on top of the boat like Pierre did. After what seemed like an interminable length of time, we finally cleared the rapids. I started making progress closing the gap between our two boats. Jean asked me, voicing our mutual concern, "Do you think Jon is all right?" As I was about to respond, Jon popped out from under the raft and crawled on top. He and Pierre sat like happy dogs, grinning at us.

I was in that same anxious frame of mind when I stood up on the dinghy scanning for Jon, hoping that, like that earlier time, he would pop back into our lives, grinning happily. I started the engine and began slowly motoring down the offshore current. Jeb and I were both half standing in the bottom of the dinghy looking seaward. My premonition turned to horror. I knew that Jon had drowned.

Then, fifty feet ahead, I saw a rectangular patch of color in a small wave. Jeb saw it at the same time. I steered for it, the slight form of a body, floating spread-eagle and face down in the water. The patch was Jon's blue-patterned bathing trunks. His pale body was just below the surface, hardly visible except for the swatch of color. I jumped over the side as we drew up next to his lifeless form. My first action was to lift his face out of the water. His eyes were open. He still had his mask and snorkel on.

Together, Jeb and I pushed and pulled from our respective positions until we had him face up in the bottom of the dinghy, with his flippered feet making a V over the bow. I pulled myself over the side and started chest compression and mouth-to-mouth resuscitation. As I pumped, I could hear his chest gurgling. First aid training from forty years before returned.

Back then I was in a school's indoor pool, and now I was in the ocean, trying to pump life back into my friend.

I was surprised how quickly Jon's color came back as I gave him mouth-to-mouth. I pinched his nostrils shut while giving rhythmic pressure on his chest, enough to hear his ribs cracking. From a gray-green pallor, his face became suffused with color. I prayed he would start spluttering and coughing any second. Jeb and I were willing life back into his open eyes that gazed dispassionately past us. Time passed, measured in hope and despair. Jeb and I alternated working on Jon. I was amazed how Jeb could perform with such composure. Occasionally he would urge Jon to life, saying, "Come on, Dad, come on."

A nearby boat had been anchored off the beach was starting to move out. We tried to attract the attention of the people aboard but it was too far away. I started the dinghy motor and we began moving toward is as it turned toward us and we met. There was a family aboard and the father helped us load Jon aboard his larger boat.

Jeb and I and the father, whose name I never got, took turns giving more resuscitation. Finally, I turned and said, "It's over, Jeb." We were kneeling on either side of Jon. We embraced and gave in to our emotions. A life gone on a beautiful afternoon.

We were now trying to work out the logistics of getting Jon's body back to Marsh Harbor. Speed was no longer a factor. Our host offered to run the body down to Marsh with Jeb. With that settled, I got back in the dinghy and motored back to *Mullet*.

As I approached the stern, Philip asked from the deck above, "Where are the boys?" When I told what had happened, I wasn't very convincing. I was still in shock, still disbelieving the event myself. It was as if I were telling him about a dream.

ALASKA

My friend David Baxter and I left for a rafting trip down the Tatshenshini and Alsek Rivers in Alaska in June 1998. The first leg of the journey from Taos was to pick up David in Colorado. I was flying my small, single-engine Piper, which, with the back seats removed, had enough room for our baggage and my mountain bike. Our destination was dinner with friends in Sun Valley, 500 miles northwest. After takeoff from Crested Butte, we climbed to 14,000 feet to cross the Rockies, and three hours later we descended into Hailey Airport, ten miles from Sun Valley.

The jet traffic into Hailey was so backed up on final approach that I was asked by the tower to give way for overtaking traffic, which I did. After landing, the pilot of the jet I had stepped aside for came over to thank me. He'd been flying a $30 million G-4, filled with executives attending a conference. I was dressed in shorts and a t-shirt, assembling my bike for the ride up the path to the resort. He was in his pilot uniform, and as soon as the G-4 was refueled, he would be on his way back to Dallas. We would each get to our afternoon destinations around the same time, but from the look in his eyes I imagined he would have happily traded places with me.

The next morning, we left for a three-and-a-half-hour leg to Victoria, British Columbia. We climbed to 12,000 feet to clear the Bitterroot Range, and then added an additional 2,000 feet as our route took us through the heart of the Idaho wilderness.

On top, at 14,000 feet, I diverted slightly west to look down on the middle fork of the Salmon River. Ten years earlier, David and I, along with our families and friends, had run the Salmon. Now, 8,000 feet above its headwaters, we could see several rafts starting their five-day journey downstream.

For the next hour we cruised across the top of the rugged wilderness. I recognized familiar spots where, on earlier trips, I had landed or rafted. The dramatic terrain of the Idaho wilderness gave way to the Snake River Canyon, and then came the wheat fields of the Columbia River Basin. The white dome of Mt. Rainier, topped with great anvil-shaped clouds, appeared in the distance. We continued up the east side of the Cascade Range until Lake Shelan, and then turned up its fjord-like valley to pass through the mountains by Glacier Peak. There we started our descent across the coastal plain to Puget Sound and the San Juan Islands.

I suggested to David that we stop at Roche Harbor, on the northwestern side of San Juan Island, for lunch. As we turned to land on a short grassy strip, I thought of the time I flew my dad and stepmother down there for lunch from Pender Harbor, where they lived, farther up the coast in Canada. Back then I ignored the formality of clearing customs. When I visited Dad, I would fly across the border and land at the local airport on the Canadian side, and do the same on the return to the U.S. Once I rode my motor scooter up from Seattle, and crossed the border on an old logging road I'd spotted from the air. A screen of firs hid the old road from the highway on the American side of the border, so it was simply a matter of pushing my motor scooter through the trees for fifty feet, walking it around a heavy chain that blocked the trail, and I was in Canada, a few miles from my father's home.

After landing, we walked to the old hotel and ordered lunch on the deck. Less than four hours from Sun Valley we were breathing the saltwater aroma of the Pacific Northwest.

The next morning, Flight Service was forecasting a low drifting onto the northern B.C. coast, bringing rain showers. High clouds were already overhead, and my planned route up the coast to Prince Rupert would be in deteriorating weather. As forecast, the clouds were lowering ahead. I could easily make Prince Rupert, but the key to longevity when flying the northwest coast is having ample fuel. I decided to land at Port Hardy to tank up and get a weather update.

We put down on an alternate strip because the main runway was closed for bald eagle traffic. Several of the big birds were practicing landings. A half hour later, we fueled up and got a current weather report for Bella Coola. Through breaks in the clouds I could see down to snow-covered peaks. The breaks were getting sparse, so I turned and picked one where I could see down to fjord water. I lowered the flaps and wheels and descended like a tightly circling rock. From seven thousand feet we descended down to five hundred, just below the clouds. We flew down the fjord to the ocean and continued northwest on up the coast to Bella Coola, where I could see that it was obstructed by clouds and rain. An hour later we landed at Prince Rupert. The airport was on an island and was served by a tiny car ferry. That night I ate halibut cheeks and sweet northern shrimp, delights not available to the timid.

By the next morning the low pressure weather system had worsened, and we had a hundred miles to go over open water to Ketchikan. I dislike flying over large expanses of water, and I suffered my first single-engine angst attack of the trip. From the airport runway it looked as if the ceiling was coming down, and shortly after takeoff I found myself flying at less than fifty feet above a gray-green, wintry-looking ocean. Rain showers brought visibility down to a half a mile, so I had David looking for the huge ten-story cruise ships that were also heading for Ketchikan. I kept my eye on the ocean surface, and looking for any fog that might suddenly materialize. I was also looking for a flashing marine warning beacon on a reef along our route. The top of the 38-foot beacon was right at our cruising altitude. Suddenly, we were inundated with the pungent smell of seal shit, and a few seconds later we passed over the beacon on the exposed reef. It was covered with seals.

Several times we diverted to avoid fog patches forming in the saturated air. About fifteen miles out, I started tracking inbound to the airport with navigational aids. Ketchikan had, as reported, a 1,000-foot ceiling, a good day for the town. Three huge tour ships dwarfed the dock adjacent to the main street. There were two 1,800-passenger ships and a slightly smaller one parked end to end on the city dock when we arrived. The two and three-story downtown buildings were dwarfed by the floating hotels.

Lines of wheelchairs descended from the ships, and the passengers scattered into a maze of t-shirt shops and kitschy art galleries, franchised in all tour destinations along the Alaskan coast and throughout the Caribbean. In the late afternoon, the ships depart for another destination that, for the passengers, will be more or less the same; another chance to buy knick knacks. Even the shop names are the same, sparing the tourists confusion. Sometimes tour buses take the adventurous to authentic 19th-century log cabins, or to a church, a salmon/ trout hatchery with a couple of maimed bald eagles, or to rustic museums with totem pole parks.

After twenty-four hours of rain in Ketchikan, the weather began breaking from the west, and we were off to Baranof Island and the old Russian capitol of Alaska, Sitka, a beautiful island and town with many remaining architectural hints of its Russian past. The southwestern coast of Baranof had many deep fjords, and it was backed by a range of snow-capped mountains. In the sixty-mile journey up the coast of Baranof to Sitka, there wasn't any indication of civilization or industrial activity; it was complete and total wilderness. A large Japanese pulp mill had even been shut down twelve years earlier to preserve the relatively untouched environment. A perfectly symmetrical volcano rose across the bay from Sitka. There was no large wharf on the waterfront, so tour boats had to long-boat the tourists in from ships anchored out in the bay. We ate lunch with a friend from Taos who had moved there to start a legal practice, a ruse to justify living in such splendor. In front of the restaurant, a flock of bald eagles fought and dove for salmon.

The next day, with clear skies, we took off for Glacier Bay, the Valhalla of tour boats. Climbing up through the Inland Passage on the north side of Baranoff, we cleared the peaks and there, a hundred miles ahead, appeared Mt. Fairweather on the mainland. It rises from the ocean to 15,300 feet. Its ice tongues begin at the ocean and the glaciated ice cap begins at 1,000 feet, so we were viewing 15,000 feet of white crenelated mountain. Not even the mountains of Nepal or northern Pakistan had prepared me for this dramatic visual experience.

We then plunged down to water level at Glacier Bay, and saw the ever-present tour boats. We flew down the bay looking for whales, got tired of that, and then climbed to skirt some snowy ridges at 3,000 feet. We found a herd of mountain goats lounging on a snowy ridge. Ahead was Juneau. The next day, for an afternoon excursion, we flew down the coast to Tracy Arm, a sixty-mile fjord into the coastal range with a perfect glacier at its end. Icebergs were calving from the ice wall at the end of the fjord, and several tour boats were underneath us going up the inlet. From Juneau it was an all-day excursion by boat, but, for us, a thirty-minute jaunt.

The next day I left David in Juneau, flew up to Skagway, and biked ten miles up to where the Chilcoot Trail began. The Yukon Gold Rush began its march over Chilcoot Pass in 1897. There had been a town of 10,000 people servicing the trail when a railway was built from Skagway, over White Pass, into the Yukon. The town was torn down for building materials and moved to Skagway. A year later, the gold rush was over and Skagway collapsed, except for the port and rail traffic that takes tourists over the pass.

The next morning, I biked almost to the top of White Pass, but was stopped by a large brown bear. He or she was contentedly scratching his or her hemorrhoids at the beginning of a guardrail at the edge of the highway, and smiling at me as I stopped fifty feet below. The bear continued undulating its ass against the rail while we sized each other up. I was hoping some traffic might interrupt this very intimate moment, and send the bear back into the forest. I wanted to continue another half mile and stand proudly on the top of the pass, but it was not to be. Instead, I turned and coasted back to the airport, and flew forty miles across the fjord to Haines to meet up with my fellow river rafters.

We would be leaving Haines the next morning for the drive to the put-in, 150 miles up the road in the Yukon, at an old trading post called Dalton Post. Except for David and his wife and daughter, the group was unknown to me; they were all friends of his from Crested Butte. We ate together at the old Haines Fort officers' quarters, now converted into a charming hotel. The good weather was still holding, but nobody wanted to discuss the odds for how long it would last. We were all experienced rafters and knew, only too well, how wretched things could get when the weather changes at this latitude.

The next morning, we loaded the gear for a float down the Tatshemshini and Alsek Rivers. An outfitter in Haines had supplied the rafting gear and food for the ten of us. The mountain of gear was loaded onto his two-ton flatbed for the trip up to the Yukon, where we were to put in at an old trading post, just five miles off the pavement, on a dirt road. On the way in we passed several fresh bear tracks in the dust; one set was from a mother bear with a couple of cubs, and we each started thinking about where we had packed our bear spray that morning.

I was designated to row one of the heavily laden 18-foot rafts. The river was fast and clear across a gravel bottom. There was lots of debris on the outside curves of the river, but it would be easy rowing, except for the snags and sheer rock walls of flinty granite that could tear up a rubber inflatable boat. Several of us learned this the hard way later that afternoon. A sudden side current carried the boat in front of me into a snag hanging twenty feet out from the shore. I had plenty of time to avoid it, but when it came time to make my move, I was helpless against the current. When impact became inevitable, my passenger and I dove for the bottom of the boat to escape getting scraped off our perches by the branches that raked across the top of our loaded raft. There were no punctures, but it was a lesson in how capricious the current would be in this fast-flowing river.

We camped for the night a couple of miles below the put-in. I was using my old green tent that hadn't been unpacked since the last time I used it, on the shore of the Arctic Ocean, eleven years before. It worked fine, although it took a while to figure out how to assemble the frame again. I was glad it wasn't raining.

In the morning, we started a pattern that would be repeated for the next ten days; after searching through coolers and boxes for menu items, we ate long breakfasts, then slowly broke camp and loaded the rafts. The trip leader optimistically suggested 9 a.m. departures, which meant 10 a.m., but we usually got underway by noon.

The second morning we entered a tight canyon, the only part of the river requiring any whitewater skill. For ten miles we were under constant pressure, rowing hard to stay off the outside curves, and looking for eddies to rest and regroup. The only incident that day was when David ripped a foot-long tear in the side of his boat. The tube almost completely deflated, but he managed to stay afloat for half a mile, until he caught an eddy and made it to shore and repaired the tear.

The tight canyon finally opened up with views to the north and south of glaciated mountains, some 15,000 feet high. We made camp by a side stream that afternoon, and spent over an hour trying to rig a rain cover over the cooking area. We each had different opinions, based on simple aerodynamics, or molecular physics, on how to attach the damned thing to the ground. Not once in ten attempts did we get it rigged correctly. If the wind blew, it became a kite. If it rained, it offered no protection from the river of rainwater that flowed off. But during the last four days, it worked well enough that we were happy to have had it.

The third day on the river was endless. Even with GPS for pinpoint navigation, we were unable to agree on our first layover camp, at the mouth of the appropriately named Sediment Creek. The river had turned to mud from an influx of side-stream silt. After giving up on alternative campsites, we pulled into the layover camp, a barren gravel bar with a couple of trees to break any wind that might develop. That night, a moderate wind blew and, like a swamp cooler, lowered the temperature by twenty degrees as it poured down from the glaciers.

The next morning we headed up the mountainside, following a bear trail/tunnel through stunted trees and impenetrable brush. The height of the tunnel indicated that the bears were not what you wanted to meet coming the other way. The Crested Butte crowd was off like a marching club. I followed behind them to eat lunch on the open ridgetop, 4,000 feet above the river. On the ridge we walked around looking at the arctic colors, the glacier-covered peaks surrounding us, and the hundred-mile view up and down the river. The last two thousand feet of the trip back down was agony on everyone's knees. I was stiff and sore for three days. That evening, I found a slough with clear water and bathed after dinner. That was fortuitous, because we never again found a place to bathe. In desperation, toward the end, I used a bail bucket to wash my hair in glacial milk. By the time we got off the river, our hair was twisted in dirty dreadlocks. The women's faces got puffier and puffier. Silt and sand were in everything. The river was so thick with silt you could almost walk on water.

The next day the river dramatically picked up speed. At the same time, it widened with lots of sand bars that, for the most part, were impossible to detect. One moment you would be in the main channel, and the next, your oar would hit bottom and then the boat would ride up on muck. We had to get out and drag the boats, trying to find deeper water.

We camped at the confluence of the Copper River. The current was so fast and the boats so heavy that unless we found dead water next to shore, there was no way we could stop. Luckily, the lead boat found an eddy below the confluence, and we were all able to land. The delta of the Copper was a mile wide and the world's largest gravel pit. The gravel banks were sometimes twenty feet high on either side of the river. The next day, in the same current with the same high gravel banks, the Tat turned west to the ocean, and the Alsek, ten times the volume of the Tat, swallowed it without a ripple. It came in from the north at a ninety-degree angle, from the high mountain country of the Yukon and Alaska. It made no effort to be a modest tributary. The Alsek would carry us west to the Pacific, beside the northern flanks of Mt. Fairweather.

So far, the weather had been almost cloudless, but that night, at the confluence, high clouds streamed in from the Gulf of Alaska. A low-pressure system was pumping moisture toward us, and for the rest of the trip we would experience a rainy Alaska.

We woke up to heavy cloud cover. Clouds obscured all the peaks up the Alsek Valley, and Mt. Fairweather was getting dimmer in the increasing mist. By the time we put in, at noon, it had started to rain. It continued all the way to our evening's destination, the Walker Glacier, which would be another layover day. The river from the confluence down to the Walker was a mile wide, and braided with channels and bars that separated our rafts, but, fortunately, no one was sucked into a dead end and forced to tow their heavy boats over sand bars.

Now the weather was like the Arctic: pervasive moisture with temperatures in the low fifties during the day. If we weren't rowing, we were cold, teeth-chatteringly cold. Mitch, the trip leader, got stuck on a mud bar and was a half hour behind us getting into Walker. He was tired and pissed off that we had left him in mid river, and that we had also overshot the campsite by half a mile. It rained all night and most of the next day. We were camped just below the end of the glacier, a fifty-foot wall of blue ice that was calving little bergs and moraine rock into the glacial pond all day and night. Huge boulders and chunks of ice kerplopped into the little lake, but it was too shallow for them to float into the main current.

The next afternoon, when it looked like it might be clearing up, we all hiked up the glacial moraine to the blue ice below the icefall. Several float planes going upriver passed overhead that afternoon, giving me hope that the weather on the coast was lifting. Might there be sunshine tomorrow?

The sound of heavy rain on my tent wall woke me in the dim light the next morning. We haphazardly repacked the rafts for the short float down to Alsek Lake, our next and last layover. The lake was formed by a giant swirling eddy of the Alsek River that swung against the bottom of three large glacier tongues, which flowed off Mt. Fairweather. The glacier's calved icebergs would either float in the lake until they melted, or drift downstream into the main current and ground on the river bottom, where they would become serious navigational obstacles.

There was a side channel that avoided the large current entering the lake, and we camped just above it. It rained all night and the wind started blowing down the river. About 2 a.m. a gust blew my tent over with me still in it. I crawled out of the debris and tried to reinvent my shelter. I crawled back into my sodden sleeping bag, cursing my fate. Our infamous rain cover blew away, along with parts of the kitchen, but the noble crew somehow re-erected it for breakfast. The rain stopped after breakfast, so we ferried one of the empty rafts down the river into Alsek Lake. The whole crew, less Mitch and his wife, were stacked in the raft, and we all took turns rowing a half mile through the icebergs. When we were in the middle of the lake the sun came out and the reflection off the ice was blinding; no one was prepared with sunglasses, so we all suffered from a little ice blindness later. Mitch was not in the raft because he and David had had a spat over who was controlling what. David was, of course, at fault. My sympathies were with Mitch, and I tried to explain to him that David was just being David and to not take it personally.

The next morning, our final day on the river, we had to tow the boats upstream a quarter mile to ensure we would have enough time to take them to the far side of the Alsek, to avoid being swept by the main current into the lake. We feared the lake's outlet might be blocked by grounded icebergs. My captaincy was usurped by two of the kayakers, who each took an oar and thrashed their way across the river with room to spare. I was quietly pissed, but I wisely acceded control for the long pull across the ten-mile coastal plain, followed by a two-mile pull against a slight current, up a slough to the takeout by a gravel airstrip with an immigration/ranger cabin. We had re-entered the U.S. from Canada somewhere upstream.

The last evening, which was dry and pleasant, we spent breaking down the equipment so it could be air-lifted back to Haines in single-engine Cessna freighters. The job of emptying the shitter went to the two kayakers, a job so onerous that I forgave them for taking over my command. In the early evening, we saw our first grizzly bear ambling across the airstrip. Several packs of wolves howled back and forth most of the night.

Except for the ubiquitous bald eagles, we hadn't seen any animals for eleven days. All the bears were hanging out down at the beach fishing, because the salmon hadn't yet started running up the river.

Because of the roaming grizzlies, we had all the leftover food stored in a small tin shed next to our camp. I would have hated to have a last-minute need to use my can of bear spray. The next morning, three Cessnas arrived on schedule at 8 a.m. I was to depart on the freight flight back to Haines to pick up my plane, then return to retrieve David, while the rest of our group flew up the coast to Yakutat to get a flight back to Juneau, and on to Colorado the next day. We started loading the gear without regard to weight or where it was placed. In a couple of minutes the plane was filled to the ceiling with rafts, frames, and cooking gear, but there was still a mountain of gear left for the next lift. The weather was deteriorating, and I was worried about getting through the coastal range to Haines and back. I chose to sit behind the pilot on a pile of gear with a pack on my lap, while another in our group sat in front. We waddled out onto the gravel strip and, in 300 or 400 feet, the severely overloaded Cessna staggered into the air.

We retraced our route up the Alsek and then followed the Tat. At the gravel confluence of the Copper we turned up the Copper River Valley to cross a 3,600-foot pass toward Haines. I kept looking over the pilot's shoulder at the plane's altimeter, which indicated that the pass ahead would be cloud-covered. We were just under the heavy clouds and still 300 feet below the pass, and the narrowing valley ahead was becoming misty in light rain. Surely the pilot knew what was just ahead, and would turn back before it became too narrow to make an emergency turn in the grossly overloaded Cessna. But he kept going and then, to my relief, we rounded a glacier-covered ridge, and just ahead was the pass with less than fifty feet of clearance. We flashed across the saddle and descended quickly to stay clear of the ragged weather ahead. The highway we had driven to get from Haines to the Tat, almost two weeks before, was visible through breaks in the clouds, and soon we were safely on the ground.

In Haines, the weather, although still raining, was flyable, and I could see across the fjord toward Skagway that White Pass was open, even sunny. But for David waiting for me on the coast, I would have been able to head south in clear weather via the Yukon. I agonized while we unloaded all the gear from the 206 and I decided to give it a try. I would follow the 206 back to the coast to pick up David. If the 206's pilot turned around before the pass into the Copper River Valley, I would as well. He, however, wasn't going to wait for me to get into the air. I had a faster plane and might catch up with him, or at least stay in radio contact about the pass being open.

I ran for my plane while the Cessna taxied for takeoff. By the time I was in the air, the 206 was well ahead. He reported that he could see that the saddle was still open, but then we lost contact. I continued up the valley, but it looked awful ahead. I was already between layers of clouds and could barely keep the road below me in sight. At some point I hoped to recognize a building that marked the U.S./Canadian border that indicated where to turn into the mountains and the critical saddle we had recently crossed. Then, through a slight breach in the clouds, I saw the building. I had already lowered my flaps and brought my speed down to a crawl, and although I was barely at 3,000 feet, I turned into the mountains hoping to pick up forward visibility. I had also glanced at my directional gyro to get an emergency reciprocal heading if the visibility didn't improve in the next few seconds. Almost immediately, the mist turned icy blue. I was heading toward a wall of ice. I cranked a tight left descending turn and fled the icy cul-de-sac I was about to impact. I was immediately back in the main valley again and thinking of that alternate route home minus David. I had turned short of the route over the pass by only a half mile because of the mist, but now, five hundred feet lower, I had much better visibility. I could clearly see the shallow valley coming in from the left, and I could just make out the pass a mile ahead. It was still clear.

I whisked over the pass and started down into the Copper drainage with visibility increasing. It continued to rain slightly all the way back to Dry Bay, where David was waiting. I landed with another Cessna coming in behind me to pick up the rest of the gear. The first plane, the 206 I had flown out in, had electrical problems so it had returned to Yakutat for repairs. David and I helped the new pilot stuff all the gear aboard the Cessna, although I doubted he would be able to make it back into Haines. The weather had turned into a steady drizzle, and I was wondering if we would be able to make it down the coast past Cape Spencer to Juneau, an hour and a half away. We took off and headed back down the coast at fifty feet to stay out of the clouds.

As long as there was no fog, we were going to make it no matter how low the cloud deck got. It was a hundred miles to Cape Spencer with the open Pacific off the right wing and Mt. Fairweather off the left. We continued down the beach at reduced speed. Bald eagles wheeled and twisted to get out of our way. The beach was littered with big brown bears. Like the eagles, they were fishing for salmon that were coming to the coast for their spawning run. We had several peekaboo vistas of glaciers tumbling off the ramparts of Fairweather right into the ocean. We passed the lighthouse at Cape Spencer and started down the Inland Passage. I knew we could make it into Juneau, just ninety more miles ahead. Weather had packed into the mountains around Juneau, and, by the time we got there, it was raining and the airport was below instrument flight minimums. But horizontal visibility was good enough to declare a sea plane approach, a ploy to make an illegal approach legal. I knew we could depart on instruments later that afternoon. The forecast was for worse weather, so after renting a room at the airport hotel to take long, hot water showers and eat lunch, we filed for Prince George, four hours southeast, but on the dry side of the mountains in central British Columbia.

We climbed out of Juneau to 13,000 feet before we broke through the clouds. Three hours later, we crossed the coastal range just north of Prince Rupert into relatively dry weather, and arrived an hour later at Prince George. A very active thunderstorm parked right over the airport. We landed with lots of air-to-air and air-to-ground lightning around us.

The day ended with congratulations from myself to myself for my Juneau departure, my return from Haines, and the beauty of the flight down the coast to Cape Spencer. I had been flying since 8 a.m. and we had arrived in Prince George after 9 p.m. David was even grudgingly appreciative. After all, I could have left him at Dry Bay in the rain with the grizzlies, and taken the route from Haines over White Pass into the Yukon in good weather.

NEPALI COAST

In June of 1998, my friend Peter invited me to join him for his annual visit to Kaalau Beach in the Nepali Coast wilderness on the island of Kauai, Hawaii. His plan was for us to slide his two sea kayaks from his grassy lawn into the Pacific, and then paddle down the coast to Kaalau in a couple of hours.

I arrived at the island's airport in the early evening. Peter and I spent the next day getting ready for an early morning departure. We packed enough food to last us a week and some minimal gear into the cargo holds of each kayak.

I had zero kayaking experience, but I owned an old, dented aluminum canoe, which I occasionally launched on a pond at Bear Paw. And I had spent some time taking my turn paddling one down the Coppermine River many years before. Those experiences confirmed my feelings about any form of paddle craft: they are tippy and prone to swamping at any moment.

Peter assured me that little skill was required. After a couple of hours paddling down the coast, I would be invested with all I needed for sea kayaking. We would have a week on the Nepali coast, exploring the valley behind the Kaalau Beach below the spectacular Kanapali cliffs.

Peter didn't over-describe the physical beauty of our destination or the ease of getting down the coast in the sea kayaks. He did, however, fail to mention the suicidal approach and landing from the open Pacific onto Kaalau Beach. The kayaks had open cockpits, with a back strap for support, and a water rudder for easing the waddle of the stern while paddling. The double-bladed paddle was for both propulsion and steerage while careening down a towering wave toward a beach.

Early the next morning we slid the two loaded vessels down his front lawn and into the lagoon, behind the protection of a reef. On the other side of the reef was the Pacific Ocean, stretching unbroken to Asia. We had to pass across a shallow lagoon with the coral only a foot underneath us. The threat of an upset in those first ocean waves, and being washed back over the coral, gave me an adrenaline rush that powered my transition to the open ocean.

We started paddling down the coast with the Nepali Cliffs clearly outlined against a cloudless sky. Except for the swell, there were no waves and hardly even a breeze. Within a mile, the offshore reef ended, and the shoreline became a tropical 3,000-foot mountainside spilling into the ocean. Except for a couple of small beaches where streams had cut steep canyons, the coastline was mostly sheer cliffs. We paddled effortlessly by, a quarter mile offshore.

Halfway to our destination, Peter suggested we explore one of the many sea caves that punctured the cliff face. We turned toward one that seemed to have the largest entrance, and blithely paddled our boats through a short tunnel into a great cavern. The cavern was approximately a hundred feet in diameter, with a domed ceiling thirty feet above. The interior was lit by reflected sunlight bouncing off the floor of the entrance, infusing our vision with dancing light. Above us was a hole in the ceiling, with a feather of fresh water and falling sunlight.

Suddenly a rush of water flooded the cavern's entrance. The Pacific rushed in, and we rose to the top of the dome. It became apparent that we might be exiting the cavern through a three-foot hole in the top of the dome. But then the upward rush tapered off and we descended.

My mind raced: What was awaiting us outside, a much larger swell? Something that would occlude the tunnel entrance and completely fill the dome? Could we be squirted out the blowhole in a geyser of water? All the horrendous options instantly became apparent. I desperately wanted to get out of the cavern.

Neither Peter nor I spoke a word, but with the downward surge and the outward rush of water through the tunnel opening, we both started paddling as if the hounds of hell were on our heels. We cleared the entrance and popped into the sunlight like two corks out of a bottle. Once outside, the open ocean swells were again benign.

An hour later, off Kaalau Beach, we were confronted by another ocean-related horror. By then the wind had substantially picked up. The swells were being compressed against the steep beach into majestic breakers that collapsed on shore with booming explosions. These were not beaches where the waves break well offshore, and surfers ride smoothly down the break. No, these waves reared up from the seemingly gentle swells and slammed down hard on the beach.

Peter explained there was a rhythm to the waves, an explanation that was lost on me. From where I sat, seaward of the monster waves, the gentle swells reared up into fifteen and twenty feet, and the beach disappeared into a crash of mist and spray. We sat there for several minutes feeling the rhythmic swells pass under us. We were trying to calculate their timing for a quick dash in on a smaller wave, but all the gentle Pacific swells looked about the same.

Finally, to end the uncertainty, we set off in a mad flurry of paddle strokes to keep up with an incoming swell. I felt the kayak accelerate as it tipped almost vertical into a death plunge toward the beach. In that half-second of free fall, I found how useless the water rudder was. Keeping the bow headed directly down the wave meant digging one blade into the water on the side that the kayak was trying to turn away. I forced the paddle into the water and, for a moment, dropped directly down the face of the wave with the boat perversely trying to turn sideways. When the wave obliterated itself on top of me, I was still pointed bow first and rushing up the steep beach in a lather of foam. I was deposited safely on the sand. I had made it. I leapt from the boat and dragged it out of reach of the next incoming wave. Peter and I had each made land and survived the horror.

During our stay at Kaalau, the midmorning entertainment was watching new arrivals and departees work their way on shore or out through the incoming waves. Many weren't as lucky as we had been. Kayaks were strewn on the beach without paddlers, especially in the case of those departing. Riderless kayaks always reached the beach before their hapless paddlers.

Peter and I camped for five days in a breadfruit forest against a rock cliff. There were other campers spread out down the quarter mile of beach; most of them were hikers and a few were squatters who lived there long-term. Whenever the rangers showed up, the squatters fled the beach for the upper valley and their hideouts and marijuana patches.

Just above the low cliffs where we were camped was a gentle valley leading up to green 1,000-foot fluted cliffs. A lovely stream with a string of pools descended from the valley. At the south end, the beach ended in a rocky cliff. At the north end was an escarpment with terraces once used for growing taro.

One morning Peter and I swam around the cliff to the next beach. It was dominated by a huge natural arch that extended from the cliffs into the ocean, and had often been used as a movie location. But now, as at Kaalau, people aren't allowed to come ashore except by swimming. Only the rangers can beach their inflatable patrol boats there when they check for permits. The only distraction from this natural paradise was the hum of sight-seeing helicopters checking out the nearby Nepali Cliffs.

On the 100-yard swim back to Kaalau, I noticed that the surf had picked up. I had fins on and I was waiting beyond the breaking waves to body surf in. When I did, I was pile driven head first onto the beach. I lay like flotsam in the sand, trying to establish that all my extremities were working.

Peter and I knew that, upon our departure, it would be our turn to entertain the beach watchers. We wanted to move down the coast to the next wilderness beach so, sooner or later, we would have to give it a go. From observing the outbound kayakers, we deduced we would have to catch the surge off the beach from a preceding wave. This required running like hell while pushing the kayak, hopping into the open cockpit, and paddling toward the incoming wave. If the timing was perfect and the wall of water hadn't yet started its collapse, the kayak might ride up its vertical face. And if you lunged your upper body forward at just the right moment, to keep from pitchpoling backward, you'd crest the wave and find yourself floating on a benign, calm ocean where your scream of joy would be heard over the crashing surf. We were lucky; we made it off the beach on our first try.

Protected by an offshore reef, we paddled down the coast to the next beach, where we spent two days relaxing before heading back north. While there, we paddled back to a rocky headland and beached our kayaks. We walked out on a sand spit that separated the beach from a canyon backed by 2,000-foot cliffs, full of taro terraces and stone ruins.

There was no beach to land on, only a boulder pile from years of flash floods. The only way ashore was to put on a life jacket backward, using its bulk for protection. We swam around the cliff with fins, waited for the right wave and surfed onto the boulders, taking the impact with the padded life jacket. After grabbing on to the boulders, I turned around and scuttled up the boulder pile on my butt before the next wave piled in. We spent most of the day exploring the canyon, where an isolated, indigenous Hawaiian culture had once existed. The return through the surf was easier than the landing.

On the evening of the third day, we started paddling back to Kaalau Beach in the wind. We made another passage through the surf, but I was flung from the boat as it started to roll over when it hit the sand. I rolled free but held on to the kayak before it was swept away by a retreating wave. It was almost dark by then, so we pulled the kayaks up onto the beach, spread out our sleeping bags beside our boats, and went instantly to sleep. We shoved out before sunrise the next morning for the paddle north, and within three hours we were back at Peter's.

BURGLED

On an early spring morning in 2001 I awoke to an intruder standing beside my bed. I became fully awake in stages; I passed through confusion, fear, and rage in mere seconds. I'd been in a deep sleep but rose to full awareness as I saw a flashlight and heard a low voice near my bed. I realized my sanctuary had been invaded. I tried to scream but couldn't produce a sound.

I was frozen, but then came a primitive roar: "OOOHHH-KAYYYYY!!!!" I bellowed as I rolled off the side of the bed. The intruder was standing right next to me, and both he and another figure turned and fled down the hallway.

I landed on my hands and knees and reached under the bed to grab a short-barreled, twelve-gauge shotgun. I pulled it from under the bed and jacked a round of buckshot into its chamber with the dust cover still on. With no thought, I tried to find the trigger with my right index finger while bringing the gun to my shoulder. The two intruders were illuminated by a small security light where the stairs descended to the ground floor. The dust cover had bunched up over the trigger guard, and, for the one moment when I could have fired eight lead pellets of 00 buckshot into the back of a man, my finger couldn't find the trigger. A dust cover had saved his life.

The intruders pounded down the stairs to the center of the dark house with four exits. The deck off the bedroom overlooked two of the exit options. I shook off the dust cover, stepped outside, held the gun up, and got ready to fire. As if on cue, I saw movement to my left; they were coming out of the sunroom. I couldn't see figures, only movement in the dim light from a quarter moon shining through scattered clouds. I fired and then jacked another round into the chamber and fired again. Once the thunderous blasts and their echoes abated, I was left standing, fully naked, on the porch in absolute calm and quiet.

I went back inside, grabbed a robe and a flashlight, and returned to the porch to scan the yard. There was nothing to see but footprints in the soft earth where I had just planted a lawn. I stood there for a few minutes, waiting for noise, maybe a getaway car's engine turning over. My nearest neighbor's house was a thousand feet away in the direction of the shotgun's blast, but it was dark; they hadn't been awakened.

As I stood there, I realized what might have been. If my finger had found the trigger while the intruder was still in the hallway, the lead pellets would have blasted a hole in his back. From forty feet up on the porch, they would have done the damage of .22 caliber bullets if they'd impacted flesh. My rage was draining away, replaced with the horror of what could have happened.

I closed and locked the door at the end of the hallway, got into bed, and went back to sleep. In the morning, I checked out the downstairs and discovered that the two guys had gotten in through the sunroom attached to the west wall of the house, where they had broken a pane of glass in a French door. From there, they had passed into the dining room, leaving a muddy trail of footprints leading to the stairs to my bedroom.

They obviously knew where they were going. I had a small safe in a walk-in closet off the bedroom, and I surmised the recently employed cleaning lady had seen it and passed its location on to the thieves. They also must have known that I was supposed to be away that night. I had canceled my proposed trip and returned home late. Brigid was dog-sitting Tex, so I had no advanced warning. Although my car was parked near the house, the thieves proceeded. I had to smile, thinking how shocked the guy must have been when he heard me roar.

I finished a tour of the house. Nothing was missing or disturbed. They had left the same way they had entered and then turned to run toward where I was standing above them on the porch. The loads of buckshot went over their heads. Their trajectory was clearly written by their boot tracks in the soft soil. When I fired, both their tracks showed that they stopped and reversed their flight. One of the guys was running like an animal with his handprints clearly visible. They ran thirty feet to and through a barbed-wire fence, toppled into a full irrigation ditch, and then, as I heard later, swam/crawled until they were clear of my property.

One of the intruders turned out to be a neighbor who knew the cleaning lady. His accomplice was later killed in a famous drug-related shoot-out at a gas station in town. Other neighbors passed this information on to me with great hilarity over the ensuing months. The thieves' struggle through the barbed wire fence left lasting mementos of their robbery fiasco on their bodies.

The law showed up later that morning. They determined that the clear boot prints in the dirt were size eleven, took photos, congratulated me on probably converting the two to a life of criminal abstinence, and left. I talked to the county DA regarding what would have happened had I brought the intruders down with buckshot. His cryptic answer was,

"Inside the house when they were fleeing, nothing. Outside the house, $20,000 for a good criminal defense attorney, and nothing." I have since changed the load for my shotgun to stinging birdshot.

ULTRALIGHT

In the early 2000s, my friend Pete offered to let me fly his Quick Silver Ultralight, an awkward-looking device powered by a loud lawn-mower-like engine. Pete had been teaching himself to fly the little beast by crow-hopping down the runway at the local airport on a high sagebrush-covered mesa. The hops were nothing more than slightly controlled bounces. After a few days of this, he wisely decided to give up. An errant wind gust had turned the machine into a crumpled pile of tubing and canvas. But days before that happened, Peter handed me his helmet and said, "Go fly it!"

With more bravado than intelligence, I donned the helmet and sat in the sling seat perched in front. Pete started the little engine by pulling a cord behind my head. It roared to life, preventing further verbal instructions. There were braces for my feet beside a tiny nose wheel. I had been told I could steer the machine on the ground by pushing them, which, in turn, would twist the nose wheel in the direction away from the one that was pressed, which is the opposite from rudder pedals in a regular airplane. If I wanted the little craft to go right, I would push on the left foot brace, and so on. But that was only while it was on the ground.

In the air, everything was controlled by an aluminum tube that was attached to the overhead wing. If I pushed forward on the tube, the contraption would pitch down. If I pressed it to the right, it would turn right.

I proceeded to taxi to the runway and practiced turning the contraption back and forth.

Ready for flight, I taxied out and very carefully placed the nose wheel on the center stripe pointing down the runway. The throttle was nothing more than a thumb lever above my head. There were no brakes, but, when power was reduced to idle, my feet could act as brakes by skidding them on the ground. The tube-and-canvas construction was as sleek as an unmade bed. The noise from the little engine made up for its lack of power. Flight instruments consisted of an air speed indicator and an altimeter. Thank God for the helmet.

My intent was to do an elongated hop down the runway, stay within safe falling distance to the ground, and, at most, remain in the air no longer than the Wright Brother's first flight at Kitty Hawk. When I pushed the thumb throttle to full power, the plane leapt forward, but changed its direction. The propeller torque swung the ultralight to the left. Panicked, I reacted as if I were in a real plane. I pushed on the right foot brace, which only increased the turn. I was also desperately trying to find the tiny throttle lever over my head, but, before I could reach it, I had veered off the runway. The nose wheel then collided with a landing light, sending a spray of broken glass, dirt, and sagebrush into the faceplate of my helmet.

Still at full throttle, the beast, with a mind of its own, continued down the two-foot deep bar ditch alongside the runway. Then it veered up and across to the other side, which launched me into the air. I had exhausted the option of landing on the runway, and there was a sea of sagebrush ahead.

My only thought was to get control and more altitude so I could maneuver the thing back toward the runway. At about two hundred feet, I leveled off and tried to make a U-turn.

Amazingly, everything worked. I was even beginning to enjoy the flight. I had managed to complete the turn, and was lined up for a landing from 200 feet. As I crossed the runway I brought the power back to idle. The response was dramatic. It was as if I had severed the wings, which weren't designed for gliding at altitude. I desperately needed power to slow my descent.

I found and jammed the throttle forward and arrested the free fall, but, when the power came on, so did the torque. The little beast touched down on the runway, but veered off again to the left. I cut the power but was already heading onto the parking ramp via another shallow bar ditch. This time I missed the runway lights, and, without power and using my feet as brakes, I came to a complete stop before I crashed into a parked Cessna.

Both the Ultralight and I were uninjured. After handing Pete back his helmet and thanking him for the chance to fly his plane, I left with a firm resolve to never attempt that form of flight again. I also departed with a new appreciation for the Wright Brothers and other early pioneers of powered flight.

A few years later, I was very sorry, but not shocked, to hear that Pete had died in an ultralight accident. He was flying along the edge of the Rio Grande Gorge on a windy day. He had just passed over some hikers and they exchanged waves and smiles. They reported that he then flipped over and crashed. Pete seemed to have been caught in a downdraft and went straight into the rocky slope below. The man said Pete didn't move after he hit the rocks, and that the mangled yellow ultralight looked like a butterfly smashed on the windshield of a car.

ROAD TRIP

The following is an example of why I should fly my forty-year-old plane cross-country at $100 per hour, instead of driving more than 200 miles away from home:

In the spring of 2004, I had an urge to buy a used car on eBay. In the past, I had bought aircraft in search of profit and adventure. The adventure part invariably turned out to be inadvertent and is recounted throughout this collection. In fact, it's the *subject* of this collection.

In this instance, I found the car of my dreams—a 2003 Ford Focus located in Sacramento. I paid the very reasonable "Buy It Now" price, contacted the seller, an English speaker with a heavy Russian accent, and booked a flight from Albuquerque to Sacramento. Two hours after takeoff, I arrived, and the seller met me at the curb in the almost-new car; it had been accurately described in every way. After a twenty-minute drive from the airport, I gave him my cashier's check. While he filled out the sales papers, I took my gleaming, almost–new car to lunch. It was now early afternoon and I was planning on hitting the road once the paperwork was completed.

After lunch, I returned to the garage, parked, and was walking to the office when I noticed that the car I was parked beside had a Mercedes star on its hood. At first glance, it was just another generic American car. I had owned a Mercedes years earlier, when appearances mattered, but the star on the hood unleashed a latent need within me for elegance. I walked into the office and casually asked my new Russian friend about the Mercedes. Moments later we were driving the little silver sylph around the block. It was virtually new with only 15,000 miles, and was spotless. I offered the Russian my now old, new car and some additional cash, hoping he would send me off in the Ford with a derisive laugh. Instead, he agreed to my offer. He told me the car had been damaged, but repaired, and was in perfect condition. Within an hour, I was on my way home from Sacramento driving a Mercedes and feeling cool.

I left Sacramento on secondary roads through the endless suburbs of California's Imperial Valley, and finally reached the lovely Sierra foothills. I drove their contoured roads throughout the afternoon—the perfect introductory ride. Although I had no idea about the instrument panel and button-laden steering wheel, or the buttons on the moon roof above, the car glided effortlessly over twisting narrow roads. Whatever damage had been repaired had, so far, held together well.

Somewhere in Gold Rush country I stopped to fill the gas tank. A moment of truth. Which side was it on? What challenge awaited me trying to open the gas panel or cap? Should I turn off the engine, and, if so, what would I do if the car wouldn't start again? I would be stranded in a gas station, miles from anywhere. But all my fears were for naught. There was no devious German trick to refueling.

I had glanced in the glove compartment and found what resembled a family Bible. It was, of course, the owner's manual that I would attend to that night when I stopped after my test drive. Of all the aircraft I have flown, I've never seen an operating manual as fat as that one.

I drove onward through picturesque little towns with historic names from the mining era until the road, heading into the mountains in broad sweeping turns, became tighter and tighter as I climbed. I reached the top of the Sierras, at sunset, on a taut twisting grade with no traffic. I crested the pass, and, ahead of me, I could see the lights of civilization. Dinner, a chance to read the manual and understand the car's buttons, and lights awaited me.

The 2,000-foot descent was steeper and even more twisted than the road up. Once in the valley, all I encountered was a huge mining operation. I drove on into the darkness on the east side of the Sierras, past Mono Lake, followed by a long descent into Bishop, where I got a ticket for doing 90 in a 65. Instead of escorting me to jail, the cop was amused by all the paperwork I handed him and gave me a warning. He sent me on my way to the nearest motel.

In the morning, after studying the manual, I could turn on the radio. I was not, however, able to set the clock, which, along with many other of the car's functions, remained a mystery for months. I hoped with another night in another motel, I would master more of the 300 pages of arcane Germanic instructions. The next day I experienced the simple joy of finding that the car started as promised.

I had a lovely early-morning drive down the side of the Sierras, as I watched the alpine glow illuminate the eastern side of Mt. Whitney up ahead. I streaked down the Owens Valley at 100 mph. While the Mercedes appeared to be ordinary and small, it had all the impressive attributes of its lineage.

An hour south of Bishop I turned east, climbed a desert ridge, then dropped 8,000 feet through sunlit fog and clouds to the floor of Death Valley. It was the end of November and slightly cloudy, only 85 degrees outside. Ahead, for miles, were hundreds of runners pounding along the side of the road. It was a surrealistic Saturday morning in California, and I was in the middle of nowhere with a long line of running zombies. I hoped that the electronic locks on the car worked.

But then, some greenery came into view. Cars were parked on the side of the road, and there was a sign: "Death Valley Marathon." Only Daisy, my daughter, at one time an endurance athlete, would appreciate this spectacle. She and her husband had run, all in one day, from the north rim of the Grand Canyon to the bottom, up to the south rim, and then back down and up again to their starting point, a loss/gain of 26,000 vertical feet. In solidarity with the runners, I stopped the car in a grove of date palms to go for a walk.

I ambled around through the trees for ten minutes before the heat got to me. Exhausted, I returned to the air conditioned car, and left Furnace Creek for the afternoon delights of soaking in Recopa Hot Springs, eighty miles south. I was still in the middle of nowhere, and saw only a couple of cars on that stretch of road, but, when I drove into the hot springs, I found them surrounded by large Harley-Davidsons belonging to the Hell's Angels.

I wisely decided there would be no soaking for me that day, and I drove on to a junction. There, a paved road led, I thought, to the east. There were no signs. According to the sun angle, it appeared to be heading east, so maybe it would connect with a road going to Needles and I-40. Once there, I would start the slog back to New Mexico on the interstate. My adventure would be over and I would be forced to submit to endless boredom across Arizona's freeways. Which is why I had brought the CD.

Just past the junction, a small historic plaque indicated that I was on "Old Cattle Drive Trail," but it gave no indication as to where it led. It still seemed to be heading easterly, so I drove on for the next eighty miles, passing over several low mountain ranges separating dry lakes. There were no signs, cattle guards, or fences. Nothing.

Finally, after starting to think I was in a time warp on Planet Dune, I saw something glistening. As I got closer, it appeared to be a tower. Closer yet, I saw truck traffic moving across the desert.

An old pickup was parked by the side of the road with a sign facing the highway, advertising "Buffalo Jerky." There was still no sign for either direction, or anything that indicated what highway I had come to. I parked and walked over to the truck where an old fellow was sitting. I told him I would buy some jerky if he would show me where I was. He got out, looked at my road map, and apologetically said he couldn't read maps. But he indicated that if I turned right I would be in Las Vegas in forty miles. I had driven due north.

Later, with a bag of jerky by my side, I passed through the sprawling half-built suburbs of south Las Vegas, heading for Boulder Dam. On the far side of the dam I parked at an overlook to further study the intricacies of the CD player, so I could listen to my book on tape. The adventure was over. I was now on a four-lane divided highway, running straight as an arrow to Arizona and I-40.

As I neared Kingman, I decided to look for a rest stop so I could pull off and snooze for a bit. But before that could happen, I awoke, with a *bang*, from an extremely short nap. I found myself heading down to the bottom of a gully, doing 85 mph, while closing in on a large concrete flood control drain that crossed under all four lanes of highway. I was on cruise control which I had also recently mastered back at the dam. Ahead and above me, at road level, was a guardrail to protect drivers from plunging into the drainage. I was instantly 200 percent awake. Without thinking about the closing geometry, I angled the car back up to the road, still at 85 mph. I had no other options. Had I slammed on the breaks, I would have slid and tumbled into the ditch. Although there was a moment when I felt as if the car was losing its grip and was going to flip, somehow the vehicle stayed upright. The Mercedes bounced back onto the highway, fishtailing slightly. I looked in the rearview mirror, wondering what I might have run off the road with my sudden re-entry, but could see nothing but dust and debris in my wake.

I had cleared the guardrail but, only by a whisker. Whatever traffic had been behind me had probably stopped and drivers were looking for wreckage in the ditch. Cell phones were probably trying to dispatch ambulances. Shaken and embarrassed, I proceeded to Kingman, where I pulled off at the first side street to hide, and inspect the remains of my once-beautiful silver chariot. I stepped out to view the damage.

There apparently was none, so I peeked under the front at the oil pan, steering controls, transmission, and gas tank. Still nothing. No oil or gas dripped from ruptured lines. No evidence of a collision. The bang that woke me, I theorized, was from hitting a sign or reflector as I left the road. The reason I didn't flip was, I think, the Mercedes' excellently engineered all-wheel drive, a feature I learned about while reading the manual later that evening.

I continued driving east, but by Flagstaff the weather had deteriorated from drizzle to sleet to snow. I began seeking shelter. I finally reached Gallup in time for a late franchised-steakhouse dinner and a bed at a franchised-discount motel. After learning about the car's reassuring all-wheel-drive function, I slept like a babe.

The next morning, after an IHOP sugar rush, I had another win: the car started in freezing weather. I went forth with confidence onto eastbound lanes of solid snowpack. Somewhere up ahead the interstate was closed. Twenty miles from Gallup, the traffic started bunching up as the pavement turned to white ice. I was only a mile short of where I was planning to turn off and head north when traffic came to a full stop. I could see the overpass I planned to take, a tantalizingly short distance ahead. The westbound lane was a solid clot of semis that looked, from where I sat, like two long aluminum tubes. The tubes extended down a slope to the median, where six semis were lying on their sides.

I noticed a few cars using the overpass to get out of the mega-jam. As I was in the outside lane, I pulled onto the shoulder to get to the exit and flee. A couple of minutes later, I was cruising north on white ice with the Mercedes perfectly tracking down the two lanes of empty pavement, deep into the Navajo Reservation. Between snowcapped red buttes and a cerulean blue sky, I ended the last extended road trip of my life. I have since resisted the habit of complaining about the high cost of flying my elderly Cessna, or the indignities of commercial airline travel. Anything is better than driving.

SIXTEEN MILES

For many years, Brigid and I enjoyed an annual custom of honoring the winter solstice by going out to the Brazos Box to cross-country ski and celebrate the first day of winter. The box is a sheer 1,500-foot canyon, carved by the Brazos River as it tumbles out of the high country of north central New Mexico and onto the eastern edge of the San Juan Basin. The box is also the halfway point between Taos and Bear Paw, another sixty miles to the southwest.

There's a shortcut that trims twenty miles off the trip, but it requires driving sixteen miles on an unimproved dirt road across the Jicarilla Apache Reservation. If weather conditions are dry and the road recently graded or plowed, this shortcut makes for an easy drive through low forested mountains. If, however, a thunderstorm has passed through, or the winter temperature has risen above freezing, or the snowpack is melting, it's imperative to take the longer, paved route.

The solstice temperature that afternoon in 2006, at 10,000 feet where we were skiing, was in the low teens. After descending to the main road, the temperature at 7,600 feet was in the mid-twenties. I reasoned we could take the shortcut, as it would undoubtedly be snow-packed and frozen. And it would get us to the ranch in time to make an all-important toast on the south-facing deck of the ranch house, a spiritually pagan ritual of witnessing the southernmost setting of the sun against the low ridge of the Continental Divide.

The dirt road across the reservation begins at the west side of El Vado Dam on the Chama River, and descends after a couple of turns onto the valley floor. We would be leaving civilization, and the pavement wouldn't start again for sixteen miles. There was no cell phone coverage, and there was seldom any traffic on the dirt track, even in the summer months.

As soon as we crossed the dam's crumbling concrete top there was a short rocky rise. It had a south-facing descent, and I was unpleasantly surprised to find the snowless road; instead, it was muddy and very slippery. We headed down the grade and immediately started sliding in six inches of greasy caliche mud. The only way to maintain control of the car was by moving slightly faster than an involuntary out-of-control skid while turning the wheel violently back and forth to keep going straight. We might have skidded a bit faster if there had been ice.

I was barely able to negotiate the two turns to the valley floor, and I hoped we would find the road frozen and firmer once we got off the slope. We didn't and it wasn't. I could neither turn back nor slow down. A heavier vehicle must have passed through earlier, as there were foot-wide, foot-deep grooves in the muddy road. I couldn't tell which way the vehicle had been going, but it didn't matter, because if I stopped, we would be stuck. We still could have walked back across the dam where there were a few summer cabins, and we might have found a phone. Instead, I decided to keep driving.

As we slithered along in the mud, I kept hoping we would find firmer footing and be able to turn around, or successfully continue south to the pavement, now only fourteen miles ahead. We continued.

I was driving an all-wheel drive Subaru that had proved to be reliable in difficult conditions. What I was encountering could only be described as impassable. The tracks in the mud ahead were from a broader and larger vehicle. I had to stay out of them while keeping my speed up to prevent bogging down. The shallow ditches on either side of the track were filled with bottomless muck. If I slid off the road we would be there for the night.

The car kept sliding across the flat valley with gentle curves and slight inclines. Traction and steering were a constant variable as I swung the wheel from one extreme to the other, hoping to stay on the road. The last five miles ahead were uphill facing north. If we ever got there, I prayed the road would be more compacted. Brigid and I hadn't spoken. She finally asked me if I was worried, and, if so, how much? I told her that on a scale of one to ten, I was at twelve, which reduced her to groans of despair.

The weather had deteriorated to light snow, and it was becoming increasingly dark. By now we had passed the midpoint and were still moving mostly forward at under 20 mph. In the twilight, I saw low-forested mountains ahead. We were closer to a telephone. Even if the car got stuck, there were ranches several miles ahead. I knew we would make it out, with or without the car. We wouldn't freeze to death or be forced to eat Tex to survive.

Although we remained lurching, flailing, and twisting along in the mud, we continued. We passed over a crest and started down a gentle grade that opened out to rangeland. Pavement was only a couple of miles ahead, and I could see a sign outlined against the darkening sky. I knew that sign; it told drivers coming from the other direction, "Unpaved Road Next Sixteen Miles, Travel Discouraged During Inclement Weather." We had made it but for a hundred feet.

Then it happened. We encountered some very deep, freshly made ruts where a vehicle coming from the opposite direction had plunged off the cattle guard into the quagmire. While trying to retreat to the pavement, it had created a bog. Our car swung sideways and came to a stop. We were still on top of the road, but also bottomed out in the mud. One way or the other, we had made it. There was a ranch house two miles down the pavement, and I wondered how AAA would respond to a call on a snowy winter solstice for a tow to the pavement thirty feet away.

But I was able, in small increments of moving back and forth, to straighten out the car on the muddy track, with the tires acting like paddle wheels in the muck. We crossed the cattle guard onto the pavement, spinning off chunks of mud in every direction. Twenty minutes later we were on the deck, champagne raised toward a red slit of light on the southwestern horizon. We also toasted our good luck and put in a request for a less-harrowing New Year.

LANDING SHORT

In early March 2009, I flew my Cessna 182 to a mechanic in Los Lunas, New Mexico, for maintenance, where I would exchange it for my Cherokee 180, which had just received its annual inspection. I invited Joe to come along. Joe had recently gotten his pilot license in the Cherokee, and, like most new pilots, he was enthralled with flying. I let him fly the Cessna down to Los Lunas while I relaxed and enjoyed the view out the window. It was a short and uneventful flight, and Joe managed his first landing in the Cessna without any trouble.

After spending time chatting with the mechanic, we took off in the Cherokee, with me, again, sitting in the right seat. Both fuel tanks indicated a quarter full, which would give us an hour of flight, not enough to make it to Taos but more than enough to get to Santa Fe, the halfway point for fuel and lunch. As we approached Santa Fe, the fuel gauge for the left tank still showed adequate fuel, and the right tank showed the as-yet-untouched quarter tank.

I told Joe that as pilot in command, it was his choice to land in Santa Fe, but I thought if the left tank held out until we had passed over we would have plenty left to get to Taos. We flew over Santa Fe, and, as expected, the left tank ran dry ten miles later. Joe switched to the unused right tank and we flew on with only twenty minutes remaining. I hoped we had at least six gallons of fuel, which meant we would land with three gallons left. I was ignoring a mandatory flight rule: never depend upon a fuel gauge or the unmeasured fuel remaining in your tanks.

Joe and I continued blithely on, cutting across the rugged terrain of the lower slopes of the Sangre de Cristo Mountains, midway between the Rio Grande and the 12,000-foot crests. Ahead was Dixon, a small village at the bottom of a tight side canyon, only a mile from the Rio Grande and just before a very rugged ridge. Once across that ridge, it was only ten miles of flat sagebrush mesa to the airport.

The last time I had looked at the right fuel tank gauge it had shown halfway between empty and a quarter, just where it should have been. Now, only minutes later, the needle was sitting squarely on empty. Surely this was a malfunction. I took the controls and banked the plane back and forth but the gauge remained solidly on E. This was a sure indication we would soon be listening to the awesome silence of a dead Lycoming engine.

Just as I couldn't see Joe's flight instruments from the right side, he couldn't see the current fuel indicator, so rather than screaming at him "Holy fuck! We're doomed, we're going to die!" I casually suggested that he jog slightly to the west and cross the Rio Grande Gorge to avoid the high ridge ahead. Although it would add a couple of miles to our flight, it would avoid the dangerous terrain ahead.

Joe obliged, and, within a few miles, we were flying over the survivable mesa. I was literally holding my breath until we passed over the gorge, but, on its west side, there was a good gravel road that paralleled it. I told Joe to keep the road off to his left wing, and I'd keep the gorge to my right. By now the airport was in sight. We'd been in the air for five minutes since I'd last looked at the gauge, and I was relatively relaxed.

If the engine was still banging away when we came abeam the airport runway, we would turn and head for it, a scant three miles away. We were 2,000 feet above the mesa, but just as I suggested that he make the turn for the runway, the fuel pressure gauge began twitching.

I told Joe we were out of fuel as the engine started to sputter. I took the controls and said, "Joe, we're going to land on the Carson road, but don't worry and please turn on the fuel pump." With that, I pulled the nose up sharply to get all the fuel that might still be in the right tank to slosh back to the engine, as there might still be a couple of quarts left that could save the day. The engine caught again, the fuel pressure steadied, and I decided to go for the runway. I turned the plane, still climbing for altitude, the engine still running steadily, the fuel pressure showing normal. We passed over the gorge and the runway was only two miles away. We had it made! Just a few more seconds and we'd be able to land, with or without power.

Then the fuel pressure went nuts again, and we were consumed by an awesome quiet. From the right seat, I couldn't see the air speed indicator. The best glide speed is around 85 mph, and I'd been climbing at 85, so things were promising. We had, at most, less than a minute before we would touch the ground, but my mental and visual calculations quickly deduced that although we were close, we weren't close enough.

Our speed was far too slow, more like 65 mph, so I quickly lowered the nose, but that only confirmed we weren't going to make the pavement. The ground was rushing up and it looked like we'd probably land in the sagebrush. I suggested that we tighten our seat belts, and then I unlatched the door. I eased the nose up and skimmed along with the perimeter fence coming up on the nose; the top strand of wire was almost at eye level.

At the last minute, I jerked the flaps down which caused the plane to balloon over the fence, but then we dropped like a stone. We wallowed to a stop in a foot of mushy snow, less than 150 feet short of a wall of icy snowpack.

We both exited the airplane with dignity, all the while congratulating each other on our fortuitous outcome. The powerless 10,000-foot glide had put us down in a 200-foot window of survivable terrain. Gliding any further might have had us crash into the icy ridge at the end of runway. A couple of feet shorter and we would've gone into a gully. As it was, the plane was untouched, we were untouched, and, except for some embarrassment, we had survived.

We walked up the runway to the little terminal where explanations were given to Kino, Joe's boss, and the airport FBO (fixed base operator). Kino was a retired Air Force pilot, and, whatever thoughts he might have had, he graciously kept them to himself. He couldn't see the plane behind the ice bank, but accepted my explanation without comment. I went into town to get my camera, and, when I got back twenty minutes later, the airport manager was chipping away at the ice ridge with a front-end loader. In another twenty minutes, we had the plane in tow and at the fuel pumps, good to go for another flight.

Years earlier, I had made another powerless landing at the same spot. I had taken the same approach coming across the gorge in a larger turbo-charged Cessna 210. I had started my descent thirty miles south of the airport from 15,000 feet. The large engine was running smoothly and the fuel gauges were showing better than half full. At 500 feet above the ground and a half mile from the runway, I lowered the flaps and wheels for landing, and added power. Then I realized I had no power and the engine had vapor locked, so I turned on the fuel pump, but got no response. I was going to impact the ground 300 feet short of the runway, outside the perimeter fence, in the sagebrush, with a dead engine. There was no time for further action and I descended into heavy sagebrush. The landing gear hit the ground with such force it caused the plane to bounce back into the air, soar over a gully and the perimeter fence, and land on the dirt outrun of the runway, where the engine roared back to full power. I tore down the runway until I brought the throttle back to idle, slowed to taxi speed, and turned off the runway to the ramp. Sagebrush was jammed into all the crannies of the extended landing gear, and one of the main gear struts was bent back and had to be replaced. Other than that, the plane was undamaged. The lucky bounce had carried me two hundred feet to safety.

DITCH

Bear Paw Ranch is a mile up the road from the village of Regina in far western New Mexico, where it straddles the transition between high desert and alpine forest. West of the ranch is an 8,000-foot multicolored ridge, the southernmost tip of the Continental Divide; while three miles to the east is a 10,000-foot ridge, at the north end of the San Pedro Mountains. Spreading south along the ridge are 30,000 acres of pristine wilderness.

Several streams tumble off the forested slopes of the plateau, to be absorbed in the high desert. In the spring, one of those streams, San Jose Creek, provides water from melting snowpack for my ponds, pastures, and a twenty-acre apple orchard. This creek passes through the ranch at 7,600 feet, but the pastures and orchard receive irrigation water from a ditch that takes it from the creek, three miles away and 1,000 feet above. The snowpack runoff irrigates the pastures and orchard from late April until the summer monsoons begin, usually in early July.

The ditch begins at a takeout where a fifteen-inch-wide steel pipe straddles the stream in a dense forest of aspen, ponderosa, and scrub oak. The top of the pipe is sliced off and rebar is welded on to fashion a crude grate to keep out forest debris. The ditch was hand dug by settlers between 1885 and 1890, to deliver irrigation water to the southeast corner of the ranch, just sixty feet above the valley floor, for seventy acres of orchard and pasture. San Jose Creek also passes through the north third of the ranch, filling three recreational ponds and two stock ponds.

On top of the wilderness, above 9,000 feet, are more small ponds, tiny streams with native trout, lush meadow, and tall stands of forest. The relatively flat plateau absorbs the summer rains and winter snowmelt, and then slowly releases it into small streams that flow into the valley. San Jose Creek is just one of several such streams, and it carries a very small portion of that stored water from the northwestern corner of the wilderness.

When the ditch was dug, New Mexico was still a territory. In this orphaned part of the state, the rules remain the same: get along with your neighbors, keep your fences repaired, and protect your historic claim to water by cleaning the ditch in the spring and irrigating the land. The watershed is still unadjudicated, which means that we must self-regulate our use of water. There are several claimants for the stream's water, and, although I am an Anglo in the multicultural mix, I am the only landowner still irrigating in the creek's natural watershed.

One other rancher with a prior historical claim on the stream takes out above me, and moves his water out of San Jose Creek into a once-dry valley for his stock ponds. This works only when we have flood runoff that lasts a couple of weeks in May. I informally regulate his water by blocking his takeout, and have suggested to him that we go to the state's water court for adjudication, based on a flimsy history of handwritten affidavits, filed in 1890 with the state engineer's office in Santa Fe by the valley's early settlers, enough to start a chain of irrigation history for my acres.

In the '60s and '70s, the prior owner of the ranch received state and federal aid to improve the property; the ponds were dug in the stream bed, and the twenty-acre terraced and fenced orchard was built and planted with 1,500 apple trees. One of the ponds is big enough to be on the federal registry of dams, which means that it now qualifies as a lake. If it was breached, the downstream flood could scour generations of trash farther down a dry arroyo. Since 2001, dams on the registry are controlled by Homeland Security.

Between my western fence boundary and the highway, there is a two-hundred-acre bog, more romantically thought of as a wetland. On the west side of the highway are the badlands of the San Juan Basin, an ancient dry seabed. The transition from alpine to high desert happens within this mile. Very little waterflow leaves the bog, but what does trickles into Arroyo San Jose, which winds south through high clay banks all the way to the Rio Grande, 130 miles away. Ten miles south of Regina, Arroyo San Jose is renamed the Rio Puerco, or Pig River. By then it deserves the name change.

Until seventy years ago, the economy of northern Sandoval County depended on agriculture and hard drinking, but then came the oil boom. People in the San Juan Basin could then survive independently of surface water. In fact, around here you're more likely to drill into oil or natural gas than into water. But the oil boom didn't change the importance of water rights or the old *acequia* ditch system. Communities borrowed money or received grants from the feds to drill deep wells and put in rural water systems. Regina received a grant from both the feds and the state to put in water lines from natural springs that flow into a large tank above the village. Now, those natural springs have been replaced by a deep well that services twenty miles of water lines and a couple of hundred homes.

In the early spring, as soon as the primitive road to the wilderness boundary is free of snow, I renew the historic right to clean and repair my ditch as it runs through the Santa Fe National Forest from the takeout to the orchard. In early April, there is usually snow on the ground by the takeout. The stream runs icy clear, but the twigs and forest litter that the stream has brought down leave an almost impenetrable mat, woven across the rebar grate where the old pipe lay across the stream. What water isn't caught by the pipe flows on downstream, and eventually ends up in the ponds and the lower wetland.

A rake is the tool of choice for this kind of work. I can get most of the clutter off the grate with one, but then I must remove the small rocks and sticks with my fingers. The fresh snow water makes my knuckles ache as I remove the debris. After the grate, the pipe passes through ten feet of the stream bank to the ditch, which was hand-dug with pick and shovel.

As the water enters the ditch, there is just enough angle cut across the ridge to maintain a current. Within a hundred yards it has left the forest and passes through a previously logged area that is lightly forested with ponderosa. Scrub oak and willows grow along the ditch bank. In places, they are laced over the ditch and slow my progress. Until I get into the heavier forest, lower down where pine needles become a big problem, there's not much debris to block the flow. I'm wearing rubber boots with heavy wool socks as I wade, pushing debris ahead of me. When this debris bunches up and dams the flow, I rake it out of the ditch and start the process again.

Cleaning the ditch is walking meditation, pure Zen. I should offer ditch cleaning as a retreat for the urban-stressed. I could lead groups down the ditch and offer mantras and pithy comments about feeling the current, the flow, the obstruction. "Concentrate on the current," I'd admonish, "how it flows around all obstacles, and always down."

And it's true. If I don't clear the obstructions with my rake, the current will disappear along with the water as it floods over the forest floor.

Sometimes I find myself getting personally irritated about the accumulated debris. Nature is chaos and my ditch is particularly uncooperative this morning. The longer needles from the ponderosa have now jammed the grate. In the recently logged area there is still heavy forest debris blocking my clearing attempts. I break the rhythm of walking in the water to lift the smaller trees and branches, unvalued timber from recent logging operations. Spiky branches catch in other fallen trees, and I must pause and think about the patterns of chaos before I can jerk the little trees free and drag them from the ditch.

I catch my irritation with my Buddha mind, and, before I know it, I'm working myself into a state of passive observance, and then quickly, to the arrogance of a simple man with a simple task. For the moment, I have filtered out the distractions of modern life. I have been transformed into a rural mystic with a rake. I will clean this ditch and then move on to others—bigger, longer, wider ones. I will have a following. They will come. I will teach. But then it's lunch time so I end my mission, walk back to my truck, and drive back to the ranch house.

Half the ditch is done, and, after lunch, I walk back up, clearing the worst jams until I get to where I left off. The ditch has now flooded a few acres of forest floor. When I break the jam, the current quickly carries a solid wedge of pine needles until it jams again. There I rake the needles out, and, within a couple of hundred feet, repeat the process again and again, as I slowly move downstream.

I come to the first of the marijuana growers' plots, and see the remains of last summer's diversion of my water to their crop, hidden in a dense pine thicket. I left them alone, thinking my complicity might earn me a couple of joints last fall, but I didn't get any. Much of the cash economy of northern New Mexico is based on small crops of marijuana. In September, this part of the state is visited by state police or DEA helicopters looking down for that special tell-tale green.

It's clouded over to the south, and I hear a roll of thunder. The wind starts blowing and, with it, large wet snowflakes are flying through the forest. The initial gusts give way to calm, but the snow keeps coming, quickly covering the forest floor in white. It's that perfect harmony of temperature and moisture that will bring down significant amounts.

Through the trees, I can see my eastern fence. The snow is still coming down but now in smaller flakes. There is texture in the clouds, which in northern New Mexico means the sun will be out shortly. A storm that looks like the beginning of the apocalypse will suddenly defer to a shaft of sunlight and a patch of blue sky. When I reach my fence and the end of the ditch, the temperature has fallen twenty degrees. Last year's dead orchard grass is coated with crystal diadems of ice, but the sun is starting to melt everything. Streams of water are running off the tin roof of the orchard shed, and, in a few minutes, the moisture will have gone to ground.

At the orchard, the ditch has done its job; carrying water three miles from the creek to the terraced trees and lower pastures. The original homesteaders cleaned the ditch for survival. I do it now to feel continuity with the land and, in my own mind, a sense of transcendence. And to practice my role as ditch guru.

RANCH DEPARTURE

One day in 2008, I was flying a single-engine Cherokee 180 from Bear Paw to Los Alamos, a short journey to the east. After takeoff, I turned eastward toward the windward side of the San Pedro Mountains. Within minutes I was enjoying a 600 feet-per-minute ascent up the steep sides of a ridge. When I reached 11,000 feet, I planned to turn east again, directly toward my destination.

Many ridges and gullies fall off the western flank of the main San Pedro ridge. On one of the more prominent ones I was skirting, I received a significant jolt of vertical assistance from a westerly wind. I swung the plane around to the right in a tight 270-degree turn to come back into the lifting air again. As I banked steeply, my visibility was blanked out by the plane's wing and nose. When I leveled the wings, I saw that I had been carried into a trough between two ridges coming off the top of the mountain, still 1,000 feet above me. I was in a classic dead-end; a forested mountain ridge 300 feet directly in front of the plane. Many pilots and their passengers have died after finding themselves flying into similar terrain.

To my right was the empty San Juan Basin, 3,000 feet beneath me. To get out of the trap I would have to increase my rate of turn, but that was impossible. Any increase in angle would bring on a stall. As it was, the stall warning light was solid red, and I could already feel a slight flutter from the ailerons and elevator indicating they were losing their effectiveness. Any increase in pitch or bank would end in what's called a wingover, as the plane asserts its aerodynamic need to maintain airspeed, which, unfortunately, would require diving into the ground. I could do nothing but keep the plane on its curving path, which now would end on the tree-covered ridge just ahead.

I couldn't drop the nose because that would merely shorten the time to impact. All I could do was verbally exhort the airplane by repeating, "Do it, baby! Do it, baby!" As I approached the sloping ridge, I could only think how stupid I was to have gotten myself in this situation. I had flown 6,000 hours of mostly mountain flying, only to be stuck in a classic confrontation with high terrain.

My wings were angled to the same degree as the oncoming ridge. I was doing 60 to 70 mph and had cracked one notch of flaps at 9,000 feet. A hundred feet from the oncoming ridge I suddenly knew I wouldn't hit it. Instead, I would hit the trees on top. With luck, I would stick the fuselage between tree trunks, letting the wings take the impact. I was wearing a stout shoulder harness. I would survive.

There were still trees coming toward me, but I could now see across the ridge and had an unobstructed view of the San Juan Basin. A second later, the trees disappeared under the nose, without impact! The knob of Cabezon Peak, an ancient volcanic core, appeared ten miles ahead, and I suddenly had 3,000 feet of space beneath me.

Yet again, pure luck or *Divina Providencia* played a major role in the happy outcome. Only two months earlier I had installed velocity generator tabs on the wings and tail surfaces, which allowed me to close my turn radius just enough to avoid impact.

LOOKING DOWN

We're barely out of Albuquerque on a short hour-plus flight to Salt Lake City, and I'm looking down at a trail of memories. The Southwest Airlines 737 is climbing through 20,000 feet and I see the western ramparts of the great Jemez Volcano, where my friend Chuck Holden was lost 30 years ago, when his plane disappeared on a flight from my ranch back to Taos. Chuck had a passenger, a lovely woman named Ripple whom he had met the night before at a restaurant where she worked. She had accepted his invitation, but had to be back in time for her evening shift. They took off in the face of deteriorating weather, never to be seen again.

Bear Paw ranch is now coming into view on the northwestern flank of the San Pedro Mountains. The San Pedros are a fifty-mile long north/south ridge, with a 30,000-acre wilderness park on the top at over 10,000 feet. Immediately to the east is the Jemez Volcano with its huge grassy caldera surrounded by a circle of peaks. Chuck and Ripple are in that jumble somewhere. As we pass over Bear Paw, now at 30,000 feet and only fifteen minutes from takeoff, I can barely make out the shape of the ranch's signature lake, a pond of about ten acres of surface water.

I can see San José Creek easily, just a fissure on the mountainside tumbling down from the wilderness. It provides the lake with snowmelt irrigation from the winter snowpack above 8,000 feet. A couple of years ago, I nearly ended my flying career there. With around 7,000 hours of flying experience, mostly in the western mountains of North America, I almost became a flying fatality. I was so close to impact that for thirty seconds I watched a forested ridge coming toward me at 70 mph. I skimmed over the trees rather than into them by mere inches.

We're now at our cruising altitude, and ahead I can see the San Juan River. West of our course is Four Corners, the only spot in the U. S. that is common to four states. Just past that, through the desert haze, the green smudge of the San Juan River's bottom land disappears into a serpentine labyrinth of red rock canyons, called goose necks. There, the river turns back on itself several times, separated by narrow red rock cliffs. This is where I started my first river rafting trip at a place called Mexican Hat. Not much was there then, or is now: a store, a gas station, and then a wall of red rock where the river disappears into the labyrinth.

In early summer 1973, Hueri and her two children and I launched a thirteen-foot boat for a three-day trip. We must have looked like a floating marshmallow—four of us, with food and camping gear, lazily drifting to where the current stops in a slop of river debris and Lake Powel begins.

Just to the right and ahead are the San Juan Mountains of Colorado. We're crossing the southwest end of that range, still with snowpack on the northern slopes above 10,000 feet. On the northeast side, just five miles horizontally and five miles vertically beneath, is the end of the Colorado Trail that roughly follows the Continental Divide.

A few of us biked a section of it several years ago. For five days, we never went below 10,000 feet. Five of us westerners joined five others from the East Coast on a guided mountain bike trip, led by a slim young woman. For us, it was probably the five physically hardest days of our lives. Two of our group had to have back surgery for ruptured disks, and three have never mountain biked again. Each night we would regroup at a prearranged site where a supply truck would deliver food and camping equipment. Each morning the lovely twenty-something would boldly lie to us: "Today we will be leveling off through open meadows filled with wild flowers. Hardly any climbing today, really." She was so beautiful. We didn't believe a word. All I remember are meadows and flowers and a trail that was always climbing.

Just to the right, we're crossing the southwest end of the San Juan Mountains, and there appears another river with many memories, the Dolores. Forty-five years ago, the river was wild and uncontrolled, with no dams. Depending upon snowpack, the Dolores was a cold spring river for floating. My first trip, a three-day float in 1974, with companions from Aspen and friends Nate and Mike from Taos. We had flown to Cortez, Colorado and hitched a ride with our raft and gear to a small bridge over the river, where there is now a dam. I had arranged to meet the Aspen group later that afternoon, fifteen miles downstream, where they had arrived by car. We were putting in, still in ranching country, before the river entered the canyon.

After hastily inflating the raft and dumping our gear into it, we pushed off into the swift current. An hour later we were relaxed and laid back on the tubes. We began trading open range for the red-walled canyon of the Dolores. The boat was doing lazy circles in the current, while we basked in the warmth of that spring afternoon. There was nothing to worry about until the boat's slow rotation brought into view some strands of barbed wire stretching across the river thirty feet downstream, which meant there were other strands of the same fence under water. After the spring runoff, the Dolores turns to a trickle and the fence is there to contain cattle.

I yelled at Mike and Nate to hang on as the boat went up against the strands of wire sideways. The boat pitched up and dumped us and all the camping equipment and food into the icy snowmelt. Miraculously, we made it through the flooded fence without getting hung up on the wire. If we'd had our life jackets on, we might have been caught passing through the strands. As it was, the boat and its contents floated downstream. Our camping gear was strewn in the current ahead of us. A watermelon, the first item to be retrieved, bobbed beside me. We dragged ourselves back into the raft, which was still right side up, and proceeded to pick up our gear that was still within reach. Our arrival, a half hour later, was not unannounced to the rest of the group. They knew we were coming because of the flotsam that preceded us.

In subsequent years, the Dolores became a springtime rite of passage. One year Linda and I introduced Daisy to the river. She would learn about the major rapid called Snaggletooth, which aptly describes it. To make the prospect of rafting the rapid more palatable to an eight-year-old, we modified it to Snuggletooth.

Now, I can clearly see terrain features fifty to seventy miles in the distance. Below is the bridge at Gateway. I had once landed my plane on its short dirt runway to start another trip down the Dolores to the Colorado River, thirty miles downstream. That excursion was the same year as the first spring trip, but the river was running out of water. Back then, we were using wooden oars, and, by the time we reached the Colorado, we'd broken most of them on the rocks. During spring flow, they would have been covered with water, but on that trip we were like bumper cars, ricocheting from rock to rock in the shallow rapids. It was July and very hot. I remember cooling down in the midday heat in the few deep pools left in the river, something unthinkable in the snowmelt earlier in the spring.

Just to the west of Gateway are the 12,000-foot La Sal Mountains on the eastern edge of Canyonlands. The La Sals climb out of hot red rock country into high forests with winter snowpack. As we fly over, the aspen trees are just going into full leaf. Streaks of snow are left in the gullies on the mountain's northern flanks. Twenty years earlier, I had surfed up the western side of the La Sals to 12,000 feet in the strong spring winds in my small Enstrom helicopter. I had been delivering the machine from Butte, Montana to Bear Paw, an 800-mile journey.

Off to the west, I can see the bottom lands of the Green River, which marks the edges of the canyon as it twists its way south to join the Colorado. Just below the confluence of these two great desert rivers, Cataract Canyon begins. On my first trip through Cataract, we put in on the Colorado just below Moab for a gentle fall float. Except for having to dodge a couple of huge boulders in the river, it was an uneventful passage followed, however, by a two-day journey down the lake, powered by a wretched little outboard engine which moved us just quickly enough to keep us in a cloud of exhaust the whole time.

The next trip was anything but placid. We were going to run Cataract during spring snowmelt. Both the Green and Colorado were running high. We had put in on the Green for two days of calm floating to the confluence with the Colorado, where we camped for the last night.

The next morning, after adjusting loads and securing life jackets, we pulled out into the current for what awaited us in

Cataract Canyon. Several years earlier the flow had been less than 5,000 cfs. We were going through Cataract this time at over 60,000 cfs. The entire river flow was a huge counter-rotating eddy filled with debris scoured from the above-normal high water mark. There was no way to scout it, as the river had covered any ledges for inspecting the horror from the shore. And it was just as well because I would never have run it had I been given time to scout. Instead, we circulated across the top of the drop in all the debris.

On the second pass, I was prepared and rowed the outside of the counter-rotating current. When I reached the point directly above the drop, I gave a couple of power strokes to pass through the debris to the downstream current. Once in the current, we pitched over into a glassy tongue and descended into a maelstrom of foam and mist. The downstream side of the hole was a huge breaking wave that built up at an erratic frequency, towered for a moment, and then collapsed back into the hole with a thunderous explosion. We climbed up the downstream side of the hole and over the top to safety, just as the wave had reached its apogee and collapsed behind us. Minutes later, we were floating in the debris-choked beginning of Lake Powell, waiting for a houseboat to pick us up for dinner and a scenic one-day motor down the lake to the marina.

With Canyonlands behind us, the pilot announces that we are beginning our descent into Salt Lake City. We are still 100 miles out and passing over Desolation and Gray's Canyon on the Green River. My first river trip with the Aspen group was there and it was where I was flipped out of my boat by a rapid. It was the Aspen group's first raft experience with our dissolute Taos dope-fiend river ways. By the end of the four-day passage, we were all bonded with the river and each other.

I can see the tram station perched atop Snowbird now as our descent into the valley steepens. Along with my son Michael, I'd been dropped off on a ridge just north of Snowbird by helicopter where we skied a steep east/west ridge that overlooked the city. Each turn across the spine landed us in either winter powder snow on the north side or in spring corn snow on the south. Skiing memories are made of a few runs that stand out, and that was one; a lovely benign run instead of something that is forever seared in memory because of a sudden adrenaline rush of fear.

Just minutes later the plane is banking to the right toward the main north/south runway in Salt Lake. As it levels before making a final to runway 18, I see that we've crossed over the southern tip of Antelope Island, where I'd landed the Enstrom on a small dock, years before.

The Southwest Airlines trip lasted a little over an hour, but I was able to look down on over fifty years of adventure, all within a 45-mile swath of a line drawn on a map, from Albuquerque to Salt Lake City.

HEART ATTACK

On September 21, 2009, I was sitting on the deck at Bear Paw, toasting the equinox sunset. I had just landed my plane after a three-hour flight from Salt Lake City, where I'd been visiting my daughter Daisy and her brand-new baby boy, my grandson. The late afternoon flight had been pleasant, although for the past three days I'd been experiencing a mild case of indigestion.

Early the next morning, I walked across the pasture below the ranch house to the orchard to pick some apples. As I was walking back up the short hill, I felt a sudden loss of energy. Virginia, the part-time occupant of the guest house and a retired ER doctor, had arrived while I'd been in the orchard. She was in the greenhouse so I went in, wondering whether I should tell her about my minor distress. I was now concerned my symptoms might indicate a long-dreaded heart attack. Why else the sweating and sudden loss of energy?

I collapsed in a chair in the greenhouse and made small talk for a few minutes, all the while thinking, *Should I mention my concern?* But that would only confirm my fear. She was a doctor! I had a choice: either tell her and drive twelve miles to the Cuba medical clinic, or walk a quarter mile to the plane, and, if I didn't die beforehand or during the flight, fly thirty minutes home to Taos. After all, I had passed my annual flight physical only ten days earlier.

I decided on the latter. I told Virginia I needed a late

morning nap, went to the house, took a couple of aspirins, and stretched out on the bed. Ten minutes later, feeling my energy return, I walked to the runway, picked up my runway rake, and leisurely walked up to the plane, scattering rocks and mole debris off to the side. The sweating was over and my strength was back, so I quickly got the plane down the runway and into the air. I cleared the 9,000-foot ridge east of the ranch, and, from there, I could see Taos Mountain, my destination, eighty miles further; the home mountain that has dominated the view from my bedroom all the years I've lived in Taos.

For reasons that now seem ludicrous, I lost interest in my symptoms after landing, and spent the rest of the day doing my usual chores in town. I went to the post office, checked my e-mail, and made telephone calls. As things slowed down in the late afternoon, my attention returned to the elephant still in the room. My symptoms were still there and Alka Seltzer wasn't curing them.

Brigid insisted that I call my friend Dr. Cetrulo for a phone diagnosis, which usually went like: "You again. Call me during office hours so I can bill you." Or, "If you can talk to me on the phone that means you're alive, so call me in the morning. I'm busy now." He wasn't home, so I called my other doctor friend, Feelgood, in Vail, and he gave me succinct instructions to get my ass to the emergency room in the following kindly manner: "You fool, you're having a heart attack!"

Shortly afterward, Cetrulo called and repeated Feelgood's instructions, and, with that, Brigid and I drove to the local hospital where we found the emergency waiting room surprisingly empty of knife and gun-shot victims, or, for that matter, any victims. I was passed immediately into the ER where I became like a newborn, cradled with endless care and attention.

I spent four hours in the Taos ER alternating between hope, fear, resignation, and acceptance. I already knew some of the hospital staff. Amy was the ER nurse that night. She and the attending ER doctor, Jennifer, sifted through the vague reasons about why I had come in. I told them my symptoms wouldn't go away after ingesting Alka Seltzer or Japanese plum balls, known cures for almost everything. Then things escalated: while an EKG showed inconclusive results, a blood analysis brought Jennifer into the ER with a serious face and news of an enzyme in my blood indicative of a recent heart attack. She promptly ordered a medivac to the UNM Medical Center in Albuquerque.

The mystery was over. What I'd been fearing was a reality. I had had a serious heart attack that morning, a seven or eight on a scale of ten. Except for mild indigestion, I was asymptomatic. I was extremely lucky to be alive instead of a smoking cinder in a puddle of melted aluminum, somewhere in the mountains I'd flown over that morning.

Cetrulo arrived at the hospital not long after I had been admitted and spent his time giving me some comfort, which seemed frightening. Concern from my longtime friend and doctor only confirmed that I was facing something serious.

Following Jennifer's diagnosis, preparation for the flight to Albuquerque began. My clothes were replaced with an open-ass gown. I was given Verced, a what-the-fuck pill, and I dissolved into velvety semi-consciousness. I was surrounded by sympathetic smiles that followed me out to the helipad, where I was bundled into a small chopper. As it lifted into the cold night sky, the smiling figures waved and turned against the rotor blast, and I was gone.

The lights of the Rio Grande Valley came over the horizon, then slowly receded behind us. We passed over Santa Fe and, after clearing La Bajada ridge, the lights of Albuquerque appeared, and we spiraled down from our one-hour flight and landed on top of the university medical center.

I was gurneyed across and through several buildings and elevators, and ended up in a room on the 7th floor, my home for the next five days. I was in a single room with a view and a bath, so I kept referring to it as the hotel room. I'd been stripped of modesty and pretension and wore a backless gown, which only serves one purpose: ego removal. I learned quickly that you must adapt to a new and absolute hierarchy with The Nurse at the top. From my bed, I became a supplicant for life's necessities, and, in turn, I was given everything I needed. When you come to terms with the new reality of your failed health, you must adjust fully. You must *surrender*. After all, what are the options? When I reached my room I was fully adjusted.

During the next couple of weeks, I made friends with and flirted with all the nurses and their aides. I became an acquiescing, compliant patient, the kind they love. I desperately wanted to be loved and healed and then go home! In return, I was fed, clothed (so to speak) pricked, punctured, defoliated, bathed, and nurtured with competence and compassion from the hospital staff, without exception. On Thursday, only a day and a half after my arrival, I was taken to surgery for a scoping and a stent. But because my major coronary arteries were fucked, I was handed over to the Aztecs—the ones with the obsidian knives and gay bird-feathered costumes drenched in gore. A couple of hours after the unsuccessful stent attempt, I met the soft-spoken Argentinean heart surgeon who would lead a six-member team in a ten-hour endeavor to transform my heart back into an efficient pump. The surgery would take place after the weekend, so I had three days to review the errors of my ways; an occasionally immoderate lifestyle and an inherited genetic predisposition to heart disease.

A highlight of the three-day prep period was a trip down to the bowels of the UNM Med Center to meet Igor. Igor's job was to sonar-map the arteries and veins that would be harvested during the Big Event on Monday. Once again, I was pushed to the elevators and down to the ground floor and then pushed for seemingly endless miles down corridors where, finally, I was left outside a door at the farthest end of the hospital. The pusher rapped on the door and quickly fled. From inside the room I could hear something scraping and wheezing toward the door. The door creaked open and there stood Igor, the sonar guy, hunched and grotesquely hairy. At one point during the sonar process he was running his wand down the inside of my left thigh and lisped, "Oh, this is a really lovely, long vein."

My grown children, Josh and Cobie, arrived from Los Angeles; and my son Michael and his wife, who live in Albuquerque, came to visit, alleviating the long weekend of waiting for surgery. Brigid, whom I'd last seen at the helipad the night before, had driven down from Taos, but, with my children in attendance, she drove home the next day to arrange for someone to care for the pets so she could return. Friends brought flowers and a fruit basket, which I traded for three pairs of hospital pajamas. Michael donated a festive Hawaiian shirt to my new wardrobe, so I tossed the backless gowns.

I was starting to grasp the nuances of the relationship between patient and staff. I exploited their unending compassion with effusive "thank-yous." I even began enjoying the hospital meals, but then again, I'm Canadian. On Saturday I was visited by the bypass team. By now I was on a first name basis with the surgeon and three of his assistants. A total of six would be attending to me, a lump of meat on a cold steel table for eight to ten hours. I asked them not to be offended if, when I recovered, I described them as ravens bent over road kill.

On Sunday, the day before surgery, Cobie and Josh took the afternoon off and returned after picking up Brigid. Early that evening, with everyone in attendance, I ate another epic hospital dinner of turkey in a sauce that resembled the soup I'd had at lunch. Then the kids adjourned for Mexican food in town, while Brigid and I spent a quiet evening together. She slept beside me on a cot.

Strangely, my state of mind was completely relaxed about the following morning's procedure. I was not to eat anything after midnight, and I passively endured the nightly routine of being awakened every two hours by staff, who verified my blood pressure and checked the ever-vigilant heart monitor over my bed to see if I was still alive. At 7 a.m. they came for me. I was freshly laundered with a special antiseptic soap I had to use while I took my last hot shower for eternity, or the next ten days, whichever was shorter. Then, denuded of my pajamas and Hawaiian shirt and back in a gown, I was laid on a gurney, given another wonderful what-the-fuck pill, and wheeled to the elevator and pre-op, where I met the jolly anesthesiologist lady. I kissed goodbye to Brigid and disappeared into oblivion.

"Breathe, Fred!" I heard a disembodied voice. I felt my chest expand with my first conscious effort in twenty-four hours. Then I thought, *I am!* For the past twenty-four I hadn't been. I felt something slithering out of my throat as the ventilator tube was pulled from my lungs, and my chest continued its rhythm of expansion and contraction unaided. My mind dispassionately observed the awakening of myself, sensation by sensation. Next came the test of conscious muscular contraction. I tried to move my index finger on my left hand. But I couldn't. I tried again, and with great mental and physical effort, I lifted it slightly. As if attached by an elastic band, the finger snapped back to prone with the rest on my hand. I lay inert, physically spent. I was completely detached from myself emotionally. I vaguely acknowledged that I was alive.

Then I saw some movement and my eyes focused on the brim of a baseball cap, which must have been attached to a head, but that was of no importance. I saw written on the edge of the cap, in very small print, a message in blue ink: "They are going to kill you!" *Who?!* With tunnel vision, I saw Brigid's face coming toward me, but I only saw her face. She absolutely needed to know about the message on the hat! But I couldn't speak. The only way I could communicate was to rapidly blink my eyes and look to the right where I'd last seen the cap. I desperately rolled my blinking eyes, then faded into nothingness.

My consciousness slowly crept back. My mind was working on the who and why of the cap's message. I mulled it around and came to the realization that *they* thought I knew where Hitler was. *They* knew that I had been in contact with Ernie Blake during the last year of his life, and with my neighbor Rumsfeld, while I had been in graduate school at UNM, so I must have been told of his whereabouts! Because of those contacts *they* knew that I knew where Hitler was. It all became clear to me. With that mystery solved, I drifted back into oblivion. As I found out later, I was under a not-so-unusual syndrome called ICU psychosis. It lasted throughout the morning with mild consequences; several spectators of my post-surgical recovery were insulted, and, because I had demanded he do so, Josh took off and gave me his shoes.

Throughout the afternoon, I became more and more aware of my body. Tubes and wires exited from my chest and neck. I noted a foot-long incision in my left arm where an artery had been harvested. Tubes and wires were draped over the side of the bed, where they disappeared into devices that whirred in a cacophony of sounds. One group sang an aquarium melody with occasional digestive burps thrown in. The monitor over the bed, fed by wires coming from my neck and chest, sighed, beeped, and buzzed contentedly. A nurse sitting in an adjacent glass cubicle paid attention to her monitor, which monitored my monitor. She occasionally awarded me a smile through the window separating us, while a parade of technicians wheeled in an apparatus and plugged me into its monitors.

Dinner arrived and I ate. Ten hours earlier I was barely able to raise a finger, and now I could sit up in bed, talk, and enjoy my recovery. There was just the mildest discomfort and very little disorientation. Twenty-four hours after surgery, I was completely aware of my surroundings and my visitors. Several members of the six-person team, who had worked over my open chest for ten hours the previous day, stopped in. We laughed and joked. As promised, I described them as crows dining on road kill. I was fully alive.

On my third morning in the ICU, she came for me, the one lovely female member of the pump team, a compassionate beauty with a tray of suspicious instruments. "We're going to start removing tubes today," she said with a smile. I had never thought about that process but was delighted to hear the news. They were like bindings holding me to the bed. I was already up and walking, but towing the bottles of elixirs and electrical leads to the traveling monitor was very complicated.

"So, which of the myriad of tubes today?" I asked her.

With a sly smile she replied, "Oh, just the little one today. The rest will come out over the next couple of days." I blanched, grabbed my crotch, crossed my legs, and whined, "No, please, not that one. I need another day to think about it. Will it hurt?" She gave me her wonderful smile and said, "It won't hurt me in the least, dear." With a deft tug, she pulled the catheter out. What an anticlimactic moment! It was over with hardly a sensation, and I never had a chance to fret.

There were still three garden-hose-sized tubes coming out of my lower chest, and a couple of electrical leads protruding through my upper chest, which I think were for jump-starting my heart should the need arise. They were pressing against the outside wall of my heart, with their ends taped off to protect me from errant currents wafting about. From my neck, a black plastic tube, called the harpoon, fed wires coming from inside my heart to the monitor.

Two days later I was out of the ICU and back in my 7th floor penthouse, being entertained by hot air balloons and their passengers passing by my window. It was Albuquerque's annual balloon fiesta.

When all the tubes had been removed, I connived to take an illegal shower. I had put up with all the hospital indignities, but I refused to remain filthy another day. My own private bathroom was two quick steps from the side of my bed, so I carefully plotted my path. I notified the hall monitor nurse station that I was going to unhook my leads while I strolled for a few moments around my bed to sit in a chair, where I would then re-attach myself. That would give me a couple of minutes of unmonitored time. Although weak and fragile, I left the bed, ripped the monitor cups from my chest, tore my pajamas off, and stepped into the shower. In a couple of seconds I was standing under a stream of lovely hot water, still trailing wires and tubes.

I soaped and luxuriated in the hot shower for no more than ninety seconds, and then emerged clean and shining, desperately drying off and reclothing myself before I was caught. I was standing in a puddle of shower water when the door burst open and there stood Big Nurse glaring at me, saying the only harsh words spoken during my stay in the hospital, "I could have lost my job over you! If those wires coming out of your chest had gotten wet you would have died, writhing, there on the shower floor!" Several student nurses were crowded behind her, wide-eyed, trying to see what was happening. Another half minute of caustic comments sent me scurrying back to my bed, mumbling apologies and promises never to be bad again, ever.

On what was supposed to be my final morning in the hospital, I awoke to the blare of the monitor alarm. I was feeling fine, but the alarm was indicating I was otherwise. Apparently, I had an arrhythmic heartbeat, thumping at over 150 beats per minute, although I couldn't feel it. For the next few hours I sank into depression. Ever since surgery, I'd been fixated on having a green chile chicken enchilada for lunch at La Chosa in Santa Fe. Today was to have been the day.

I was put on another IV drip elixir for the next twenty-four hours, but they released me at noon the next day. The last act by my lovely hose-removing angel was to gently pull the electrode wires from my heart and through my chest wall. Then, with my son Michael driving, Brigid and I were on our way to La Chosa at last for the meal that had kept me hopeful and alive. I would live another day as a *very* lucky, very grateful, no-more-risk-taking, voluptuary.

ACKNOWLEDGMENTS

The author wishes to thank the many people who read the manuscript and offered helpful suggestions for *Surviving Myself*, among them Bonnie Black, Alan MacRae, Steve Fox, and Theresa Webb. Many thanks to Barb Scott for formatting, to Helen Rynaski for expert copyediting, and to David Perez for recommending Helen. Special thanks to my wife, Brigid Meier, for coming up with the title and for ushering the book through to completion.

Made in the USA
Columbia, SC
26 September 2017